For Shelly

Contents

PART II
ASSESSMENT AND DIFFERENTIAL DIAGNOSIS

PART III
CLINICAL CHALLENGES:
ENACTMENTS, COUNTERTRANSFERENCE,
AND NARCISSISTIC DEFENSES

Acknowledgments

I am primarily indebted to the many children and their families who allowed me the privilege of entering their lives. While this book may often emphasize the hidden pain within children, it is also intended to celebrate a child's capacity for pleasure, joyfulness, and love.

I am deeply grateful to those contributors who graciously allowed me to republish their papers in this volume, as well as to those who took this opportunity to add to the literature on narcissism in children.

I am very fortunate to have been in a peer group for the last fifteen years with Madelon Sann, Susannah Shopsin, Esther Savitz, Marjorie Slobetz, and Leni Winn. The nurturance of this group has been unflagging, as has its dedication to the child's emotional and physical well being.

I also want to thank Delia Battin, Carolyn Ellman, Arlene Richards, Lynne Rubin, Rebecca Shanok, and Irving Steingart, who discussed this project with me and offered me their thoughts and suggestions. A special thanks to my mother, Sonja Lerner, who always encourages my endeavors. Catherine Monk was there when the idea for this volume evolved and Michael Moskowitz, publisher, and Judy Cohen have helped bring it to fruition, and I thank them all for their thoughtfulness and gracious help.

My very special thanks and gratitude is reserved for my husband, Sheldon Bach, whose talents include being able to make me sit down at the computer but, more important, who has always been there for me and helped me in more ways than I can describe.

Contributors

Agi Bene   Faculty Anna Freud Center; Member, British Psycho-Analytical Society. (Deceased)

Phyllis Beren, Ph.D.   Fellow and Faculty, Institute for Psychoanalytic Training and Research (IPTAR), Training and Supervising Analyst, New York Freudian Society, Supervisor and Faculty, Institute for Child, Adolescent and Family Studies (ICAFS).

Marion Burgner, B.A.   Training and Child Analyst, British Psycho-Analytical Society; Faculty, Anna Freud Center. (Deceased)

Judith Fingert Chused, M.D.   Clinical Professor of Psychiatry and Behavioral Sciences, George Washington University School of Medicine; Training and Supervising Analyst, Washington Psychoanalytic Institute; North American Chair, International Psychoanalytical Association, Committee on Child and Adolescent Psychoanalysis.

Rose Edgcumbe, B.A., M.S.   Training and Child Analyst, British Psycho-Analytical Society; Faculty, Anna Freud Center.

Allan Frosch, Ph.D.   Member, Institute for Psychoanalytic Training and Research (IPTAR); Co-Director, IPTAR Clinical Center.

Erna Furman   Child Psychoanalyst, Hanna Perkins Center, Cleveland, Ohio.

Robert A. Furman, M.D.   Training Analyst, Cleveland Psychoanalytic Institute, 1962–1992; Director Emeritus Hanna Perkins Center.

Walter Joffe, M.D.   Vice-President, International Psychoanalytical Association; President, British Psycho-Analytical Society; Training and Supervising Analyst, British Psycho-Analytical Society. (Deceased)

Louise J. Kaplan, Ph.D.   Editor of *American Imago* and associate editor of *The Bulletin of the Menninger Clinic*; private practice in psychoanalysis and psychotherapy, New York City.

Marsha H. Levy-Warren, Ph.D.   Associate Director, Institute for Child, Adolescent, and Family Studies (ICAFS); Clinical Associate Professor of Psychology, Postdoctoral Program in Psychotherapy and Psychoanalysis, New York University; Training and Supervising Analyst, New York Freudian Society.

Margaret Mahler, M.D.   Clinical Professor of Psychiatry Emeritus, Albert Einstein College of Medicine; Visiting Professor of Child Psychoanalysis, Medical College of Pennsylvania; Faculty Member, New York and Philadelphia Psychoanalytic Institutes. (Deceased)

Andrew Morrel, Ph.D.   Clinical psychotherapist in private practice in New York City; Supervisor, National Institute of Psychotherapies (NIP).

Corliss Parker, Ph.D.   Faculty and Supervisor, Institute for Child, Adolescent and Family Studies (ICAFS); Member and Faculty, Institute for Psychoanalytic Training and Research (IPTAR); Member, New York Freudian Society.

John Rosegrant, Ph.D.   Member, New York Freudian Society; Adjunct Assistant Professor of Psychology and Education, Teacher's College, Columbia University.

Joseph Sandler, M.D.   Professor of Psychoanalysis Emeritus, University College London; Past President, International Psychoanalytical Association; Past President, European Psychoanalytical Federation; Training and Supervising Analyst, British Psycho-Analytical Society.

Susannah Falk Shopsin, C.S.W.   Member, New York Freudian Society; Supervisor and Faculty Postgraduate Center for Mental Health, Child, Adolescent and Family Program; Supervisor, Metropolitan Institute, Child and Adolescent Program.

Phyllis L. Sloate, Ph.D.   Member and Instructor, New York Freudian Society; Supervisor and Faculty, Institute for Child, Adolescent and Family Studies; Professional Associate and Clinical Instructor of Psychology in Psychiatry, New York Hospital-Cornell Medical Center, Westchester Division.

Introduction

In 1980 Donald Rinsley noted that

> the literature devoted to the treatment of children with borderline and narcissistic disorders is, to say the least, scanty. . . . One reason for this state of affairs is the yet unsettled nature of the diagnostic nosology of borderline and narcissistic disorder. Another related reason is that vast numbers of children with borderline disorder are labeled as suffering from one or another variety of "hyperkinetic syndrome" or "minimal brain damage," hence are treated largely or exclusively with drugs. Further compounding the problem is the trend away from the use of long-term intensive psychotherapies. [p. 160]

This statement is perhaps more true today than it was in 1980, with attention deficit disorder being the currently popular version of "hyperkinetic syndrome." And Rinsley's "trend away from the use of long-term intensive psychotherapies" has now almost become a fact. With our increased reliance on drugs and brief therapeutic interventions, children are now at even greater risk for misdiagnosis and mismanagement.

For various complex reasons, both conscious and unconscious, many adults have difficulty understanding and attending to a child's inner pain. Children do not make the task easier, since they communicate primarily through nonverbal and behavioral means. Although psychopharmacology and behavioral modification certainly do have a place in our therapeutic armamentarium, we seem to rely increasingly on drugs and behavioral modifications to treat the troublesome child, as we do the troublesome adult, and perhaps not always to their best advantage.

Morrel, in this volume, takes up this point when he suggests that the definition of attention deficit disorder (ADD) has been quietly but systematically expanded in the last few years to include a wider range of behaviors. A troubling aspect of this expanded definition of ADD is that it obscures or invalidates psychodynamic approaches to this and other childhood disorders. Ultimately, the biobehavioral model of ADD ignores the profound impact that relationships have upon every aspect of a child's development. In his contribution, Morrel proposes a model for an understanding of the etiology of ADD that fully incorporates both biological and dynamic factors.

The overall aim of this book is to refocus our interest on the inner life of children, including both their internal conflicts and their reactions to the environment, while acknowledging the integral role of the family system. The more specific focus will be on the many disorders of narcissism that occur in the children, adolescents, and parents whom we see today.

It is beyond the scope of this introduction to review the theory and controversies surrounding the use of the terms narcissism and narcissistic personality. This has been taken up at length since Freud first used the term in 1910 in a footnote to the "Three Essays on Sexuality" (1905, p. 145), and there is an abundant literature on the subject. There are also some excellent review articles, two of which I cite here (Akhtar and Thomson 1982, Rothstein 1979). This introduction will therefore focus on certain authors, some included in this volume and others unfortunately not, who have contributed to our clinical and theoretical understanding of narcissistic disorders in children and adolescents.

It is rather common today to see children who present with a preponderance of narcissistic vulnerabilities expressed in feelings of injury, shame, and humiliation, with accompanying feelings of powerlessness, helplessness, and rage. These children pose unusual challenges by their frequent provocations and enactments, their omnipotent and grandiose fantasies and their formidable defenses that aim to control the therapist by keeping him at arm's length. Their parents may also pose a particular challenge for the child therapist because they too frequently suffer from narcissistic disturbances, often lack empathy for their child's distress, and have a great need for the child to remain an extension of themselves. Because of these complex dynamics, their cooperation with their child's treatment is often extremely variable. The therapeutic task, therefore, necessitates a special form of attunement and a particular treatment stance and attitude that take into account the not always obvious sensitivities and painful feelings that lie beneath the surface for both child and parent. An understanding of these narcissistic vulnerabilities will better inform the treatment and help to modulate the countertransference feelings that almost always arise. The contributors to this volume, as their detailed case reports show, have demonstrated enormous patience and courage in tolerating the confusion, ambiguity, and chaos that seem to arise when treating a child with a narcissistic disturbance.

Conceptualization of Narcissistic Disorders in Children

Children and adolescents who are suffering from some form of narcissistic disturbance present with major disturbances in areas of self-regulation. These include difficulties in such areas as the regulation of self-esteem, the regulation and modulation of affects, and the regulation of the body and bodily orientation in time and space, among others. A narcissistic disturbance also usually includes strong defenses against significant object relationships, frequently accompanied by illusions of omnipotence and self-sufficiency (Kernberg 1975, Modell 1975, Novick and Novick 1991). But it also includes a deep conscious or unconscious longing for such an (idealized) relationship. This emphasis on self-display and self-sufficiency, which is paradoxically accompanied by longing for an idealized object, has been conceptualized by Kohut (1971) as marking normal phase developments revealed in the mirroring and idealizing transference, or as the overt and covert faces of two varieties of narcissistic disturbance seen in adults (Bach 1985, 1994). These shifts between overemphasis on the self and overemphasis on the other seem to correlate with the disturbances of the normal separation-individuation sequence that Mahler and Kaplan discuss in this volume. Bach (1994) has also described some typical problems associated with narcissistic disorders in adults, many of which are also found in children and adolescents. Some of these are: disturbances of self and object continuity and constancy, disturbances of separation and the sense of separateness, difficulties with the transitions between subjective and objective awareness, and difficulties with contextualizing and taking multiple perspectives on situations. All these writers seem to agree on the apparent lack of empathy and the tendency to enactment in these children and on the strong countertransference feelings that this evokes. Similar difficulties in the parents only compound the problem and may serve as an antidote to one's own narcissistic therapeutic ambitions.

In discussing narcissistic issues in children, we are not necessarily speaking of an established personality disturbance, although in some cases this may be so, but rather of narcissistic concerns that occur on all psychosexual and developmental levels.

In Chapter 1 Joffe and Sandler evaluate disorders of narcissism in children while at the same time extending the theoretical framework to include the concepts of libido distribution and primary and secondary narcissism. They point out how auxiliary concepts have been used either explicitly or implicitly by various authors, including Freud, who used such terms as self-regard, self-love, and narcissistic libido interchangeably. In their opinion, a clinical understanding of narcissism and its disorders should start from the viewpoint of deviations from an ideal state of well-being, in which emphasis is placed on affective and ideational aspects rather than on drive-energies. However, they still regard the instinctual drives as the most potent factors in maintaining or disrupting the ideal state, and believe that the ideational and affective contents of this ideal state are profoundly affected by the sensorimotor components of instinctual wishes. Their definition of a narcissistic disorder includes the existence of an overt or latent state of pain which must constantly be dealt with by the ego. The activities an individual employs that are aimed at coping with or preventing this pain may take the form of seeking narcissistic supplies or overcompensating in fantasy, as well as identifications with idealized and omnipotent figures, pathologically exaggerated forms of narcissistic object-choice, perversions, and so forth. Joffe and Sandler also believe that when these defensive maneuvers fail, the individual is left feeling hopeless and helpless in the face of this pain and may then develop a depressive reaction. This view places depressive reactions within the broad spectrum of narcissistic disorders.

In Chapter 2, Mahler and Kaplan consider the interlocking strands of narcissism, psychosexual development, and object relations in the separation-individuation process. They view each subphase as making its particular contribution to healthy or pathological narcissism, and think that narcissistic reserves continue to be built up by subphase-adequate mothering in the later subphases. They describe the diametrically opposed vicissitudes of infantile omnipotence, body-self love, self-esteem regulation, and self and gender formation in two children, and, by contrasting these children's subphase development, they demonstrate how the assessment of narcissistic and borderline personality disturbance may be anticipated.

In Chapter 3, the Furmans look at a particular type of parental dysfunction which they describe as "intermittent decathexis." This dysfunction is characterized by the parent's interrupted investment in the child at critical developmental periods of the child's life. It may later be manifested by the child's difficulty in forming an integrated body image, and in maintaining a libidinal body investment sufficiently consistent to seek appropriate need fulfillment and to protect itself from harm. One might consider some eating disorders as being rooted in this form of interaction between child and parent.

The Furmans also note serious damage to secondary narcissistic investments of the self. The child's low self-esteem is sometimes warded off by infantile narcissistic overestimation and/or is accompanied by lasting narcissistic rage at the decathecting parent. This in turn interferes with appropriate libidinal distribution between self and objects, handicaps instinctual fusion, and precludes the development of considerate relationships. In children who had experienced this form of decathexis, the Furmans also noted a fear of sudden and total object loss that made it impossible for them to master phase-appropriate physical separations, such as entry into nursery school.

Until recently, many theoretical discussions aimed at defining narcissistic pathology had been centered around the issue of deficit versus conflict. Deficit was usually taken to imply a developmental arrest that would necessitate treatment geared to a holding or corrective emotional experience with the child, while conflict presupposed that the child had reached a level of oedipal development that would allow him to make use of interpretation in the context of verbal or play therapy. But the literature on children with narcissistic pathology often seemed to suggest that unresolved problems of a pre-oedipal nature were predominant, at least initially.

Our tendency to dichotomize these issues seems to be diminishing with the realization that conflict and deficit entail each other and that holding and interpretation need not necessarily be mutually exclusive. So much seems to depend on how we understand these terms and on the clinician's sensitivity that we might well agree with Hamlet: "The readiness is all." How and in what way we hold the child—and how we cultivate and judge the child's readiness for insight—now seem to be the more important issues that engage us. The large number of clinical reports in this volume is intended precisely to demonstrate, along with more theoretical discussion, just how gifted clinicians are going about doing this today.

A related issue and one that at times has also tended to be seen in a dichotomous way is the distinction between the exclusive need for a dyadic relationship versus the capacity to have a triadic relationship, which is generally considered the hallmark of the oedipal phase. In Chapter 4, Edgcumbe and Burgner differentiate between preoedipal and oedipal aspects of phallic development. The phallic phase, although perhaps this is not the best term to describe this particular stage, does hold an important place in any discussion of narcissistic development. In the preoedipal part of the phallic phase, which Edgcumbe and Burgner refer to as the phallic-narcissistic phase, the one-to-one dyadic relationship is still dominant and the real or fantasied use of the genitals to gain the admiration of the object serves primarily narcissistic and exhibitionistic ends. It is in this stage before the oedipal dilemma itself that children are in the throes of coming to terms with the difference between the sexes. They are in a heightened state, greatly needing confirmation of their sense of self and especially desiring affirmation and admiration of their bodies and their gender. This phase is crucial for the building of body-self representations, the processes of identification, and the acquisition of a sexual identity. Children with narcissistic disturbances frequently present with some gender confusion, have difficulties in identification with the same-sex parent, and have a particularly difficult time sharing the object.

This predominance of unresolved narcissistic issues has far-reaching consequences for oedipal development and oedipal resolution. In Chapter 5, Beren suggests that it is an achievement for a child to be able fully to experience the oedipal drama as outlined by Freud, because this presupposes that the child has attained a sense of self. This implies that the child experiences feelings of separateness, autonomy, and effectance, has gained phase-adequate mastery over sexual and aggressive impulses, and has developed certain superego precursors including the capacity for empathy. It also presupposes that the parents have been there as reliable, affirming caretakers who have encouraged and taken pride in the child's developing autonomy, sexuality, and sense of self. When narcissistic issues predominate, these children are instead preoccupied with utilizing narcissistic defenses to deal with fears of separation, loss of autonomy, effectance, and control; they dread the loss of love and admiration, and they are confused about whether they are really loved for themselves.

Adolescence has sometimes been celebrated as a second chance to work through unresolved preoedipal and oedipal issues. Levy-Warren, in Chapter 6, once more draws our attention to adolescence as a period of great transformation. Children derive a good deal of healthy narcissism from their caregiving environment. Adolescents have the task of changing from a primarily outward focus to a primarily inward one in order to achieve a continued sense of healthy narcissism, a difficult task at best. Levy-Warren describes how her male adolescent patient, because of events earlier in his life, did not achieve the self-focus required to meet the challenges of adolescence, so that his healthy narcissistic development was impaired. In her detailed report of the therapeutic process she suggests what was derailed in his earlier development and how the therapeutic relationship offered this young man the second chance that is again possible in adolescence. Her contribution also gives us the opportunity to consider aspects of both healthy and pathological narcissism.

Assessment and Differential Diagnosis

Kohut (1971) first drew our attention to types of transference formed by patients with narcissistic personalities as compared to the transference found in the analysis of neurotic patients. Bene, in Chapter 7, building on Kohut's view that narcissistic disorders imply psychological problems centered on an insufficiently consolidated self and in turn give rise to the narcissistic transference seen in adult analyses, raises the question: Why are so few child treatments reported in which the nuclear pathology is in the realm of narcissism or in a specific developmental failure of the self? She feels that predominantly narcissistic pathology is insufficiently recognized for two reasons. By pursuing the object-libidinal kind of interpretation alone, a narcissistic type of treatment relationship is precluded, so that this kind of pathology is neither allowed full expression nor recognition. Another suggested reason is that the parents of such a child, because of their particularly intense involvement with the child, cannot tolerate the treatment and so prematurely interrupt it.

Beren, coming at this problem from a slightly different vantage point in Chapter 9, observed that certain children who at first glance seem ideally suited to psychoanalytically oriented treatment do not respond in the anticipated manner to the standard therapeutic interventions. Instead, treatment with these children may end in a therapeutic stalemate or fall short of treatment goals despite what appears to be a relatively benign initial diagnosis and a good therapeutic prognosis. These children frequently present the therapist with unusual countertransference reactions such as feeling bored, ineffectual, or doubtful about the usefulness of the treatment. Beren postulates that there are children who present with problems that seem to fall easily into the neurotic range, but that this may be a misdiagnosis. She proposes a set of criteria for the diagnosis of narcissistic pathology and offers suggestions for a particular treatment approach that differs from the interventions used with neurotic children.

Narcissistic Defenses, Enactments, and Countertransference

As one reads the case descriptions in this volume, one becomes cognizant of the emergence of similar concepts, parallel themes, and coinciding characteristics that seem relevant both to the etiology of narcissistic disturbances and to the technical challenges posed by these young patients and their parents. The disturbance of the early object relationship, the ubiquitous utilization of omnipotent and sadomasochistic defenses, the enactments, and the distinctive qualities of the countertransference all play a prominent role in therapy with the child who suffers from a narcissistic disturbance.

Characteristics such as precocious ego development or an early history of unusual sensitivities are not uncommon in a significant number of children with this disturbance. With respect to precocious ego development, it is not unusual to find the parents using the child's particular gifts as extensions of their own narcissism, overly emphasizing achievements while remaining unattuned to their child's emotional needs. Unusual temperamental endowment also places a high demand on the parents, requiring particularly intensive nurturance or devoted parenting to successfully manage the challenges posed by these youngsters. In meeting this challenge, the parents' own level of maturity or their particular unconscious conflicts may also present some difficulties.

Attachment research and mother–infant research have increased our understanding of the importance of the earliest interactions of the dyad in the overall development of object relationships. A "good" fit or its opposite, a "misalliance" in the dyad, may well influence later narcissistic disturbances in the child. In Chapter 10, Parker's detailed account of her psychotherapeutic journey with a 7-year-old boy allows us to compare and contrast her attunement to him with the lack of attunement between the boy and his parents, particularly his mother. Unlike healthy narcissism, in which mother and child feel a mutuality of love, in pathological narcissism there is a sense of misalliance, distrust, and union in pain.

Treatment of this boy became a precarious balancing act in which Parker had the task of creating a safe environment for the child to open up and trust her, while at the same time dealing with the mother's enormous rivalry and envy of her. This case also demonstrates that a child's curiosity and overt preoccupation with sexual fantasies is not necessarily evidence of oedipal phase dominance or oedipal object relationships.

Sloate makes use of the findings from infant research to illustrate the part played by early developmental processes in the formation of pathological narcissism and the genesis of auditory defenses. She proposes that severe disruptions of early object relations, in which mutual affect regulation plays such a central communicative role, may promote a pre-symbolic substructure that predisposes to the pathogenesis of narcissistic disorders. Hearing, like gaze, may then undergo developmental distortions that will later become part of an entrenched defense organization. In Chapter 11, Sloate describes her work with a boy whose treatment began at age 5, at a time when his parents were in the midst of a bitter divorce and custody battle. The treatment, in which audition played a pervasive role in the child's defensive repertoire, resulted in a partial resolution of this boy's severe narcissistic disturbance. The case also illustrates the interactive mutual regulation of the mother–infant dialogue, in this instance as a matrix for masochistic pathology. The mother's words were often a source of narcissistic injury to this child, conveying cruel and emotionally unrelated meanings whose content made no sense within the boy's psychic reality. Hearing her words became an experience of pain and devastation, as opposed to one of joy and acknowledgment as when one is responded to by an emotionally attuned other. The therapist's challenge was to find a way into this boy's world and to become a significant source of meaning for him.

Enactments in the therapeutic process are very much in evidence in almost every case described in this book. Chused's contribution to the subject holds a very important place in our contemporary understanding of the concepts of countertransference and acting out. We have come to accept that enactments are ubiquitous in the analysis of adults, although often very difficult to capture because they occur in the realm of nonsymbolic and nonverbal communication. Child therapists are very familiar with enactments, since so much that transpires in the treatment of children occurs in action and the nonverbal realm. Chused notes this fact in Chapter 13, when she chooses the analysis of a latency-age girl to illustrate the concept of enactment, its profound impact on the analytic dyad, and its overall implications for analytic technique and understanding.

Enactments are defined as symbolic interactions between analyst and patient which have unconscious meanings for both. Enactments occur when an attempt to actualize a transference fantasy elicits a countertransference reaction. The analysis of this latency-age girl revealed many characteristics typical of children with narcissistic disturbance, and the challenge posed to the analyst was to manage the countertransference feelings aroused by the intensity of the child's rage, contempt, and lack of empathy for others. Also seen here, and not unusual in such cases, was the analyst's growing awareness of the parents' contribution to the disturbance by their often inappropriate use of the child. Chused notes too, as many have observed, that the need for therapy is frequently experienced as a profound narcissistic injury, one that poses unusual challenges to the therapist in working with such childen.

The case of a 6-year-old boy described by Shopsin in Chapter 12 highlights Mahler's and Kaplan's discussion of the interlocking strands of narcissism, psychosexual development, and object relations in the separation-individuation process. Shopsin's focus is on the here-and-now relationship between the child and the therapist, and on the particular demands placed on the therapist as she deals with avoidant, grandiose, and omnipotent defenses that are primarily expressed through action. She shows how the child's play does not so much symbolically portray underlying conflicts as graphically actualize these conflicts directly in the relationship with the therapist. In order for the therapy to move forward, the therapist has to find a means of preserving the child's narcissism while at the same time presenting herself as a separate object that the child can gradually tolerate. Understanding the enactments in such a treatment becomes an essential part of the therapy.

The contributions by Chused, Rosegrant, and Frosch in Chapters 13 to 15 are representative of work with children whose narcissistic disturbance is expressed primarily through what Rosegrant calls a perverse play style, which is further characterized by a highly charged anal-aggressive mode of relating to the analyst. In addition, this type of case can also be most challenging because it involves the therapist directly in sadomasochistic enactments.

Bach (1994) has suggested that many narcissistic disorders in adults share a developmental origin in what he calls the anal/depressive/rapprochement/bisexual phase. This is the pregenital phase that includes Freud's anal stage, Klein's movement from paranoia to reparation and whole-object love, Mahler's rapprochement subphase, and the bisexual flux characteristic of this period. Bach notes how in this phase the toddler is first gaining objective self-awareness and the ability to view himself from someone else's perspective, an experience which makes him particularly vulnerable to feelings of shame and humiliation. He suggests that because of these developmental origins, sadomasochism is ubiquitous in the narcissistic disorders (pp. 33–34). This also seems true of narcissistic disorders in children, where omnipotent defenses are a way of dealing both with loss and with unbearable shame and humiliation.

Rosegrant describes how, by means of playing, he enters the anal psychic world of a 6-year-old boy. What he gains from entering into these perverse enactments is an understanding of how this anal world was created as a defense against fears of separation, loss, and castration. Unable to acknowledge sexual and generational differences, the boy strove to eliminate them by pulling the therapist into his regressed anal universe. Rosegrant offers some ideas about what enabled this boy to make gains in his analysis. Initially, he employed the child's anal language—the only language this child could understand at the time he entered analysis. Through this shared language the child felt understood, and was able eventually to develop a positive transference. Rosegrant suggests that their partial mutual enactments were therapeutic because they helped the boy deal with the conflict between his regressive desire to stay in the anal world and his progressive desire to move toward the adult world. The particular mode of interaction between therapist and child gave the boy opportunities to observe that the boundaries between the adult world and the anal world were crossable; if the therapist could step down and then back up again, the boy could also step up.

Frosch begins his chapter with an association between his young patient and Richard III: "deformed, unfinished . . . lamely and unfashionable so that dogs bark at me as I halt by them." Frosch notes Richard's overcompensation: "Since I cannot prove a lover . . . I am determined to be a villain." Richard's mother says of her son: "A grievous burthen was thy birth to me. Techy and wayward was thy infancy." As with Richard, something went awry in the early bond between Frosch's patient and his mother. This boy's mother reported that her milk was "bad" and that she was overly preoccupied with her work when her child was born. Frosch sees this as a metaphor for the mother's lack of libidinal connection to her son and suggests that this failure in infancy and early childhood was met with by a mobilization of aggression on the boy's part. At the time of entering treatment, this latency-age child presented with a full-blown sadomasochistic organization. His primary mode of getting attention from others was through exercising his aggression, both verbally and behaviorally. Like Richard III, if he could not be loved he would at least be feared. Frosch, like Rosegrant, describes a treatment filled with enactments where the principal mode of relating was to engage in a perverse relationship characterized by intimate and highly charged anal-sadistic expressions. Frosch describes his own therapeutic journey as he tries to understand the intense countertransference feelings evoked by the treatment of this child, whose need to humiliate and control him was the boy's only defensive means of staying alive.

Re-reading the papers gathered in this volume, one is struck by the intensity of feeling aroused in these treatments, both on the part of the child and the therapist. The child acts as if his very life were at stake, and he defends himself by any means available. The therapist too seems to get caught in this struggle, but her self-awareness often happily allows her to use this for a therapeutic purpose. The therapist's developing self-awareness seems to elicit the child's self-reflection, and sometimes vice versa. The factors of mutual interaction and regulation seem much more prominent in these cases than they appear to be in the treatment of neurotic children. But this may not be surprising when we recall that dysregulation of the mother–infant dyad has been postulated as one of the probable causes of later narcissistic disturbances.

References

Akhtar, S., and Thomson, J. A. (1982). Overview: narcissistic personality disorder. *American Journal of Psychiatry* 139:12–19.

Bach, S. (1985). *Narcissistic States and the Therapeutic Process*. New York: Jason Aronson.

——— (1994). *The Language of Perversion and the Language of Love*. Northvale, NJ: Jason Aronson.

Freud, S. (1905). Three essays on the theory of sexuality. *Standard Edition* 7.

Kernberg, O. F. (1975). *Borderline Conditions and Pathological Narcissism*. New York: Jason Aronson.

Kohut, H. (1971). *The Analysis of the Self*. New York: International Universities Press.

Modell, A. H. (1975). Narcissistic defense against affects and the illusion of self-sufficiency. *International Journal of Psycho-Analysis* 56:275.

Novick, J., and Novick, K. K. (1991). Some comments on masochism and the delusion of omnipotence from a developmental perspective. *Journal of the American Psychoanalytic Association* 39:307–331.

Rinsley, D. B. (1980). The developmental etiology of borderline and narcissistic disorders. *Bulletin of the Menninger Clinic* 44:127–170.

Rothstein, A. (1979). An exploration of the diagnostic term "narcissistic personality disorder." *Journal of the American Psychoanalytic Association* 27:893–912.

I

Thinking about Narcissistic Disorders in Children and Adolescents

1

On Disorders
of Narcissism

Walter G. Joffe
Joseph Sandler

An increasing amount of attention is being paid in psychoanalysis to the assessment and treatment of "disturbances of narcissism" in both children and adults. While originally the term "narcissistic disorder" was used by Freud (1923) to refer to the psychoses, the term has nowadays come to be used in connection with a much wider field of clinical disturbances, a field that encompasses a variety of conditions reflecting major disturbances in attitudes towards the self and in the regulation of well-being and self-esteem. These disturbances, which include depressive reactions in children as well as adults, show in their pathology not only conflict over drive discharge but also substantial intrasystemic ego disturbance connected with the maintenance of self–object relationships and problems of self-regard and identity.

Thus while we may, for example, assess a child who has problems over exhibitionism from the point of view of neurotic conflict over the discharge of exhibitionistic drive impulses, we also include the consideration of the function of exhibitionism in connection with the maintenance by the child of a particular type of object relationship, and its function as a possible technique for gaining admiration and praise in order to do away with underlying feelings of unworthiness, inadequacy, or guilt. Thus, for example, it is well-known from psychoanalytic work with adults that actors may not only be attempting to sublimate their exhibitionistic impulses in their work. Acting to an audience can also have an important function from the point of view of maintaining an "identity in action," an identification with some "ideal" self-image that may serve the function of defending against an underlying painful ego state, a state that can originate in many different ways.

Hartmann (1950) has pointed out that it is essential to distinguish clearly between ego, self, and personality if we are to examine problems of narcissism within a structural framework: He proposed that narcissism be defined not as the libidinal cathexis of the ego but of the self-representation; in this sense, narcissism could be contrasted with the libidinal cathexis of an object representation (object cathexis). Hartmann's formulation retained Freud's (1914) view that narcissistic libidinal cathexis can be transformed into object cathexis and vice versa. A higher degree of narcissistic (i.e., self) cathexis was seen to imply a lower level of object cathexis and, similarly, an overinvestment of the object representation with libido meant that the amount of narcissistic investment must be correspondingly low.

That there is an assumption of a fixed quantity of libido contained in Freud's original formulation is borne out by the following remark in the "On Narcissism" paper (1914): "We see also, broadly speaking, an antithesis between ego-libido [we would now say libidinal cathexis of the self] and object-libido. The more the one is employed, the more the other becomes depleted" (p. 76).

When we come to apply the concept of libido distribution to clinical material, we find that certain difficulties arise. For example, a child may have intense feelings of inferiority, appear to be very insecure, and show marked dependence on the attitude of his objects for his well-being. From this, one might be tempted to infer that the level of his narcissistic cathexis of his self-representation is low. However, the same child may show a high degree of self-interest and self-preoccupation in one form or another. He may, for example, indulge in many daydreams in which he figures as the hero, he may be concerned about his physical health, and so on. The constant attention that he pays to his objects may be predominantly in relation to the use he makes of them to gratify his need for admiration, support, or praise. Indeed, he may present the features of what is often referred to as a "narcissistic character," and we might accordingly be inclined to assess him, from this point of view, as having a high degree of narcissistic cathexis. We have here an immediate problem if we attempt to encompass these phenomena in terms of the distribution of libidinal cathexis between the child's self and object representations.

The opposite case raises similar problems. We may see a child who appears to be extremely secure, who maintains a basically constant state of well-being in spite of adverse environmental conditions. We might confidently say that he has an adequate and sufficient degree of narcissistic self-cathexis. We might be surprised at any suggestion that such a child's narcissism was depleted. Yet it is usually precisely such children who are capable of more mature types of object relationship, who show consideration, love, and concern for their objects, and who would have accordingly to be assessed as the possessors of a high degree of object cathexis.

We take such clinical states for granted, but if we are to apply metapsychological formulations to the clinical material meticulously, it seems clear that a simple statement of the distribution of libidinal cathexis between self and object representations is at best insufficient for our purposes, even if we allow for the assumption of differences in quantity of libido in different children. We are all, of course, in dealing with the sort of clinical material that we have attempted to subsume under the heading of "disturbances of narcissism," compelled to use what are in fact highly sophisticated qualitative descriptions that are not adequately encompassed by drive-energic formulations. While it is true that dynamic, structural, genetic, developmental, and adaptational considerations are usually taken into account, it is worthwhile exploring the extent to which the concept of energy distribution can remain useful if we extend our theoretical framework.

The first thought that comes to mind is that a distinction between primary and secondary narcissistic cathexis of the self might be of value. We could say, for instance, that if there is a low degree of residual primary narcissism and the quantity of secondary narcissism is high, then this would fit the picture of the insecure and dependent child who may nevertheless be referred to as "narcissistic." However, it must be evident that if such a formulation is to be satisfactorily applied, then additional *qualitative* assumptions are necessary. The inadequacy of a description in terms of a distinction between primary and secondary narcissism in this context becomes clear if we remember that we are dealing with the addition and subtraction of quantities of libido. Once secondary narcissistic cathexis is added to primary narcissism, we cannot, *from the point of view of quantity alone,* differentiate between them. To do so would be as difficult as ascertaining, from the total amount of money in a bank account, how much was derived from capital and how much from income.

What we have said does not mean that there are no differences between the *states* that we call primary and secondary narcissism; of course there are, but they have always been described in terms that are not simply statements relating to energy distribution. Existing psychoanalytic theory certainly does make allowances for qualitative distinctions, and we shall touch on some of these later. For the time being, however, we shall be concerned with rigorously pursuing the "energy-distribution" aspects of narcissism in order to "test the limits" of its application.

It seems possible to make a step forward in the application of the libido distribution concept if we take into account the fact that different aspects of the self-representation—different self-images—can be regarded as being cathected by different quantities of libido. We can conveniently speak in this connection of different *shapes* of the self-representation, and say that the child might invest a high degree of libidinal cathexis in that "shape" that is "ideal" self, and a low amount in that image that is his perception or apperception of the actual state of his self at any time. The same considerations would apply to different images of the object, and we can differentiate between "ideal" and "actual" object representations, the first being assumed to receive a greater quantity of libidinal investment than the second. We are now in a position to apply such a model to the hypothetical cases that were cited earlier. We might say, for example, that the first child has a low degree of libidinal cathexis of his "actual" self-representation, but a high investment in his ideal. Similarly, the representation of his "actual" object might have a low object cathexis, and that of the ideal object may be substantially invested with libido.

Although this may seem at first sight to be a considerable step forward in the application of the energy-distribution concept, the increasing importance in our metapsychology of aggression and of aggressive cathexis must lead us to give it an equal place alongside libido in our consideration of narcissism. Jacobson (1954) has demonstrated very convincingly that the discussion of primary and secondary narcissism must, if it is to be profitable, be considered along with primary and secondary masochism. Primary masochism may be regarded as the very early cathexis of the self with aggression, and secondary masochism the turning of aggressive cathexis from object representations to the self-representation.

If we expand our scheme to include aggression, we would have to take into account that each and every representation of self or object may receive quantities of libidinal and aggressive cathexis. The system of self and object representations must also include ideal selves and ideal objects as well as "actual" self and objects. But this is not all. Kaplan and Whitman (1965) have drawn attention to the role of so-called negative ideals that represent the "introjected negative standards of the parents and of the culture" (p. 183). The "negative ideal" represents the "self-I-do-not-want-to-be." These negative ideals have clearly to be taken into account, but if we do so in relation to quantities of libido and aggression, we may then find ourselves in a position of such complexity in regard to clinical assessment that it would take a mathematician to disentangle us. And even with all this refinement, we cannot be at all certain that we have encompassed more than a small part of the relevant aspects of our clinical material in an adequate theoretical fashion.

It must be abundantly clear by now that concepts that are auxiliary to those of energy distribution must be called upon if we are to account for the state of an individual's "narcissism" in a meaningful way. What we propose to do now is to examine the way in which such auxiliary concepts have been used, either implicitly or explicitly, in the work of various authors. We may begin with Freud who, although he defined narcissism in terms of libidinal investment in 1914, stated at that time that narcissism was the libidinal complement to the egoism of the instinct of self-preservation (p. 74). His descriptions in this connection always involved statements referring to attitudes of what later came to be called the ego as we now understand it. Thus he made statements such as the following: "The libido that has been withdrawn from the external world has been directed to the ego and thus gives rise to *an attitude* which may be called narcissism" (p. 75, our italics).

Throughout his writings, even after the abandonment of the theory of ego instincts, Freud used such terms as "self-regard," "self-love," and "narcissistic libido" interchangeably.

Jacobson, in her valuable paper on "The Self and the Object World" (1954), elaborated the intimate connection between the psychoeconomic processes of narcissism and masochism on the one hand and affective experience on the other. On this basis she goes on to make such statements as: "He is apt to undergo experiences of realistic physical and of mental hurt accompanied by feelings of inferiority which clearly manifest an increasing cathexis of the self-representation with aggression turned away from the love objects" (p. 92). "The rising cathexis of the [whole self] manifests itself in general feelings of increased self-confidence" (p. 94).

In speaking of people who relate well to the object world, she says: "The wide and rich affective scale, the manifold and subtle feeling shades, the warm and vivid emotional qualities . . . point to the predominance of object-libido and the variety of its fusions with more or less neutralized energy" (pp. 96–97).

Jacobson introduced a great many sophisticated ideas into her consideration of narcissism and object love, and she demonstrated unequivocally both in her 1954 paper and in her book (*The Self and the Object World*, 1964) that any attempt to link such concepts as affects, values, self-esteem, and self-devaluation with quantities of energy must indeed be extremely complicated.

Fenichel had, in 1945, made use of the concepts of narcissistic *needs* and narcissistic *supplies* without deeming it necessary to define these in terms of quantities of energic cathexis. Thus he says:

> The full capacity for love not only changes the relations toward other persons but also the relation towards one's own ego. The contrast between object-love and self-love again is a relative one: in primary narcissism there is self-love, *instead* of object-love; in secondary narcissism there is a need for self-love (self-esteem) which overshadows the object-love. With the capacity for object-love another, higher, post-narcissistic type of self-respect becomes available. [p. 85]

As early as 1928, Rado had remarked that frustration during the oral phase lowers feelings of security and the self-esteem of the infantile ego. Bibring took this a step further in 1953 when he equated lowered self-esteem with the ego state of depression.

Fenichel equated self-esteem with self-love, and also defined it as the expression of closeness to infantile omnipotent feelings (1945). Jacobson's formulation was that self-esteem was "expressive of the discrepancy or harmony between the self-representations and the wishful concepts of the self" (1954, p. 123).

Lampl-de-Groot (1936, 1947) drew attention to the importance of maintaining a sufficient level of self-esteem, both for the child and for the adult, and illustrated the way in which threats to self-esteem affect ego functioning.

Annie Reich, in her paper on "Pathologic Forms of Self-Esteem Regulation" (1960) applied Jacobson's definition of self-esteem and demonstrated its usefulness in the understanding of certain types of narcissistic disorder. Her clinical formulations are couched in terms that refer to ego states—ego attitudes and defensive formations.

With all these formulations, we find ourselves, with the authors quoted, unequivocally in the sphere of feeling states of the ego. It would seem that a full understanding of narcissism and its disorders must take into account all that we have learned in psychoanalytic theory—and much that we have not yet learned—about feeling states and their modes of regulation. It is striking that when we come to describe clinical states in which the relationship between self and object is important, we tend to phase our formulations in terms of feelings and attitudes. When, however, we speak of love or hate of an object, or love or hate of the self, and go on to characterize this clinical state metapsychologically in terms of energy distribution, we are certainly in danger of obscuring and blunting both our clinical and theoretical formulations.

Freud was, of course, well aware of this problem, and he attempted to deal with the clinical manifestations of differences between, for example, crude sensuality and tenderness, by postulating a process of aim inhibition of the instinctual drive. Later writers, particularly Hartmann, Kris, Loewenstein, and Jacobson, have also been aware of the difficulties involved and have dealt with it by extending Freud's theory of sublimated or desexualized libido to the aggressive drives as well (Hartmann et al. 1949), postulating degrees of neutralization of drive energies in addition to a primary neutral energy.

In all these approaches there is either the implicit or explicit assumption that feeling states mirror, either functionally or genetically, the cathectic distribution of the various energies.

Consider, for example, the following quotation from Jacobson (1954):

> Hence disturbances of self-esteem may originate from many sources and represent a very complex pathology: on the one hand, a pathology of the ego ideal and of the self-critical ego and superego functions; on the other hand a pathology of the ego functions and of the self-representations. Increase or decrease of libidinous or aggressive discharge, inhibitions or stimulation of ego functions, libidinous impoverishment or enrichment of the self caused by external or internal factors, from somatic, psychosomatic, or psychological sources, *may induce or enhance the libidinous or aggressive cathexis of the self-representations and lead to fluctuations of self-esteem.* [pp. 123–124, our italics]

However, Jacobson has herself pointed out that there are difficulties in the way of linking affects entirely to drive concepts (1953), and it seems likely that the difficulties remain even if we bring neutralized energy into the picture.

We would like to offer, in this chapter, an alternative approach to the problem of "disturbances of narcissism," an approach based on the view that Freud's formulations of the pleasure principle really referred to *two* aspects of the organism's functioning, namely the regulation of energic homeostasis on the one hand, and the various experiences that accompanied this regulation on the other. That there is an intimate link between these two aspects in early infancy is indisputable, but this should not obscure the difference between feelings and instinctual drives. Schur has treated this topic in some considerable detail in a monograph (1967).

From the point of view of the simple biological animal, the principle of energic homeostatis may be useful and adequate. However, from the moment the infant becomes a psychological being, from the moment it begins to construct a representational world as the mediator of adaptation, much of its functioning is regulated by feeling states of one sort or another. The demands of the drives, and the reduction of these demands, have a major influence on feeling states, but they are not the only influence. Feeling states are produced and influenced by stimuli arising from sources other than the drives—for example, from the external environment; and it is an oversimplification to assume that the vicissitudes of the development of affects are a direct reflection of the vicissitudes of the drives.

In addition to his condensation of the energic and experiential aspects of the pleasure principle, Freud did not distinguish pleasure accompanying drive discharge from the state of satisfaction, of well-being, that follows it. The double meaning of the term "gratification" was pointed out years ago by Waelder (1933) when he spoke of the "fatal equivocation resident in the word 'gratification' (Befriedigung)." Waelder, Bühler, Hendrick, Hartmann, and others have also drawn attention to the existence of "function pleasure" and its role in mental activity, and it is difficult to see how this type of feeling experience can be encompassed by a simple pleasure principle.

It must be self-evident that the feeling experiences of even the very young infant include not only feelings of pleasure and unpleasure but also feelings of well-being associated with the somatic states that follow instinctual gratification. While it is true that well-being may be the feeling state that accompanies drive quiescence in the neonate, it is by no means certain that it is equally a reflection of drive quiescence in the older child or adult. While we may link pleasure, unpleasure, and well-being with the state of the instinctual drives in the very young infant, there is evidence that the newborn infant is able to distinguish feelings of pain from the unpleasure associated with unsatisfied instinctual urges. Thus, for example, it has been demonstrated (Lind 1965) that the newborn infant produces a different cry when it is hurt than when it is hungry, and we can perhaps infer that its subjective experience is also different in the two conditions. As the child develops, so its organization of affective experiences becomes increasingly complex and more removed from its actual bodily state.

It is obvious that a formulation such as that of the pleasure principle (and its descendant, the reality principle) cannot alone do justice to the processes whereby these experiential states (we include here both conscious and unconscious experience) are brought about and regulated. For example, it is evident from clinical work with both children and adults that the need to preserve well-being and safety may take precedence over the wish to gain sensual pleasure. The striving for sexual pleasure is, as we all know, readily sacrificed in the interest of preserving feelings of safety. Any attempt to explain all of this as a reflection of the disposition of drive energies within the whole mental apparatus is obviously bound to be unsatisfactory. Feelings, we have suggested, do not only reflect fluctuations in the drives, although genetically there may be a close (but still far from complete) connection.

Freud drew attention to the function of the affect of anxiety as a signal that initiates special forms of adaptive activity (1926), and we believe that there is a strong argument in favor of the idea that all adaptive activity, defensive or otherwise, is instigated and regulated by the ego's conscious and unconscious scanning and perception of changes in its feeling states. We can assume that, from the very beginning of life, the development of the individual is influenced not only by the search for pleasurable experiences and the avoidance of unpleasurable ones. The striving to attain states that embody feelings of well-being and safety is, we suggest, of cardinal importance.

The implication of all this discussion is that we take the view that the states that are important in any consideration of narcissism are not only determined by the state of the drives nor can they be more than partially understood in terms of the hypothetical distribution of energic cathexes. We would suggest that the clinical understanding of narcissism and its disorders should be explicitly oriented towards a conceptualization in terms of a metapsychology of affects, attitudes, values, and the ideational contents associated with these, from the standpoint of both present function and genetic development.

It seems to us that it is possible to approach narcissism and its disorders from the viewpoint of deviations from an ideal state of well-being, in which emphasis is placed on affective and ideational aspects rather than on drive energies, however transformed, modified, or neutralized these may be. And in order to avoid any possible misunderstanding on this point, we wish to make it perfectly clear that we regard the most potent factors in maintaining or disrupting the ideal state to be the instinctual drives, and that the ideational and affective content of what we refer to as the ideal state (or indeed, any other affective state of the ego) are profoundly affected by the sensorimotor components of instinctual wishes.

During the course of development, affective experiences become increasingly integrated with ideational content, and aspects of both self and object representations become linked with affective qualities, often of the most complicated sort. In this connection, the notion of an *affective cathexis* of a representation becomes meaningful and valuable; and affective cathexes can range from the most primitive feelings of pleasure and unpleasure to the subtle complexities of love and hate.

In another work we pointed out that the term "idea," in this context, refers to an affective state of well-being. This was seen as the feeling component linked with primary narcissism, and it was considered that many of the dynamics of ego functioning could be understood in relation to the ego's motivation to preserve the dynamic homeostasis associated with the mainte-nance of a state of well-being. A connection was made with the concept of the representational world, and it was emphasized that the developing child's system of self- and object representations includes both images and affective states.

It follows from this that the state of psychological well-being can be said to exist when there is a substantial correspondence between the mental repre-sentation of the actual state of the self and an ideal "shape" of the self. This formulation is, of course, similar to Jacobson's (1954), although her view is presented in terms of self-esteem. It seems to us that the basic form of unpleasure in disturbances of narcissism is an affective experience of mental pain (Sandler and Joffe 1965). Mental pain, in the sense in which we are using the term, reflects a substantial discrepancy between the mental representation of the actual self of the moment and an ideal shape of the self. Lack of self-esteem, feelings of inferiority and unworthiness, shame and guilt, all represent particular higher-order derivatives of the basic affect of pain. These higher-order derivatives are determined and influenced by the manifold and complex elements that enter into the formation of the ideal self.

At this point we are in a position to make a step toward the definition of narcissistic disorder. We would regard its central feature to be the existence of an overt or latent state of pain that has constantly to be dealt with by the ego; and that the defensive and adaptive maneuvers which are responses to it can assume pathological proportions. The developmental causes of the state of pain may be many and varied, and the major part of the individual's activities may be directed toward coping with it or preventing its occurrence. These activities may take various forms: the so-called seeking of narcissistic supplies, overcompensation in fantasy, identification with idealized and omnipotent figures, pathologically exaggerated forms of narcissistic object choice, the compulsive pseudosexuality characteristic of nymphomania, many aspects of homosexual activity and other perversions, and the like. Various forms of self-punishment may be seen, particularly when superego factors predomi-nate in causing pain. Self-demanding and self-denigrating activities may be sexualized and reinforced by masochistic trends.

If the individual's adaptive and defensive maneuvers fail, and he is left helpless and hopeless in the face of the (conscious or unconscious) state of pain, he may then develop a depressive reaction; this view places the depressions in the wide realm of narcissistic disorders.

Important in all of this is the role played by the particular *values* attached to various representations of the self, and the genesis and pathology of these values. We have suggested elsewhere that enduring and constant attitudes to objects differ from more primitive need-satisfying ones by virtue of the object representations being invested not only with drive-related pleasure and unpleasure cathexis, but also with an enduring affective ego cathexis of *value* (cf. Hartmann, 1939, 1947). By "value" in this connection we do not refer specifically to moral value, but the term is used rather in the sense of feeling qualities that may be positive or negative, relatively simple or extremely complicated. It is these affective values, sign-values so to speak, that give all representations their particular significance to the ego. Thus in studying the narcissistic disorders, we are involved in questions of attitudes to the self that are intimately bound up with the enduring affective value cathexes attached to self- and object representations. Thus the self-representation can be invested with an enduring affective value cathexis of love or hate in the same way as object representations can be; like objects, the self may be ambivalently loved and hated. And these value cathexes can be attached to all the extensions of self and object that the various activities of the individual may come to represent.

References

Bibring, E. (1953). The mechanism of depression. In *Affective Disorders*, ed. P. Greenacre, pp. 13–48. New York: International Universities Press.

Fenichel, O. (1945). *The Psychoanalytic Theory of Neurosis*. London: Routledge and Kegan Paul.

Freud, S. (1914). On narcissism: an introduction. *Standard Edition* 14:69–102.

———— (1923). Two encyclopaedia articles. *Standard Edition* 18:235–259.

———— (1926). Inhibitions, symptoms and anxiety. *Standard Edition* 20:77–175.

Hartmann, H. (1939). *Ego Psychology and the Problem of Adaptation*. New York: International Universities Press, 1958.

———— (1947). On rational and irrational action. In *Psychoanalysis and the Social Sciences*, 1, ed. G. Roheim. New York: International Universities Press.

————— (1950). Comments on the Psychoanalytic Theory of the Ego. *Psychoanalytic Study of the Child* 5:74–96. New York: International Universities Press.

Hartman, H., Kris, E., and Loewenstein, R. (1949). Notes on the theory of aggression. *Psychoanalytic Study of the Child* 3–4:9–36. New York: International Universities Press.

Jacobson, E. (1953). The affects and their pleasure-unpleasure qualities in relation to the psychic discharge processes. In *Drives, Affects and Behaviour*, ed. R. M. Loewenstein. New York: International Universities Press.

————— (1954). The self and the object world: vicissitudes of their infantile cathexes and their influence on ideational affective development. *Psychoanalytic Study of the Child* 9:75–127. New York: International Universities Press.

————— (1964). *The Self and the Object World.* New York: International Universities Press.

Joffe, W. G., and Sandler, J. (1965). Notes on pain, depression and individuation. *Psychoanalytic Study of the Child* 20:394–424. New York: International Universities Press.

Kaplan, S., and Whitman, R. (1965). The negative ego ideal. *International Journal of Psycho-Analysis* 46:183–187.

Lampl-de-Groot, J. (1936). Hemmung and narzissmus. *International Zeitschrift fur Psychoanalysis* 22.

————— (1947). On the development of the ego and superego. *International Journal of Psycho-Analysis* 28:7–11.

Lind, J. (1965). *Personal communication.*

Reich, A. (1960). Pathologic forms of self-esteem regulation. *Psychoanalytic Study of the Child* 15:215–234. New York: International Universities Press.

Sandler, J., and Joffe, W. G. (1965). Notes on childhood depression. *International Journal of Psycho-Analysis* 46:88–96.

Schur, M. (1967). *The Id and the Regulatory Principles of Mental Functioning.* New York: International Universities Press.

Waelder, R. (1933). The psychoanalytic theory of play. *Psychoanalytic Quarterly* 2:208–224.

2

Developmental Aspects in the Assessment of Narcissistic and So-Called Borderline Personalities

Margaret S. Mahler
Louise J. Kaplan

We believe the outstanding feature of narcissistic as well as borderline person-alities is that they do not proceed in the ordinary way through the develop-ment process that culminates in a well-defined Oedipus complex and in neurosis. We agree with Rangell (1972) that the Oedipus complex—the core of neurosis—may be regarded as the fourth psychological organizer. Its shape, resolution, and mode of dissolution can restructure earlier develop-mental events. The Oedipus complex represents the acme not only of infantile psychosexual development but also of object relations. It transforms the previous mainly external regulation of narcissism into internal self-esteem regulation by the superego.

Many of our colleagues have found the symbiosis and separation-individuation frame of reference useful in their work with child and adult patients in general, and narcissistic and borderline patients in particular. Nevertheless, although we have delineated the subphases of separation-individuation and come to some general hypotheses about subphase vulner-abilities, we are increasingly aware of the need to be more precise and detailed in our evaluation of what we call subphase adequacy. Such an extension can only be achieved by consideration of the interlocking strands of narcissism and psychosexual development (Spruiell 1975), in addition to that of object relations of the separation-individuation process. We hope that this broader perspective of the subphase theory will facilitate the assessment of narcissistic and borderline personality organizations.

Eventually it should be possible to determine the progressive subphase adequacy in all three areas of development and in the second half of the third year perhaps gauge whether the preconditions for normal oedipal development and the infantile neurosis prevail. These preconditions entail that self-constancy, that is, individual entity and identity, should be achieved at the end of the rapprochement subphase, in addition to a level of object constancy that facilitates triangular whole-object relations cathected with neutralized libido and aggression. In the psychosexual sphere an emerging and flexible narcissistic genital orientation should be evident. Repression is the main defense mechanism in these important developments.

As we emphasized in the book *The Psychological Birth of the Human Infant* (Mahler et al. 1975), a predominantly observational study of the preverbal and primary-process phases of development, the subphase-related progress in object relations could be fairly reliably studied through its *referents*. These referents were furnished by observation of interactive behaviors of the mother–child unit over the course of time, polarized by the two partners of the dual unit. In contrast to progress in object relations, the building of a cohesive, separate, and whole self-representation is elusive. What the infant feels subjectively eludes the observing eye; that is, behavioral referents are barely existent. We may assume, however, that the earliest perceptions are those of bodily sensations. Freud (1923) described the ego as "first and foremost a body-ego" (p. 27).

What we have in mind then is to consider the subphase adequacy or subphase inadequacy of all three strands of preoedipal development. Consideration of the traditional hierarchic psychosexual stages is implicit in the separation-individuation-subphase theory; here we will stress this issue somewhat more than previously.

As for narcissism, in our observational study and later in our film analyses we noted episodes in which the differentiating 5- to 8-month-old, surrounded by approving and libidinally mirroring friendly adults, seemed electrified and stimulated by this reflecting admiration. We recognized that an important source of narcissistic libido, the quantity and quality of libidinization of the body ego or body self, is dependent upon early narcissistic supplies. These supplies are contributed in the symbiotic phase as well as in the differentiation and early practicing subphases by fueling by the environment. Imbalances in fueling by the environment will be described in our two sample cases.

Each subphase makes its particular contribution to healthy or pathological narcissism; narcissistic reserves are still being built up, to a great extent, by subphase-adequate mothering in the later subphase. *The autonomous achieve-*

ments of the practicing subphase are the main source of narcissistic enhancement from *within*. Most infant-toddlers of the practicing stage show three contributories to narcissism at their peak. These are (in an exaggerated way and in individually different proportions): self-love, primitive valuation of their accomplishments, and omnipotence. During the rapprochement subphase, prior to and dependent on the resolution of the rapprochement crisis, narcissism (particularly omnipotence shaken by the coming of age of representational intelligence) is subphase-specifically vulnerable.

We shall describe below the diametrically opposite vicissitudes of infantile omnipotence, body self-love, self-esteem regulation, and self- and gender formation in two children. These two case studies illustrate what we mean when we speak of the broad spectrum of borderline phenomena. Furthermore, these examples point out the relevance of the subphase hypothesis for the understanding of both borderline and narcissistic phenomena in future investigations.

The sketches of Sy's and Cathy's development have been drawn from *carefully processed*, voluminous observational data of their first three years of life, occasional follow-up material of their nursery and kindergarten and school years, and finally a more systematic follow-up study undertaken at latency age and early adolescence, respectively. We shall not of course regard our project as satisfactorily terminated until we have had the opportunity to analyze two to three children and at least one mother.

Sy

We begin with the subphase developmental history of one of our study children in whom, by the middle of the third year, we already found such severe disorders in all three aspects of the separation-individuation process that we predicted borderline personality development (Mahler et al. 1975, p. 200).

Sy's innate ego endowment was better than average, as our controlled observational data and the developmental tests unequivocally indicated. From his sixth or seventh month until the last quarter of his second year, Sy's life was a saga of daytime attempts to extricate himself from his mother's suffocating envelopment and intrusiveness. During the night, on the other hand, he behaved or was seduced into behaving as the "child-lover at the breast." At 7 to 9 months, when normally the specific bond with mother is at its peak and stranger anxiety appears, Sy strained *away* from his mother's body when she held him.

Sy's slow locomotor maturation complicated matters. Moreover, the mother discouraged every attempt at locomotion as well as other autonomous functions. Phase-specific stranger anxiety was replaced by *stranger preference*. By 12 months of age Sy used his newly emerged ego function of crawling to crawl rapidly away from mother. And if a stranger and mother were to beckon simultaneously, he would unhesitatingly go to the "non-mother." As soon as Sy mastered rapid crawling, Sy's mother redirected his course incessantly—intruding and forcing him to interact with her continually.

Sy had no opportunity to experience the obligatory forms of separation reactions that the other children showed at subphase-adequate times. His differentiation, practicing, and rapprochement subphases were rudimentary and distorted and the subphase characteristics highly confused.

Sy's symbiotic phase pervaded the differentiation process; it interfered with and crowded out the ego-building contributions that the practicing and rapprochement subphases furnish to psychic structuralization. *It was the all-important, almost purely maturational, species-specific emergence of free up-right locomotion, as late as at 17 months, that made Sy suddenly aware that he might suffer object loss.*

The sudden onset of the rapprochement conflict, which Sy experienced without his ego having been prepared for functioning separately (in a clearly delineated practicing subphase), was one of the roots of his deviational development. The absence of a definitive practicing subphase deprived his ego of the capacity to mitigate gradually the impact of his pregenital instinctual drives and deprived him as well of *both* the internal source of narcissism derived from the autonomous ego sphere and the narcissistic enhancement afforded by the normal active, aggressive spurt of practicing.

The period from his seventeenth to twentieth month was a particularly unstable and stormy one. At the beginning of his rudimentary rapprochement subphase, Sy would go to his mother somewhat more often with requests and demands. More often than not his mother completely ignored these requests. At 17 to 18 months Sy refused the breast, and promptly developed a sleep disturbance, which allowed his mother to rationalize the reintroduction of her dried breast—a "giant pacifier." At the same time the need for mother increased. Sy clung to her after each nap, cried in the morning, and continued to have difficulty in falling asleep.

By his twentieth month, whatever relation Sy had developed to the object world at large became actively split off as all "bad." He became aggressive to the other children and suspicious toward those at the Mother–Infant Research Center who were previously his friends. Up to then he had been fairly exuberant and trusting. Now he became somber, depressed, and moody.

From the moment he weaned himself, Sy's separation-individuation process was corroded in all three areas previously cited by his excessive castration anxiety, which later amounted to mutilation anxiety. This anxiety was so overwhelming because his ego did not experience the obligatory and normal subphase-adequate fears of object loss, stranger anxiety, separation anxiety, and fear of loss of the object's love at subphase-adequate times. In the psychosexual sphere anal concerns and severe castration anxiety overlapped. Such overlapping was augmented by massive, visual exposure to the sexual organs of nude men, his father's included, in the locker room. At the same time, Sy was permitted to perceive in equally traumatic proportion sights that brought home to him, out of phase, the danger of castration. He would go to urinate in the bathroom but instead would masturbate. He was unable to sit down for fear that his feces, and possibly his penis, would be flushed away. His predilection to expose his penis and frequent utterances, such as "nice penis," "you nice people," indicated, among other signs, the precocious onset and prolonged adherence to the narcissistic-phallic phase of libido development.

The father's dictum was: a baby belongs to the mother as long as he wants her breast. As soon as the son rejects the breast he belongs to the father. Sy's castration anxiety increased significantly in his third year when Sy's father took him over, body and soul. The father duplicated the mother's overstimulation of the first two years. The father's behavior was described thus: "He at once threatens and cajoles, manhandles and caresses, slams about and seduces Sy. When the father's rage reaches a peak, he switches to seductive kissing and tickling. The whole thing is sadistic, sexualized, and hysterical." At the birth of his brother in Sy's thirty-fourth month his mother was in the hospital for a prolonged stay and his father was his only caretaker. Sy was in a frenzied, panicky state. He talked incessantly in gibberish, expressing primary-process ideation.

By age 4, Sy had turned violently against his mother and emulated his father's degrading of her. He totally rejected her in his attempt to become big and manly like his father. Sy began to vomit food his mother wanted him to eat and developed an eating problem. During Sy's struggle with identification with father, he turned all his crude aggression against his mother—kicking and biting and shouting at her. In the midst of this turnabout in Sy's fifth year, another fateful traumatization occurred. Sy's father exchanged him for his younger brother, who was at the very age at which the father had taken Sy over from the mother. Whereas Sy had been aggressive, elated, and rather manic in nursery school, now at kindergarten age everybody noticed that the sparkle in his eye was gone. Sy turned once again to his mother and became her quasi satellite, in an anxious but subdued alliance against the younger brother and father.

Sy's subphase developmental history was characterized by prolongation up to his twentieth month of the nocturnal "child-lover-at-the-breast" symbiosis. This, without more than a nominal experiencing of the practicing and rapprochement subphases of separation-individuation, was overlapped by and continued as a bizarrely frank oedipal relation with his mother and later with his father.

From the time he weaned himself and walked, Sy was treated by the mother as her "man," with reciprocal behavior on his part. It is a demonstration *in statu nascendi* and step by step of what Kernberg (1967) describes as the genetic-dynamic analysis of the borderline personality's Oedipus complex. He says: "What is characteristic of the borderline personality organization . . . is a specific condensation between pregenital and genital conflicts, and a *premature* development of oedipal conflicts. . . ." (p. 678).

We could follow, in the second part of Sy's third as well as in his fourth, fifth, and sixth years, the vicissitudes of the failure of the ego's function of normal repression. There were many instances of this failure, but for lack of space we cannot elaborate on them. An example might suffice: Sy remembered minute details about the Center, which the other children had completely repressed. These details were syncretically retained by his ego's pathological memory function.

Sy's behavior at times seemed a caricatured emulation of his mother; at other times he seemed a bizarre diminutive replica of his father. Instead of repression, the extensive splitting operations described by Kernberg resulted in a morbidly combined father–mother image. There was hardly any opportunity for his ego to identify selectively with desexualized and deaggressivized paternal or maternal traits. We observed an unusual confusion between the paternal images and dissociation and lack of neutralization of his erotic and aggressive impulses.

It is very difficult to conceptualize Sy's ego ideal or his identifications and self-representation. The unassimilated introjective identification of part images of mother and father was predominant at the expense of transmuting internalization.

We believe that the positive qualities that saved Sy from psychosis were his excellent endowment, for example the way in which he made up for his slow locomotor development by becoming extremely proficient in gymnastics (his favorite activity was acrobatics). From material gained from him, his mother, and teacher, one can surmise that Sy liked to be away from home. He was the least homesick when the class went to camp. The mother also told of times when Sy did not come home from school but went to his teacher's house instead. He had obviously succeeded in creating an island for himself where his ego developed without constant intrusion and interference by his disorganized, disorganizing, and aggressive environment.

Sy's intrapsychic conflicts can be only guessed at, of course, and we would like to get Sy into analysis, but both parents are opposed to it.

Follow-up home and school interviews of Sy in his eleventh year described him as faring much better than we would have predicted. His academic achievement in an honors class in a local public school is excellent and he is fairly popular with his classmates. The teachers, however, could not suppress their irritation with Sy and his family. They described Sy as a fresh, sexually precocious child who bragged and engaged in disruptive, exhibitionistic clowning and crudely inappropriate sex talk. Moreover, the teachers felt that the parents overestimated Sy's creative and intellectual potential, very often insisting that he be treated specially.

The psychological tests, which were administered without knowledge of the follow-up interviews or the early developmental history, revealed a diagnostic picture of borderline personality organization at the lower level of the borderline spectrum. When tested, Sy's characteristic posture was hunched over and limp, as though his body were totally devoid of muscle tone. He handled the examiner's test materials in a way that suggested that he was appropriating and possessing them—but without active intentionality. In his passivity there was a decided blurring of the boundaries between yours and mine.

Even though Sy's behavior betrayed no signal or social anxiety, he was apparently in a *state of overwhelming anxiety*. The palms of his hands would sweat profusely, leaving moisture on everything he touched. His hands would shake and he looked helpless and vulnerable. Alternately, Sy was often able to pull back and take an active, more rationally bound view of reality. At these times his body was firmly erect and alertly mobilized. His mental functioning also improved and toned up. He concentrated actively and sharpened his previously vague responses. He then smiled happily and even tried to show off.

Such unpredictable alternation in affect states, body posturing, and modes of responding typified Sy's Rorschach responses. Most often, Sy would be pulled into the cards—his loss of distancing was prominent. Repeatedly he would confuse his inner bodily feelings with external perceptions. He yawned, for example, and then said the wolf on the card was tired. Now and then he would project his impulses and then become inundated by the anxiety aroused by his own projections. He experienced the projected impulse simultaneously with the fear of the impulse. Primitive denial and externalization were prominent defenses. Notably absent during the testing were any indicators of shame or guilt and there was very little signal anxiety—only overwhelming primitive anxiety.

When Sy is able to extricate himself, put distance between himself and the stimuli of external reality, he is able to maintain fantasy-reality distinctions. Secondary-process thinking and logic were evident in many of Sy's responses, although it was abundantly clear that his mode of thought organization was subject to easy regression.

In his eleventh year, Sy's good basic endowment has allowed him to extricate himself and create distance, analogous to the way he actively pushed, crawled, and turned away from the engulfing mother–child symbiosis—and thereby escaped outright psychosis. Nevertheless, the prolonged symbiosis has cast its shadow over all future subphases of separation-individuation. It continues as a grossly erotic, overly aggressivized, out-of-phase oedipal constellation which has left an indelible stamp on Sy's body representations.

On the tests, the ego-inundating nature of Sy's castration anxiety was apparent in his body-mutilation fantasies and the fragmented quality of his body representations. Moreover, in Sy's perceptions body parts merged with one another, were interchangeable with one another, and were in fact interchangeable with the inanimate objects of reality.

Cathy

By way of contrast, we will briefly describe the separation-individuation process of Cathy, a child whose development proceeded along more or less neurotic lines, but who at 13 showed signs of a narcissistic disturbance.

Cathy joined our project at 12 months of age. She immediately conquered our mother–infant room with her spectacular self-assurance and verbal precocity, without the slightest "stranger" and "strangeness" reactions. Her mother—a somewhat colorless, depressive woman—seemed to enjoy Cathy greatly as the narcissistic, glamorous extension of "her self."

Cathy had mastered walking by 11 months. Her exuberance, however, did not include the usual abandon and daring observed in other children in the practicing subphase. Cathy's much praised and encouraged "independence" had been bought at the expense of bodily closeness, that is, libidinal supplies of her body self. Mrs. C., who stressed that Cathy was not a cuddly baby, never picked her up except for brief comforting followed by distraction tactics.

At around 19 months Cathy's mood definitely deteriorated. Mrs. C. complained about Cathy's crying, temper tantrums, and often incomprehensible behavior. Her toilet training had been uneventful and she was practically trained by 19 months without coercion. The mother, however, complained, "She doesn't want me to touch her, to dress her, to put her on the toilet, although she will let others do so." We felt that at this point a "bad" and dangerous maternal part representation was actively split off from the "good object representation." We may also assume that Cathy's moodiness indicated dissociation of aggressive and libidinally invested part-self representations.

We watched our radiant, narcissistic "queen-bee" of the nursery become — intermittently — a petulant, hard-to-understand, and for the moment very aggressive little girl. Not only were we faced with a full-fledged rapprochement crisis, but with a sudden and abrupt collapse of Cathy's omnipotent grandeur. Only many weeks later were we able to piece together the events that culminated in this intense and prolonged rapprochement crisis. Between her sixteenth and eighteenth month Cathy often visited a little boy from the nursery. One day this boy's mother bathed the two children together and Cathy came home declaring that the little boy had *two* belly-buttons.

Six to seven weeks after Cathy's discovery of the anatomical sex difference she became extremely aggressive, pulling the hair of other children in our nursery. The mother recalled that when she took Cathy into the shower to facilitate washing her long, fine hair, Cathy pulled at her mother's pubic hair. *Cathy's desperate search for a penis was quite clear.* Disturbances of both sleep and toileting followed. We felt that Cathy's aggressive provocativeness represented a demand to her mother to make amends for her anatomical shortcoming (even at 27 months of age she asked for a penis for Christmas!).

At 2½ years Cathy briefly wanted mother, father, and herself all to be together. We thought this was to be the beginning of a true phallic-oedipal relation. Cathy, however, soon preferred exclusive dyadic relations, vacillating between selection of *either* father *or* mother. From then on and throughout her second to fifth year, Cathy alternated between weakly energized forays into a triadic relation which included both the mother and the father and frantic claims for exclusive dyadic relations.

Also at 2½ Cathy attempted to give up the bottle, but was unsuccessful.

Her mother declared that "the bottle was the only thing that Cathy was really attached to." Her overestimation of her transitional object—the bottle—betrayed a certain pathology, in Winnicott's (1953) terms. From her third year on, Cathy required a mirroring, exclusively dyadic relation in order to maintain her ideal state of self. The search for shifting dyadic relations became a major theme in Cathy's life.

When Cathy entered nursery school at 3, she turned with her unspecific object hunger to the nursery-school teacher as a mother substitute—entwining her, seeking her exclusive attention. A crisis soon occurred involving child, mother, and teacher. Unable to cope with Cathy's intense need for exclusive attention, the teacher sent her home to her mother. Mrs. C.'s reaction was one of angry depression directed toward the teacher and also toward her own daughter. Cathy, as never before, clung to her mother's body—clutching her thighs. Mother extricated herself by angrily pushing her off. Cathy responded to this dual rebuff by engaging in compulsive talking to an imaginary audience from whom she anticipated mirroring admiration. It was as though Cathy were trying to recapture the ideal state of self she experienced in her twelfth to nineteenth month when she was the omnipotent "queen bee" of the nursery. Even though Cathy's clinging behavior declined, we felt that Cathy had abandoned hope rather than resolved the rapprochement crisis. We believe that the ambivalently loved, needed and hated object, who regarded herself and Cathy as failures, was at this point split off and externalized, in favor of an internally retained, differentiated, negatively cathected self-representation.

Cathy's later school experiences continued to be disappointing. She hated school and at 6 declared that the children hated her and would not play with her. From her sixth year on Cathy blamed her mother for all the ills of her life, calling her "the worst mother in the world."

In Cathy's seventh year an interview with the father revealed a complex and ever-worsening sadomasochistic relation between his wife and Cathy. He said, "They are more like sisters than a mother and daughter." He also felt that Cathy often daydreamed. He thought it quite natural, however, that Cathy, like daughters in general, should be closer to her mother than to her father.

The outstanding impression conveyed by follow-up interviews, school and home visits when Cathy was 13 was her sense of her personal inadequacy and low self-esteem. Although her full-scale IQ was 134, her school achievement was in the B minus to C range.

When Cathy was tested her voice was barely audible and she tried to keep her head positioned so that her hair would cover her face. The omnipotent, self-assured, exhibitionistic toddler had become an adolescent who seemed to want to disappear. Whereas the follow-up testing of Sy revealed some of the inner dynamics of borderline personality organization, in the personality picture of Cathy at 13 we recognized what is typically called obsessive-compulsive personality organization. *Repression* was evident and the additional defenses of reaction formation and isolation were well maintained without evidence of decompensation. Her excessively exalted ego ideal led to easy self-devaluation and to continuing prominence of anxiety and shame. Nevertheless, in contrast to Sy, the affect of guilt was the major regulator of instinct defense activity. Overwhelming panic and diffuse anxiety did not replace *signal anxiety*.

Cathy perceived bodies as hidden, blocked in action, slouched down, and trapped. These images represented her basically *masochistic* orientation. In hindsight we can now hypothesize that these hidden and trapped bodies echoed Cathy's ungratified longings for bodily libidinal supplies during practicing and rapprochement. In turn, the sudden shattering of her omnipotence—her desperate demands for the undoing of her anatomical shortcoming—added to Cathy's growing predisposition to disparage herself and her femininity.

Whereas Sy's body image was distorted, fragmented, and confused with the inanimate, Cathy's body image was intact and well bounded. Nevertheless, Cathy's self-image, her dissatisfaction with herself and with her feminine gender identity was evident. She was disappointed in herself and expected disappointment and defeat in her relations with others.

In Sy we noted perilous regression and the disorganization of secondary-process thinking by condensations and contaminations. Cathy's reality testing was excellent. However, even temporary regressions were forbidden and when things were not "just so" she gave up rather than taking the chance that she might be wrong.

In Cathy's case, we believe that neither the overidealized and overidealizing, all-good, admiring mother-image nor the grandiose, omnipotent ego ideal were gradually adjusted to reality. The infantile self-object image was never cut down to size so that the real mother would be able to match that image. Nor did the ego ideal become reconciled with the realistic potential of Cathy's autonomous actual self-image.

The characteristic and unique feature of Cathy's struggle was her seeking substitutions in the outside world in order to approximate the highly overestimated, exceptional, and exclusive self-object representation unit. She sought these substitutions in dyadic relations that would match the idealized self-object image of her longed-for omnipotent past.

Cathy's mother's inability to provide a balance of libidinally satisfying, intermittent body closeness and to recognize Cathy's hunger for physical contact during practicing led to an intensification of the splitting mechanisms which characterized Cathy's rapprochement period. The narcissistic reserve, which might have enabled Cathy to overcome later narcissistic hurts, was depleted on two fronts during practicing. The excessively exalted ego ideal and the absence of practicing phase-specific libidinal refueling laid the groundwork for inflexible ego ideal and superego structures which would not allow for an adaptive tolerance for ambiguity and ambivalence. Furthermore, during rapprochement itself, Cathy's coercive wooing behavior was once again rebuffed by her mother. But, although Cathy was not prepared to experience a fully developed oedipal constellation, we know that some aspects of an advanced oedipal solution were achieved. This solution was character-ized by a repression of the instinctual preoedipal and oedipal strivings. Cathy's narcissistic grandiosity was replaced by masochistic self-disparagement, but whole-object relations remained dominant, even though there seemed to be a potential for homosexual development.

Conclusions

Our aim in this brief presentation was to adumbrate the explanatory power that full utilization of the symbiosis and the separation-individuation-subphase theory contributes to the assessment of later personality organiza-tion, provided its complexities are taken into account. Rather than presenting a coordinated system of subphase-related failures in one subphase of the separation-individuation process with a corresponding specific form of nar-cissistic or borderline personality organization, we have tried to avoid over-simplification and closure.

In our assessments of the personality organization of narcissistic and borderline child and adult patients, the overriding dominance of one sub-phase distortion or fixation must not obscure the fact that there are always corrective or pathogenic influences from the other subphases to be considered. In Sy's case, for example, the luxuriation of the symbiosis prevented later subphases from making their specific *positive* contributions to personality development. In practicing, Sy was deprived of the internal source of narcis-sism derived from the autonomous ego sphere as well as the shaping influence of the normal aggression spurt. At the same time the age-appropriate separate self- and body awareness of rapprochement was inundated by castration anxiety and overstimulation of fantasy life. The distorted nature of Sy's oedipal constellation cannot be understood merely from the perspective of the symbiotic phase.

In Cathy's case the rapprochement theme of the search for exclusively dyadic relations to mirror her lost ideal state of self predominated. Yet the specific shape of Cathy's oedipal resolution cannot be adequately understood unless we include the dramatic imbalance in which Cathy's exalted omnipotence was not matched by the necessary body-libidinal supplies to her narcissism during the symbiotic, differentiation, and practicing subphases.

References

Freud, S. (1923). The ego and the id. *Standard Edition* 19:12–66.

Kernberg, O. (1967). Borderline personality organization. *Journal of the American Psychoanalytic Association* 15:641–685.

Mahler, M. S., Pine, F., and Bergman, A. (1975). *The Psychological Birth of the Human Infant*. New York: Basic Books.

Rangell, L. (1972). Aggression, Oedipus, and historical perspective. *International Journal of Psycho-Analysis* 53:3–11.

Spruiell, V. (1975). Three strands of narcissism. *Psychoanalytic Quarterly* 44:577–595.

Winnicott, D. W. (1953). Transitional objects and transitional phenomena. *International Journal of Psycho-Analysis* 34:89–97.

3

Intermittent Decathexis—
A Type of Parental Dysfunction

Robert A. Furman
Erna Furman

For many years now, the Cleveland group of child analysts has been using the concept of a particular type of parental dysfunction, best described as intermittent decathexis of the child by his parent. This has proven to be a helpful concept which, although reported in prior publications by one of the authors (E. Furman 1975, 1978), has not as such been the subject of a paper, at least to the best of our knowledge. Anna Freud (1967) did address one aspect of what we wish to consider at length here.

It would seem appropriate to introduce the topic with the clinical examples that served as our introduction. A number of years ago a young latency boy was in analysis who could be characterized as having deviant ego development, a child we would call "atypical." By "atypical" we mean, descriptively in this instance, that he presented a mixture of ego defects, such as in reality testing and cognitive functioning despite a normal intellectual endowment, defects not comprehensible within the framework of typical development, defects that coexisted with neurotic conflicts, represented by such symptoms as night fears and enuresis. While he attended the Hanna Perkins Nursery School he was described by his teachers as "constantly out of touch, always on 'cloud nine.'" When he could be engaged, he was insatiable in his demands for attention. Reality testing, simple verbalization of feelings, peer relating, all lagged well behind age-appropriate expectations. When he received a gift from his teachers for his sixth birthday, during the first year of his analysis—a set of rubber stamps for making various pictures—he opened the package and put the stamps in his mouth one by one. When asked what he was doing, he replied, "I am looking at them."

A striking characteristic of his during his analytic hours was to stand very close to his analyst and with his hands take the analyst's head and turn it so that they were in direct eye contact. He stood so close that, with the analyst's emerging presbyopia, it became hard to focus clearly on him. No explanation could dissuade him from his behavior and no efforts at its understanding were successful. When his mother was asked about it, she initially had no insight to assist in its elucidation.

One day his father was questioned about this behavior. He understood at once and explained it. He said his wife had a peculiar characteristic in that, unless she was looking directly at you and talking with you, you could never be sure she was paying any attention to you. "If I want to ask her something or tell her something and she is, for example, reading the paper, I go and take the paper out of her hands and sit in front of her to talk. If I don't do this, she will respond as if she had listened to me but it will soon turn out she had not heard a word I said."

When this new observation was shared with the mother, she immediately confirmed it and told a painfully poignant story—painful to the listener, more puzzling or interesting to her as a description of a particular trait of hers. When the patient was but 18 months old, she gave a rather large evening party on behalf of some friends, inviting many people whom she did not know. About 10:00 P.M. the doorbell rang and she opened the door to be greeted by a stranger she assumed was yet another of her guests she did not know. It took her some moments to understand what he was trying to tell her. He was explaining that he had found a toddler in pajamas wandering the sidewalk in front of her house. He had been driving by and had stopped to try to help the child, and was wondering if she knew where the boy lived. Only at this point did she see the child whose hand the man held. "Would you believe that at first I did not even recognize my own son? I was so absorbed in the party, I just did not see or recognize him."

It should be noted that this was not a clinically depressed woman. She always seemed warm and appropriate in her contacts with her child as these had been observed at our school.

It should also be noted that during the boy's analysis his "constant need for attention" was stressed by all his subsequent teachers and could be understood in relation to his mother's problem. His withdrawals to "cloud nine" also became more clear as a combination of an identification with his mother and a passive-into-active defense, decathecting others as she had him, as well as a now internalized attitude to himself. This was demonstrated in a withdrawal of self-investment and self-awareness which showed in an inability to keep himself safe—he endured many accidents and self injuries—and in an inability consistently to cathect his various ego functions. Analytic understandings that could lead to improvement in reality testing or a wish to learn at school, for example, rarely led to permanent gains as they could simply disappear without warning in response to some small stress.

At the same time a young adolescent was in analysis who had a period of reluctance to leave the office during his hours to make occasional trips to an adjoining bathroom. The discomfort he felt some mornings as a consequence of his apparent inhibition finally served as the impetus to analyzing the difficulty. It turned out he was afraid that if he left the room the analyst would forget what they had been talking about, might in fact just totally forget him. As he put it, "Out of sight, out of mind." This could then be traced as a transference reaction to his father, who could forget a promise moments after a separation, could even forget his son when the boy accompanied him on routine business trips. Coming back to the car, he would be surprised to find his son there, apparently having totally forgotten the boy who had been waiting, sometimes for well over an hour.

These examples of parental dysfunction can be contrasted with many instances of the more usual parental functioning of uninterrupted investment in a child. Many mothers express this when they say, "Go see what the children are doing and tell them to stop." Though the children are out of sight, the mother's investment in them has never wavered and a change in sound pattern or an absence of sounds from them indicates a need for closer scrutiny and supervision. Recently one of us had to interrupt a kindergarten class to have a few words with the teacher, then responsible for a group of about five youngsters. As we talked and she was fully involved in the conversation, her eyes focused on her visitor, she calmly and clearly said, without turning her gaze, "John, come down off the bookcase. You know that is not for climbing on. We'll be going outside in just a few minutes." John, who had been out of her direct line of vision, was heard to mutter, "Gee, she's got eyes in the back of her head!"

In her lecture to the medical students at Case Western Reserve many years ago, Anna Freud (1953) gave a lovely example to explain to the predominantly young male audience how a mother's investment in her infant operates. She likened it to a young man's investment in his car. Sounds which have no meaning to another, are not even heard by another, are immediately perceived by the young driver without his consciously listening for them and are recognized at once as indicative of the functioning of the automobile.

A few years ago there was a consultation with the director of a day care center who wished to review her decision to discharge a teacher. She described that the teacher in question left the classroom for her breaks by the clock, regardless of what was going on with the children. The group was always least in control when she was in charge. When the concept of decathexis was explained to the director, she was immediately relieved, not just to understand the shortcoming of this particular teacher, but to have conceptualized one of the cardinal attributes that she knew she was always seeking in hiring new staff: the ability to maintain constant investment in the children for whom that staff was responsible.

Constant investment in one's children is simply taken as a given by most parents. With older children it leads parents to call home at the appointed hour, often without checking their watches, to make certain a teenager is home safely from an evening's outing; or never to forget for a moment the child away at college who, in a last letter or phone call, had reported a minor illness or a difficult exam just ahead.

The ability of parents to maintain a constantly available investment in their children varies widely. It may be helpful to think in terms of a spectrum. At one end parents are anxiously preoccupied with their children; theirs is an unhealthy investment, deleterious to the child's development. At the other end of the spectrum would be parents unable to enter the developmental phase of parenthood (E. Furman 1969), unable to invest in their children, causing the child severe deprivation. Between these extremes are those parents who by and large enter the developmental phase of parenthood and invest themselves in their children. Their parental investment may, however, be subject to various forms of interference. One such, namely intermittent, near-total decathexis, is the form we have been describing.

What causes this dysfunction? How is the phenomenon to be explained? Are we correct in our characterization of it as decathexis? Is this a psychoanalytically sound designation? What are the effects on the developing child of being decathected? To seek answers to these questions we would like to explore the relationship of decathexis to depression and to aggression first, then discuss its manifestations in adult analysis, before contrasting the phenomenon we are presenting with more familiar examples of decathexis.

One of our first insights into the relationship of decathexis to depression came from a nursery school girl of 3 whose mother had recurrent episodes of depression which were manifest to the child in periods in the afternoon when the mother would become physically inactive, lying down on her couch at home to rest. One day at school the children were describing what they were going to do at home that afternoon. The little girl in question said that she would "lie down with my Mommy to be with her in her sadness." Our work with this mother showed that she was emotionally available to her daughter, and did not decathect her, although the nature of their relationship had an unhelpful effect on the little girl's development.

This offered a contrast to the little boy described at the start of this chapter who was in analysis at about the same time and whose mother did decathect him but who did not have a discernible depression. We had always heretofore assumed that when a mother was depressed, she would withdraw from her child, and that this was perhaps the main pathogenic factor in a mother's depression. Such obviously is not always the case. Our conclusion was that a decathexis of her child was a frequent but not universal component of a maternal depression and could exist all on its own without a depression (E. Furman 1975).

Such thinking was recently confirmed by an adult analysand, well familiar with what she called her mother's "being disconnected" at times of depression. She had described one day her husband's "depression about his work," a sad, worried and somewhat helpless state of preoccupation that resulted from recent frustrations and reversals at work. She told of complaining to him about household and family matters and of getting no response. The analyst interjected here that such behavior must have painfully recalled the times of her mother's being "disconnected" when depressed. "Oh, no," was the response. "You see, when he is depressed, he never disconnects. Within half an hour he came upstairs with a cup of tea for me, said he had been thinking about the troubles I had told him about and sat down and discussed them. His depressions are different. He never disconnects in his, whereas Mother always did in hers. They feel and are totally different."

The relationship of decathexis to aggression is a bit more complex, but perhaps helpfully so. Analyses of children and adults who were decathected have shown that being treated as nonexistent constitutes a major narcissistic injury. This can engender fury in the decathected person and lead him to attribute an aggressive intent to those who decathect him. An adult male analysand, recurrently decathected by his mother as a child, had periods himself as an adult parent and spouse of what he characterized as "withdrawals." These his wife complained about as manifestations of his aggression. Analysis revealed that on one level she was correct: that he could withdraw when he was furious. First he became aware that he withdrew to protect the objects of his wrath, later we learned that his withdrawals could also express anger, as he abandoned the objects of his fury as a means of demonstrating his displeasure with them.

At other times analysis revealed that his wife's complaints were not valid, in that episodic periods of decathexis could be unrelated to his aggression. His wife, of course, was at these times still abandoned, felt this to be an expression of his anger, and was furious in turn, and it is quite possible some projection found a ready niche here. What was so instructive in these latter instances was the analysand's lack of awareness of these times when he was decathecting, which had not been so true when the mechanisms had been in the service of his aggression. Now, instead, we would have vague complaints about periods of loneliness, reports of his wife's displeasure coming days or weeks after the event. He was just unable to report the episodes immediately on their occurrence and his usually excellent self-observing function was apparently not operative. Another adult analysand, almost simultaneously dealing with the same problem, supplied the answer: "How can you expect me to report to you, even though I so much want to do so, those times when I respond to people as if they weren't. I don't know when I am doing it. If I did know, I would not be doing it. That is just the problem. When I treat people as a 'nothing,' there is nothing to report." This was a most helpful insight, leading to a more active pursuit of the phenomenon in adult analyses, beginning with a more tenacious seizing of these reports, so often fleetingly given, that "others say I am so withdrawn."

Another aspect of the relationship of decathexis to aggression was reported by an adult in analysis who described his mother's dreaded "icy stare" which was followed, if he did not humble himself to her at once, by her closing her eyes, looking away and then not speaking to him or acknowledging his existence until her anger had abated. In frequent angry arguments between his parents they could go for days ignoring each other, not speaking to each other, both pretending the other did not exist.

This is not too unusual a way for aggression to be demonstrated, although one is struck at once with a certain lack of maturity in this particular mode of expression. We believe this is a simulated decathexis, a consciously instigated one, that differs from the instances of decathexis as a parental dysfunction which is an unconscious process, one not necessarily related to aggression.

In relation to aggression, therefore, it would appear that a form of decathexis can be used as a consciously utilized mechanism of discharge or as an unconscious defense against aggression or as an unconscious expression of aggression. The parental decathexis we are describing is not intrinsically related to aggression. Rather, as with depression, decathexis may appear as if closely associated with aggression or appear totally separate and on its own.

Understanding the adult analysands' great difficulty in observing their decathecting served as a helpful start to clarify what had been a puzzle to us: why our introduction to parental decathexis had come from child analysis. A child who is the object of an active, ongoing decathexis manifests this in his emotional response and/or in the symptoms which can be traced to it. An adult primarily manifests his having been decathected by his parents by decathecting as a parent, and is unable to observe this in himself in its active manifestations. There is, however, also another explanation for the puzzle. In the initial example reported of the 6-year-old analysand, it was mentioned that he had internalized his mother's attitude to him by decathecting himself and some of his functions which contributed significantly to the severity of his pathology. Several other child patients' serious personality disturbances proved to be similarly related to extensive parental decathexis. When a factor plays such a major part in the etiology of a disturbance and leads to such striking manifestations in personality functioning, it is easier to pick up in the analytic work. All these child patients were so ill that as adults, without prior treatment, they would never have achieved the position in life to enable them to manage an analysis.

Once we had become aware, however, of the phenomenon of parental decathexis, we could more readily appreciate its presence and effect in patients—children and adults—who suffered less severely from decathexis and did not sustain such serious and widespread damage to their personalities. It appeared that sometimes these patients could utilize the analyst's constant availability and investment as a present force to assuage any sense of decathexis, even some of its present manifestations, while the analysis was ongoing. Let us therefore describe first the marked effects of parental decathexis in the severely disturbed children and then the more subtle indications of its presence in the adults.

In some child patients the effect of decathexis manifested itself primarily in a difficulty in forming an integrated body image and in maintaining a consistent sufficient libidinal investment in it to protect themselves from harm and to seek appropriate need fulfillment. Serious damage to secondary narcissistic investment of the self was another striking outcome. The patients' low self-esteem ("I am a nothing") was sometimes warded off by infantile narcissistic overestimation and/or accompanied by lasting narcissistic rage at the decathecting parent. This in turn interfered with appropriate libidinal distribution between self and objects, handicapped fusion, and precluded the development of considerate relationships. At the same time the constant fear of sudden and total loss of object made it impossible for these children to master phase-appropriate physical separations, such as in entry to nursery school, or developmental losses, such as relinquishing infantile forms of relationship (e.g., toilet mastery), entering latency, and coping with adolescent object removal. The identification with the decathecting parent here contributed also to the fear of inner loss, the fear that a parent not fully needed and engaged in reality might be lost as an internal object representation. Periods of decathexis of the analyst and of the analysis were marked in some instances, and presented major technical problems. In the severest cases, the effect of parental decathexis on the lability of ego functions, on their lack of secondary autonomy, has already been mentioned. It needs to be stressed, however, that the synthetic function, in all its aspects, was interfered with even in the less disturbed patients. Of course, parental decathexis was not the sole determinant of these difficulties, and there was considerable variation in the extent to which the children had been exposed to it and in the areas where it had most affected them.

If the analyst starts to seek evidence of the mechanism of decathexis in the analyses of adults, there are other clues that can be used, besides the reports that others find the analysand often withdrawn. For the first of these let us return briefly to work with children. In evaluating children for admission to the Hanna Perkins School and in working with them and their families, we have become acutely aware of the preschooler who has been seduced or raped. Perhaps some will recall that in the Hanna Perkins follow-up study (R. Furman and Katan 1969), there were a number of instances of children for whom treatment by way of the parent had not been fully successful and where subsequent analysis revealed a previously undetected seduction about which the parents had no knowledge or even suspicion, at least consciously. Close attention to these children focused our group on how frequently the parent of a seduced preschool child was a parent with the particular dysfunction at issue here. Although many factors enter into early seductions, we find that parental decathexis often plays a significant role, operating in a number of ways. Children this young are rarely left in situations that will eventuate in a sexual molestation if their parents have an unremitting investment in them. Children whose secondary narcissism has been compromised have trouble valuing their bodies sufficiently to make them unavailable for use by others. Children who are repeatedly decathected in the presence of their parents are at those times exposed to recurrent episodes of being overwhelmed by their drives. When left inadequately supervised with a potential seducer, they can readily become instinctually flooded and vulnerable. Occasionally a decathected child who is then overwhelmed by his own drives discovers that the ensuing loss of control attracts his parents' cathexis back to him, and he thus learns to use an instinctual approach to adults.

Our experience is the same in regards to "lost children." Even the child who runs away may, by turning passive into active, be responding to a decathexis. Children who repeatedly get lost do so because the parent responsible for them has lost them, has decathected them. Years ago, in trying to help a mother find neutral activities to share with her not yet 3-year-old daughter and because of an apparent mutual interest, it was suggested that they garden together. The suggestion was a miserable failure as the mother reported back that whenever she went out to the front of her house, located on a busy street, to work on the flower beds there with her daughter, the child just drifted away. Both she and her neighbors had wearied of their concern for the child's safety, of constantly having to return the girl to her mother. The mother, in decathecting her daughter, never noticed when the girl left. "I would turn around and she would just not be there. I guess she is not ready for that yet."

In addition to the clue available in adult analysis mentioned above, the fleeting reports that others find the analysand withdrawn, we can now add clues available from historical reports of early seductions or repeated childhood episodes of being lost, and reports that the analysand's own children were seduced or tend to get lost. Another such clue may exist when an analysand is reluctant to use the couch. This, of course, may have many determinants. In at least two instances that come to mind, analysands have ultimately corrected an initial explanation of "I must see how you are responding to me," to the more accurate explanation of "I must see *if* you are responding to me. I cannot know unless I can see that you do."

Another manifestation of the adult who experienced parental decathexis as a child, who is a decathector, is his sensitive ability in analysis to detect correctly those transient moments when his analyst may withdraw full attention because of preoccupation with his own, that is, the analyst's, affairs. An interesting variant of this occurred when one such analysand was not distressed in an instance when the analyst missed a sentence or a thought the patient had just expressed. When asked about this, he explained, "I knew you were distracted with what I had said earlier, did not hear me because you were thinking about me. That's all right; that's different."

A connection has also been found with a silent patient whose silences were ultimately understood to indicate a decathexis of the analysis on the part of the analysand in response to what had felt to him in the transference as a

decathexis by the analyst. This presented a technical problem until the mechanism was clarified. The analyst sensed at the outset of the analysis that silences
that were allowed to go on past a few moments meant an irretrievably lost
hour, an irretrievably lost patient, an overwhelmed patient unable to analyze.
When a suggestion was made about not allowing the silences to go uninterrupted, the patient confirmed that this felt correct. Without at first knowing
why, they agreed that the silences would be interrupted by the analyst. When
the issue was finally clarified and analytically understood as a transference
reaction involving decathexis, a transition period ensued during which the
analyst asked each time whether he should interrupt the silence. Much later
on, the silences could be allowed to run their course without interruption by
the analyst.[1]

A further clue to the unreported presence of this phenomenon in adult
analysis, perhaps the one of greatest analytic significance, may be in those
instances where analytic insights and gains which seemed well understood
and integrated subsequently disappear in response to the least stress. In this
respect these adults are like the little boy described at the start of the chapter,
and similar to the one reported by one of us in a previous publication (E.
Furman 1975).

Implicit in what has been said about the occurrence of decathexis in adult
analysis is something that should be made explicit. We take it as a truism that
anyone decathected as a child will, as an adult, likewise be a decathector. This
will certainly be true in his role as a parent and, depending on the severity of
his exposure as a child, can influence many aspects of his personality. Evidence
of having been decathected is, therefore, taken as presumptive evidence of the
active utilization of this mechanism in adulthood. This issue can be clouded in
instances of multiple parenting, some of the parenting coming from people
who did not decathect, but even in these cases, it will be present. It seems that
an identification with a decathecting parent is something one is helpless to
avoid.

Two aspects of this identification should be mentioned at this point for
clarification. One concerns the parent, the other the child. As to the parent, it
should be noted that many well-functioning parents occasionally decathect
their children. The tendency to decathect in small measure does not entail a

---

1. Katan (1981) reported another indication of an adult who had been decathected
as a child. The patient talked incessantly to assure herself of the analyst's unwavering
investment or attention.

major disturbance in parental functioning and does not lead to a major disturbance in the child. Even rare instances of decathexis, however, differ from the more usual fluctuations in parental investment, as was pointed out by Katan (1981) in her discussion of this paper. For example, a mother distressed by her husband's illness or loss of job may diminish her investment in her child, but would either be aware of it or readily notice its effect on the child and attempt to correct the situation. Parental decathexis by our definition would be unconscious and near total rather than partial.

As to the child, one may well wonder why his identification with the decathecting parent does not include the aggression the child experiences, his own in response to being decathected and the presumed aggression of the parent perceived as rejecting or humiliating. According to our findings, decathected children tend to manifest both types of identification, one of simple decathexis (of themselves and of others) and one of "aggressive decathexis," as in the earlier described adult patient.

Let us now turn to nomenclature, where analysts are often their own worst enemies, contributing to confusion, inaccuracies, and misunderstandings. Care must be taken in our choice of the word for the parental dysfunction we are describing. This means first looking to a dictionary and, next, checking where this word or phrase has been otherwise used in psychoanalysis. We want to make sure that our term accurately describes the psychological situation, at least as far as it is possible to judge at our current level of understanding.

In a dictionary sense (*Random House Dictionary of the English Language*, Unabridged Edition, 1966), we may well be all right. "De" is defined as a "prefix used to indicate privation, removal, separation, negation." "Cathexis" denotes the investment of psychic energy in a mental representation (Moore and Fine 1967).

The next question is where and how this term is currently used psychoanalytically. For Cleveland child analysts (E. Furman 1974) the answer to that would be with one aspect of the process of mourning: the painful, slow, laborious, never fully completed psychological task of decathexis, dictated when the demands of reality indicate that a loved one is no longer alive. The next instance that comes to mind is the process of object removal Katan (1937) described so long ago, when an adolescent removes his sexual investment from his parents to free that energy to be available for falling in love with an age-appropriate object. This is also a painful process, the adolescent's painful sense of internal loneliness relating to his decathexis of the object representations. Again it is a slow process that proceeds over many years, often by well-defined phases, and is in health ultimately a reasonably complete process, though perhaps no more so than with mourning. It would seem that a transitional object is also decathected in a gradual process as progressive development favors investment in new relationships, interests, and activities. This process of decathexis, so well described by Winnicott (1953), is also never fully completed. Although it is not associated with as much emotional pain, its success, like that of the other two instances of decathexis, is in the service of the health of the personality.

A final example of decathexis may be found in the defense analysis that is a part of every psychoanalysis. Defenses can be said to receive an investment that sustains their existence and availability, that is a source of the counter-cathectic activity intrinsic to their functioning (Hartmann 1955). As defenses are analyzed, as the impulses they seek to ward off are made conscious and coped with in other ways, as conflicts are resolved, and genetic origins pinpointed—at each of these steps in the mastery of a defense, its deactivation involves a withdrawal of cathexis from it. With characterological defenses whose existence long outlasts their usefulness, the slow nature of this cathectic withdrawal is perhaps most clearly seen. We believe that the work of defense analysis is also an instance of slow, gradual decathexis. It too is often incomplete and proceeds in treatment despite the distress and unpleasure engendered by the need to find new solutions to old conflicts.

What do these four examples tell us about the meaning of decathexis in current psychoanalytic usage? Many factors are shared by all or almost all of these examples. The process is a slow one; an investment once made seems difficult to undo, and the decathexis is often associated with pain. The process is initiated by, and endured at the behest of, the realities of further development, be it in mourning, preparing to return to the world of the living; or in adolescence, preparing for a mature, fully adult sexual relationship; or with a transitional object whose surrender indicates readiness for different life experiences; or in an analysis, trying to gain emotional health through defense analysis. The process in all these instances is adaptive, the ego well in charge. And finally, the process is never complete in all these examples. Who does not feel a sadness for his own past losses when attending a funeral where his involvement of the moment is minimal? Who has forgotten his teddy or blanket? Who cannot run into trouble in adulthood from oedipal feelings not fully resolved? Who, under stress, cannot recall into service defenses he would be better off without, defenses presumably fully analyzed? All this is in keeping with Freud's (1915, 1926) emphasis on the difficulty in giving up libidinal cathexes and on the pain associated with the hypercathexis which immediately precedes and accompanies decathexis. Freud (1937) returned to this concept later in a different context when he described the "adhesiveness" of libido as an obstacle to personality change in analysis and contrasted this with patients who readily relinquish old investments but are similarly likely to give up newly acquired therapeutic gains. Hartmann (1955) speaks of the lasting investments the ego makes, utilizing more or less neutralized energy, a process which contributes to the stability of secondary autonomy and which he relates to ego strength.

Decathexis as a parental dysfunction shares with the others in being an unconscious process, but there the similarities seem to end. This decathexis is more complete, the investment being apparently totally, albeit transiently, withdrawn; it occurs in the span of a moment; it is not associated with pain; it does not appear to be adaptive; it is not undertaken at the behest of reality, of furthering healthy development.

Let us examine the nature of the energic investment first. The fact that the parental investment in the child can be withdrawn so readily, so speedily, and to such an extensive degree, betrays a fluidity of the investment, an ability for the investment to fluctuate quickly, a lack of permanence, a lability of the investment, that reminds very much of primary process and speaks to relative lack of secondary autonomy. Fluctuations of cathexis occur every day for all of us, but never to this extent or to this degree. Moreover, they are usually in the service of the ego. For example, concentrated attention implies a partial decathexis of other mental contents, of inner and outer stimuli which would interfere with the task at hand. Lability of cathexis is also usually in the service of the ego, such as in the process of creativity, in the appreciation of art, and in free association, the basic rule of psychoanalytic procedure. The decathexis of the parental dysfunction is in all these ways much closer to the id, much more primitive than that which is operative in the other examples of decathexis described.

With the other examples of decathexis, the mechanism was adaptively at the service of the ego, under the sway of the reality principle. They occurred despite the pain associated with them in three of the examples. Parental decathexis is not adaptive, for example, in the way it can leave loved ones exposed to distress and even danger. It is not reality based, for example, in ignoring appropriate parental responsibilities and expectations. It serves neither ego, reality, nor superego, often afterwards exposing its employer to the guilt of failure of parental functioning. In whose behest then does the process we are describing operate?

We are proposing that the decathexis of parental dysfunction is an unusual defense, a very primitive one, that operates in the service of the pleasure principle and is close to primary process. When a parent decathects his child, he avoids a competition between his wishes and the child's needs, and avoids the unpleasure of the delay in gratification of his wishes. The narcissistic distribution, in these instances, is not sufficiently weighted toward the child to counteract the need for self-gratification. The parent's interest is pursued, his child treated as if nonexistent.[2] The ensuing abandonment is almost total for that period of time. The defense is unusual as it does not involve the taming of an instinctual demand under the pressure of ego, superego, or reality. This maneuver seemingly obliterates those demands to effect an id gratification. And when the patient is made aware of it, he or she does not experience anxiety, the usual motivating force for defensive measures, but puzzlement or discomfort and unpleasure. Countercathexis, as usually seen with a defense mechanism, is not operative. Instead we have a primitively most economic withdrawal of cathexis from all the demands associated with parenting, which include demands from ego, superego, reality, and even some id demands connected with the instinctual investment of the child.

For these reasons we view the decathexis we are describing as properly named, representing a primitive defense. Hartmann (1955) pointed out that differences between instinctual and neutral energy go parallel with differences between primary and secondary process. Although secondary processes are characteristic of the ego functions, "there are differences in mobility also between various ego functions" (p. 23). These can be, in part, correlated with degrees of neutralization and, in part, are probably related to bound and mobile cathexes. It may be the primitive nature of the defense, its closeness to the id and to primary process, its service on behalf of the pleasure principle, that makes its acquisition by identification with a decathecting parent so compelling. It may be this nature of the defense that makes it so resistant to analytic mastery, even when the identification with the decathecting parent has been worked and reworked. Its primitivity may be just what so opposes the conscious wishes of those analysands who are aware of their mechanism and want to overcome it. It may be what makes the task of these analysands so long and difficult. The id and the pleasure principle can hardly be considered the best allies of analysis.

---

2. Katan (1981) finds in her analyses of mothers who are gross decathectors that these are often women with very low self-esteem who must focus on replenishing their own narcissistic needs at the times when they decathect their children.

At the time of the first presentation of this chapter Katan (1981) called our attention to the recently published discussions of the mechanisms of defense, primarily between Anna Freud and Joseph Sandler (1981a,b,c). Several points raised by them have direct bearing on our topic. Anna Freud notes the closeness of some defenses to primary process, especially those which occur in dreams (1981b) and those which are used in the earliest stages of personality development (1981c). She states, "The person who first develops primary and then secondary process is still the same person, and the earliest defence mechanisms of the ego are based on primary processes. The experience gained by the individual from his primary processes is used by him in the elaboration of the defence mechanisms. Of course, later defences are much more sophisticated and much more under the influence of the ego . . . The primitive id processes get taken over only later by the developing ego as a defence mechanisms" (1981c, p. 154). Anna Freud also comments on defenses being directed against anxiety *or* unpleasure (1981a).

In "The Project," Freud (1895) described the withdrawal of cathexis due to the threat of unpleasure in his discussion of "primary defence" and its relationship to its biological underpinnings. "Primary defence or repression" refers to "the fact that a hostile [painful or unpleasurable] mnemic image is regularly abandoned by its cathexis as soon as possible" (1895, p. 322).

It seems to us probable that the form of decathexis we are describing originates in the earliest phases of development, when id and ego are marginally differentiated, secondary process inadequately established, the ego still utilizing instinctual or barely neutralized energy.

Is the form of decathexis we are describing a primary process mechanism, a defensive maneuver or a defense mechanism? According to the Hampstead discussions (1981b) it does not qualify as a defense mechanism on a historical basis. Clinically it is not an intrinsic part of a hysterical or obsessional neurosis. We have, however, seen a number of patients whose primary difficulty, whose basic problem, related to the consequences of having been decathected by their parents and having acquired the predilection to utilize decathexis in such a variety of ways that it became the core of their disturbance. With adult patients the clinical picture included a complex mélange of hysterical and obsessional features. With the more severely affected child patients the disturbance was of an atypical nature.

In functional terms decathexis is, we believe, used by the personality in a variety of ways: adaptively (e.g., mourning), developmentally (e.g., object removal), and defensively. The first two are instances of decathexis at the service of a mature ego. A mature ego may also use various forms of decathexis defensively, as we have described with aggression. The decathexis that arises from parental dysfunction is used by an immature part of the ego, is close to primary process, and may perhaps best be described, in reference to the Hampstead discussions, as a primitive defensive maneuver.

We hope, however, that focus on the precise psychoanalytic characterization of this phenomenon will not distract from what we believe to be its clinical and theoretical significance.

In concluding this introductory report some final observations may be clarifying, the first concerning two ways in which some children try to protect themselves. One is by confrontation. A 3-year-old, for example, once told his mother, "Be careful, Mommy, you almost lost your little boy," when she was in the process of decathecting and losing him in a supermarket. Other children have responded to the removal of the mother's investment by a precocious reversal of roles, the not unfamiliar "mothering in order to be mothered." This also requires a somewhat older child, say certainly of 3, and a mother who can be relatively easily recalled to responsiveness.

Another observation concerns a comparison between what we are describing and what Winnicott (1958) has reported, such as in his paper on "The Capacity to Be Alone," where he refers to failures of what he calls a mother's "ego-relatedness." Initially this might seem an identical situation, but closer scrutiny, we believe, reveals he was speaking to a constant and much more often partial failure of an ego investment. The parental dysfunction we are focused on is intermittent, much more total in a quantitative sense for the time it is operative, and qualitatively would appear to involve all aspects of investment in the child, not just the ego investment.

Analysands decathected as children often have an immediate understanding of, and empathy with, Winnicott's concept of a holding environment and the significance of the capacity to be alone in the presence of another (Winnicott 1958, 1960a,b). In being decathected they have experienced aspects of what he describes. In some of our decathected analysands we have observed the development of the false self he reports. In this paper, however, we have not focused on this aspect of the patients' difficulties. Suffice it here to mention that, in our patients, the development of a false self has not been caused by intermittent total parental decathexis but by continuous decathexis of parts of the child's personality. Although we use very much Winnicott's descriptions of the mother's role, particularly in early normal development, it appears we are reporting a different pathological way in which these developmental processes can fail from the maternal side, with different consequences.

The consequences of parental decathexis we have tried to emphasize are the inevitability of a child's identification with his parent's use of this primitive mechanism, the part it plays in early childhood seductions and in repeated episodes of a child getting lost, and, most significant of all, the frequently ensuing failure of reality-based ego adaptedness and the lasting lability of cathectic investments which interfere with relationships, with integration, with secondary autonomy of functions, and with the ongoing utilization of the insights accruing from a psychoanalysis.

Recently a 16-year-old was experiencing one of those moments of profound insight that can make adolescents so interesting and rewarding to work with. He was protesting being pushed a bit to do something in his analysis and in his life about his somewhat lagging relationships with girls. "Look," he said, "I'll be able to love a girl, truly love a girl, when I can truly love myself. Maybe what the analysis is really all about is straightening out this loving myself by understanding how I was loved."

In effect, this is what we are saying about emotional investments, about cathexis. We invest in others, in things outside ourselves, as we invest in ourselves and we invest in ourselves as our parents initially invested in us. It may be that it is the nature of those investments that ultimately determines the mature harmonious functioning of the personality.

Summary

This chapter describes a type of parental dysfunction—intermittent decathexis—which apparently has not previously been reported although it occurs frequently, to varied extent. The dysfunction is introduced by some of the clinical material that originally brought it to the authors' attention, and is contrasted with the more usual parental investment in their children. Its relationship to depression and then to aggression is next clarified. Examples of the manifestations of having been intermittently decathected are offered from both child and adult analyses as well as the impediments it provides for a child's progressive emotional development. Finally, the evidence is presented which led the authors to conclude that metapsychologically intermittent decathexis is a primitive defensive maneuver.

References

Freud, A. (1953). Some remarks on infant observation. *Psychoanalytic Study of the Child*, 8:9–19. New York: International Universities Press.

———— (1967). About losing and being lost. *Psychoanalytic Study of the Child*, 22:15–19. New York: International Universities Press.

Freud, A., and Sandler, J. (1981). Discussions in the Hampstead Index on the ego and the mechanisms of defence. *Bulletin of the Hampstead Clinic*.

(a) II—The application of analytic technique to the study of the psychic institutions. 4:5–31.

(b) III—The ego's defensive operations considered as an object of analysis. 4:119–143.

(c) IV—The mechanisms of defence. 4:151–201.

Freud, S. (1895). The Project. *Standard Edition* 1.

———— (1915). Mourning and melancholia. *Standard Edition* 14.

———— (1926). Inhibitions, symptoms and anxiety. *Standard Edition* 20.

———— (1937). Analysis terminable and interminable. *Standard Edition* 23.

Furman, E. (1969). Treatment via the mother. In *The Therapeutic Nursery School*, ed. R. A. Furman and A. Katan, pp. 64–123. New York: International Universities Press, 1969.

———— (1974). *A Child's Parent Dies*. New Haven, CT: Yale University Press.

———— (1975). Some aspects of a young boy's masturbation conflict. In *Masturbation from Infancy to Senescence*, eds. I. M. Marcus and J. J. Francis, pp. 185–204. New York: International Universities Press.

———— (1978). Use of the nursery school for evaluation. In *Child Analysis and Therapy*, ed. J. Glenn, pp. 129–159. New York: Jason Aronson.

Furman, R., and Katan, A. (1969). *The Therapeutic Nursery School*. New York: International Universities Press.

Hartmann, H. (1955). Notes on the theory of sublimation. *Psychoanalytic Study of the Child*, 10:9–29. New York: International Universities Press.

Katan, A. (1937). The role of displacement in agoraphobia. *International Journal of Psycho-Analysis* 32:41–50, 1951.

———— (1981). Discussion of this paper at the Scientific Meeting of The Cleveland Psychoanalytic Society, 20 November 1981.

Moore, B. E., and Fine, B. D., eds. (1967). *Glossary of Psychoanalytic Terms and Concepts*. New York: American Psychoanalytic Association.

Winnicott, D. W. (1953). Transitional objects and transitional phenomena. *International Journal of Psycho-Analysis* 34:89–97.

———— (1958). The capacity to be alone. In *The Maturational Processes and the Facilitating Environment*. New York: International Universities Press, 1965, pp. 29–36.

————— (1960a). The theory of the parent–infant relationship. In *The Maturational Processes and the Facilitating Environment*. New York: International Universities Press, 1965, pp. 37–55.

————— (1960b). Ego distortion in terms of true and false self. In *The Maturational Processes and the Facilitating Environment*. New York: International Universities Press, 1965, pp. 140–152.

4

The Phallic-Narcissistic Phase

Rose Edgcumbe
Marion Burgner

Our previous work on early object relationships (1972) led us toward the understanding of development from the viewpoint of object relatedness as well as from the more classical viewpoint of the drives. The *psychological* capacity for object relatedness progresses through levels of maturity, developing out of the infant's biological and self-preservative needs for the libidinal object into gradually more complex relationships. We view these developments as *levels* of object relationships and distinguish them from the *phases* of drive development, though in optimal conditions the two proceed in parallel lines, smoothly and congruently.

In our consideration of later phases of development from this dual viewpoint of object relatedness and drives, of particular interest to us was the phallic-oedipal phase of development. Our examination of the literature disclosed a tendency to assume that entry into the phallic phase is accompanied by the *simultaneous development* of oedipal relationships, so that the terms phallic, oedipal, and phallic-oedipal are often used synonymously. *Yet close scrutiny of clinical and observational material reveals distinct differences in the forms of drive derivatives and in the nature of the child's relationships in the preoedipal phallic phase as compared with the phallic-oedipal phase.* In the preoedipal phallic phase, exhibitionism and scotophilia are the most pronounced drive components. In the child's object relationships, correspondingly, the real or fantasied use of the genital serves primarily exhibitionistic and narcissistic purposes, to gain the admiration of the object. In the preoedipal phallic phase, the one-to-one relationship is still dominant, since the rivalry of triangular oedipal relationships has not yet developed.

Many authors have described the changes in drive aims and relationships involved in the move into the oedipal phase, as well as the stages and vicissitudes within that phase (Brunswick 1940, Deutsch 1930, Freud 1923, 1924, 1925, 1931, Lampl-de Groot 1928, 1952). The assumption that a phallic child is also an oedipal child is in part a legacy from the historical growth of psychoanalytic theory. The concept of the Oedipus complex was formulated by Freud as early as 1897, several years before his first formulations of the drive theory (1905) and the even later formulations of phase development which Freud added to the "Three Essays on the Theory of Sexuality" in 1905. In fact, Freud did not differentiate between the phallic and the oedipal phases; for instance, in 1924 he wrote that the phallic phase, in which he saw the male genital organ as taking the leading role, "is contemporaneous with the Oedipus complex, does not develop further to the definitive genital organization, but is submerged, and is succeeded by the latency period" (p. 174).

In his more general formulations of object choice, Freud described the anaclitic nature of the early development of libidinal drives in relation to the object who satisfies the child's earliest self-preservative needs. Since at that time his primary emphasis was on drive development, he did not explore all aspects of the development of relationships through all developmental phases. Thus, he examined the object mainly from the viewpoints of finding an object for drive gratification and the changing expressions of drives toward the object. It is of interest to note that in his description of the Oedipus complex he spelled out in more detail than in other phases the various relationships involved.

In order to clarify the development of relationships to self and objects during the early part of the phallic phase, we think it helpful to separate out the preoedipal phallic phase from the oedipal phase proper, since such a separation will enable us to examine in detail the development of object relatedness and drive development in these two phases. Further, we consider it appropriate to trace in more detail both the development of the body representation as an integral part of the developing self-representation, and the processes of identification affecting these representations. This development of self and body representations and of identifications makes a crucial contribution to the establishment of a differentiated sexual identity, to the narcissistic valuation of the sexually differentiated body, to the development from a two-person relationship to the triangular relationship of the oedipal phase, and to the organization of phallic drive aims in regard to the objects concerned.

The Phallic-Narcissistic Phase

The Main Tasks

We shall refer to the early, preoedipal part of the phallic phase as the *phallic-narcissistic phase*,[1] and reserve the term *oedipal phase* for the later part of the phallic phase when triangular oedipal relationships are established.

Psychic organization in the phallic-narcissistic phase is complicated by the presence of two factors not encountered in the oral and anal phases: first, the child has to attempt to come to terms with the differences between the sexes in the physical formation of the genitals, the dominant erotogenic zone of the phallic phase; second, the child is faced with the task of recognizing and accepting the immaturity of his or her own genital apparatus and functioning. Normal development in the phallic-narcissistic and oedipal phases therefore requires a gradual divergence, in boys and girls, of drive derivatives, fantasies, sexual identifications, and modes of relating to the object, as well as a difference in the sex of the object to be chosen for the oedipal relationship. Every child has the task of consolidating his or her sexually differentiated body image, renouncing the sexual role not appropriate to his or her own sex, and accepting, relative though such an acceptance may be, the indefinite postponement of full adult genital functioning.

The Development of the Body Representation and of Identifications

The establishment of the body representation has to be traced back to its starting point in the first weeks of life when diffuse, experiential awareness of polarities of feeling gradually differentiates into localized sensory perceptions belonging to specific parts of the body. When the infant starts to distinguish between what is external and what is internal, what belongs to his own body and what is given or taken in from the outside, the body representation has begun to be structured. Such localization of body parts, a process which may

---

1. We are indebted to Anna Freud for this term.

be seen as beginning at approximately 3 months with mouth-hand integration, serves to build up and establish the mental structure of a body image (Hoffer 1950. In the second year of life, with the rapid development of cognitive and affective responses, this body representation becomes firmly integrated with the self representation, and we may surmise that the same mental structure serves both the body= and the self-representations; subsequently, these representations remain as an established and integral structure (Sandler and Rosenblatt 1962). It is this representation of body and self which receives the narcissistic investment of the child, an investment which is in part determined by the objects' attitudes toward him (Joffe and Sandler 1967). The child is aware of sexual differences prior to the phallic phase, but the narcissistic investment of sexually differentiated aspects of the body assumes particular importance with entry into the phallic phase, and with the consolidation of a sexual identity.

The process of acquiring a differentiated sexual identity rests largely on the child's capacity to identify with the parents of the same sex. We understand the process of identification as a modification of the self representation with the aim of acquiring some attributes of the object representation (Sandler et al. 1963, Sandler and Rosenblatt 1962). And we define the acquiring of a sense of sexual identity as a process starting during the child's second year, continuing through the anal phase, and reaching its peak within the phallic phase.

We choose to restrict the term identity[2] quite particularly to one aspect of the child's self-representation—the child's growing awareness of his or her sexual identity, an awareness which is intimately linked with the identifications with the parent of the same sex, as well as with the upsurge of phallic sexual drives with the entry into the phallic-narcissistic phase. Thus we see in the boy the precursors of his oedipal masculine attitudes toward the mother, while the girl[3] similarly manifests precursors of feminine oedipal attitudes toward the father.

Mahler (1958) describes "two critical phases of identity formation: (1) the separation-individuation phase; (2) the phase of resolution of bisexual identification" (p. 136). With regard to the latter, she is reported to have said:

---

2. The concept of identity is a problematic one; it is sometimes used interchangeably with the concept of self representation, for instance, by Erikson (1950, 1956) who describes in careful detail the genetic sequence involved.

3. While it is misleading to use the term "phallic" for the girl, at present we are at a loss for a more satisfactory one.

The second crucial period of integration of feelings of identity extends from three years to latency, most significantly during the phallic phase with its massive concentration of libido in the sexual parts of the body image. Body-image representations now emerge from pregenital libidinal positions and bisexual identifications to firm establishment of sexual identity. Here not only successful integration of prior pregenital phases, but successful identification with the parent of the same sex and the emotional attitudes of both parents to the child's sexual identity are of paramount importance. Thus, the distinct feeling of self-identity hinges on solution of the oedipal conflict. [p. 138]

We differ with Mahler in regard to timing, because we attach great importance to the phallic-narcissistic (preoedipal) phase as the time in which the child may be expected to acquire and to shape his own sexual identity; having done this, the child is then better able to enter the oedipal phase of development.

Sexual Activity and Fantasies

When the genital area first becomes a source of erotic pleasure, there is little difference between boys and girls in the way this pleasure is achieved; both stimulate themselves autoerotically by rubbing or squeezing their genitals; and if sexual pleasure is sought from the object, the child envisages it as taking the same form. Examples of this abound in the literature, starting with Freud's accounts (1909) of Little Hans who, at the age of 4¼ years, asked his mother to touch his penis because, "It's great fun"; and of a 3½-year-old girl who, while her mother was testing the fit of some new drawers, closed her thighs on her mother's hand, saying, "Oh, Mummy, *do* leave your hand there. It feels so lovely" (p. 19). This kind of masturbatory activity indicates only that the child has reached or is entering the phallic phase of drive development. It cannot be taken by itself as an indication that the child has attained the level of oedipal relationships: this can be determined only by the nature of the accompanying fantasies about and attitudes toward the object.

If at this early stage the child engages the object in some form of game indicating a wish for mutual sexual activity, there is little role differentiation between self and object. For example, early in treatment, Derek, a 3-year-old boy, wanted his therapist (a woman) and himself to have toy cars, which were made to chase, bump, touch, and drive over each other as well as their owners. Derek was visibly excited and his game was a thinly disguised form of a masturbatory wish to touch and to be touched. But at this time there was no clear differentiation between the roles of the two participants. Although Derek was already acutely aware of and anxious about bodily differences between the sexes, these had not yet assumed importance for him in terms of *differing sexual roles*, so that it was not yet possible to discern a fantasy of the penis penetrating the woman.

Intercourse fantasies during the phallic-narcissistic phase show a similar lack of differentiation of sexual roles: characteristically they are expressed in terms of activities belonging to earlier drive phases, e.g., oral impregnation and anal birth, or the mixing of urine or feces produced by two people, but with no clear differentiation between the activities of the partners.

For example, Jane, aged 3½, made use of her therapist in the transference situation to reenact her infantile sexual theories of impregnation and birth; one such reenactment concerned her wish to urinate and defecate in the therapist's company so that they could make a baby together. There was, however, no clear indication in the treatment material that this activity involved the displacement of a rival, or that the partners had differing sexual roles.

It is characteristic of the child's relationships in the phallic-narcissistic phase that sexual wishes and fantasies toward an object are expressed within what is still essentially a one-to-one relationship. The third person may be seen as an unwelcome intruder in this exclusive relationship, as in earlier prephallic phases of the mother–child relationship, but this intruder has not yet been awarded by the child the full status of the oedipal rival.

The distinction between phallic-narcissistic and oedipal phases applies equally to normal and neurotic children, from whose clinical material we shall give examples. Our observation of such normal children in the nursery school[4] and family settings suggests, however, that their consolidation of oedipal relationships is achieved more quickly and decisively as compared with neurotic children, whose conflicts interfere with the transition between the two phases.

For example, in the treatment of Stella, who began analysis at about 5 years, there was a long period when phallic drive derivatives were sufficiently abundant to indicate phallic dominance, while her relationships remained essentially on a preodipal, need-satisfying level. Play with dolls which at first sight appeared to be indicative of oedipal fantasies turned out to be only an expression of her own longing to be well-mothered. A reported early attach-

---

4. The Hampstead Clinic Nursery School; Mrs. M. Friedmann, Head Teacher.

ment to her father, at about 2½ years, proved to have been part of her search for a substitute for her disappointing preoedipal mother, rather than a turn toward an oedipal father. Although Stella was preoccupied with sex differences and penis envy, her concurrent relationships continued to center on her intense wish to be mothered until the end of the first year of treatment; then there appeared some indications of negative oedipal attitudes toward her mother. Only toward the end of the second year of treatment, when Stella was nearly 7, did full-fledged positive oedipal attitudes and wishes toward her father become firmly established.

Exhibitionism and Scotophilia

We have found from observations of children in the nursery school and in analysis that during the phallic-narcissistic phase the most noticeable component drive wishes are exhibitionism and scotophilia; either parent (and other people) may be the object of these wishes. Exhibitionistic trends in the anal phase are particularly characterized by the child's demands for his body products to be admired. The move into the phallic-narcissistic phase is, in contrast, characterized by the child's demands that his objects admire his entire body self. The demand, "Look at what I've done" changes into "Look at what I am and look at what I'm able to do." The admiration demanded of and given by the object for the child's body and physical prowess is an important source of narcissistic gratification; the gratification received from the object is subsequently internalized.

The child's curiosity develops as an aspect of ego functioning in the prephallic phases, and usually includes interest in sexual matters among the many situations in the world that the small child seeks to understand. With the entry into the phallic-narcissistic phase, however, curiosity becomes sharply focused, under the pressure of phallic drives, on questions of sexual differences and sexual activities; the wish to look now has the urgency of a drive derivative, which distinguishes scotophilia as a sexual activity from more general curiosity. It is well known that this is an important period of development for the child's future learning capacity; in favorable circumstances the scotophilic drive component can boost the child's ego functioning, increasing his wish and capacity to learn; whereas unduly severe conflicts over scotophilia can result in generalized inhibition of curiosity and can later in development drastically reduce his learning capacity.

Castration anxiety occurs during the phallic-narcissistic phase, but it is of a different order from the oedipal castration anxiety. In boys whose castration anxiety and conflicts over competing in the phallic phase are not too severe, the exhibitionistic component normally remains quite marked through the oedipal phase, when it becomes part of the boy's masculine pursuit of his mother. It also continues into latency, though the derivatives normally become further removed from the object, the emphasis shifting to such pursuits as physical prowess in organized games, skill in handicrafts, and achievements in intellectual activities.

In girls, normal development is less smooth since they have to contend with a much greater blow to their narcissism than boys. Exhibitionistic and scotophilic activities make the boy aware of the small size of his penis, whereas the girl is made aware of her complete lack of a penis; and, unlike the boy, she must abandon the idea that it will grow. Our observations suggest that the phase of indiscriminate exhibitionistic and scotophilic activity directed toward objects of either sex is shorter in girls than boys, since girls are so quickly plunged into the problems of penis envy.

Differences Between Phallic-Narcissistic and Oedipal Manifestations

Boys

A brief clinical example may serve to illustrate the differences between the phallic-narcissistic and oedipal phases of development. These differences can be seen in the levels of relationship to self and object, in drive activity, and in the content of castration fears.

At the beginning of treatment Derek (mentioned above) was 3;1 and Peter was 3;10. Both boys had reached the phallic-narcissistic phase, and in both analyses there was for a long time a central preoccupation with the penis and castration fears before the appearance of triangular oedipal relationships (either in or outside the transference). Both boys were envious of the man's big penis and anxiously aware of the woman's lack of one. Both had fantasies of stealing the man's penis and of having stolen the woman's penis. Each boy consequently feared both the father's anger and the deprived mother's envy; castration was thus feared at the hands of male and female objects. In each boy's analysis there was a phase in which the central theme was the wish to gain the object's admiration through the exhibitionistic demonstration of the penis and its possession, and the protection of the penis against loss by castration or theft. During this phase women were experienced as frighten-ingly envious and castrating objects. Only in a subsequent phase of treatment did mother (or her substitute) become the desired sexual object whom the boys wished to possess, impress, dominate, and care for in a masculine way. Concomitantly, male objects became rivals for possession of the female, not merely for possession of the penis. Fear of castration by the female grew less, sympathetic concern for her lack of a penis appeared, and a wish to impress and excite her sexually with his own penis was seen in each boy, with a concomitant shift in the intercourse fantasies.

This material shows that as the boy moves from the phallic-narcissistic to the oedipal level, changes occur in all areas: following the consolidation of his sexual identity, he experiences the full intensity of the triangular relationship of the oedipal level, with concomitant changes in the content of castration anxiety and in the aim of the phallic drive. At the phallic-narcissistic level, the boy's penis becomes a highly valued body part, his main source of narcissistic and autoerotic gratification, and the focus of his phallic exhibitionistic wishes. He may fear its loss, or wish to be a girl, thus defensively anticipating its loss. Such responses may indicate his expectation of envious attempts by females to take away his penis or of talion punishment from father, or fear of having damaged his penis himself through masturbation. Fears of father's retaliation at the phallic-narcissistic level differ from those at the oedipal level both in content and intensity; at the oedipal level, the boy anticipates punishment for his wishes to castrate and banish father in order to take his place as mother's sexual partner.

This schematic outline of processes during the phallic-narcissistic and oedipal levels tends to obscure an important ongoing process, namely, the boy's developing positive identifications with and his love and admiration for his father.[5] These positive aspects of the relationship with father are main-

---

5. It is worth commenting that apparent regression during the phallic phase to earlier modes of relating may not be indicative of regression in either drives or relationships. Rather, it may be due to distortion of identification with specific sexual aspects of the parents who themselves have marked prephallic fixations. Derek, for example, showed a marked persistence of oral modes of drive expression: phallic excitement was often expressed in his mealtime behavior. Analysis showed that one of the determinants of this behavior was identification with his parents, especially his father, who used demands and complaints about food to get his wife's attention. Both parents used to get up in the middle of the night to eat. Derek clearly showed a wish for a continuation of the overindulgence he had experienced from his mother in the

tained and developed alongside the oedipal rivalry; they are not to be confused with the negative oedipal relationship to the father, which may alternate with the positive oedipal relationship to the mother.

As the boy's sexual identification at the phallic-narcissistic level proceeds, he may at times defensively deny his awareness of sexual differences in objects; such defensive maneuvers may result from a valuing, or even over-valuing, of the phallus, with a consequent fear of its loss and a defensive bid to generalize such a prized attribute onto others. In the oedipal phase these defensive maneuvers must be distinguished from the fear of retaliatory cas-tration by father. This denial and confusion must also be distinguished from those manifestations belonging to prephallic phases when he has not yet fully discovered the important differentiating sexual characteristics of his objects and integrated them into his self and object representations. At this earlier stage the child does not defensively deny sexual differences, but merely generalizes from his experiences of his own body and assumes that other people have similar bodies. In the prephallic phase many children are curious about the differences between the genitals of boys and girls, without this necessarily being an indication of castration anxiety. While the penis seems to become a valued object when the boy is still in the anal phase of development, his interest in the penis is allied to a general curiosity about bodies, their functioning and their differences.

For example, John became interested in whether or not adults possessed a penis when he was about 2¼ years old, and firmly in the anal phase. He repeatedly asked his father and mother whether they had a penis, and then his interest spread to other adults whom he began to differentiate according to their possession or lack of a penis. At this time he appeared quite able to accept his parents' explanations about such bodily differences. In the course of toilet training John occasionally evidenced some fear that his penis, like his feces, might be lost, but he was able to reassure himself by means of observing the reality and by reasoning. By the time he was 3 years old, entering the phallic-narcissistic phase, and establishing a sexual identity, however, the increasing importance of his penis made it necessary for him to resort to defensive denial of his mother's lack of penis. At this time, he asked increasingly sophisticated · questions about conception, pregnancy, and birth. He was given simple

---

oral phase. But when, in the phallic phase, he began to identify with the phallic, sexual aspects of his father and father's sexual activity, this identification also reflected the father's own oral fixation and mode of relating to the mother.

answers, but was now unable to accept his parents' explanations as readily as he had done previously. Instead, he maintained in conversation with his mother: "When I was born I came out of your penis." At the same time, he made active attempts to master his castration anxiety; for example, he wanted to be allowed to use the bread knife. The prohibition of this activity, as well as of others, enhanced his awareness of being little, and made him long to be "a big man" like father.

Such examples demonstrate that during the anal phase the boy does not yet regard his penis as a confirmation of his masculinity. This confirmation takes place with the move into the phallic-narcissistic phase and consequent drive investment in the genital organs. It is in this phase too, or even earlier, that the boy may envy mother's possession of breasts and her capacity to have babies, but these feelings are partially counteracted by his growing masculine identifications.

Girls

While most authors are prepared to conjecture, or to extrapolate from later analytic material, about the formation of the body representation and identifications in boys, they are far less forthcoming about similar processes in girls. To our understanding, the process of establishing a constant representation of the body self follows exactly the same pattern in girls and has the same time sequence as that of the boy prior to the phallic-narcissistic phase. Only after a well-defined self-representation has been attained, can the girl, by virtue of her developing ego capacities, begin to make comparisons between her own body and the body of the male. As Brunswick (1940) puts it: "The active wish for a penis of the little girl arises with the observation of the difference between the sexes and the determination to have what the boy has. This original basis is narcissistic" (p. 276).

The girl experiences feelings and fears of castration different in nature and in complexity from those of the boy. She has to come to terms with the differences between her body and that of the boy; depending upon her narcissistic organization, level of ego development, and interaction with the important objects in her environment, she begins to a greater or lesser degree to accept her female body, a process which is not completed until the end of adolescence, if at all. Unlike the boy, the girl has no external organs to indicate to her the future capacity for achieving female adult functioning; such a prospect has to be realized principally by the adaptive process of identification with the mother and the later positive oedipal fantasies and wishes toward the father.

In examining the course of the girl's development in the phallic-narcissistic phase, we have to consider that envy in the girl may start prior to this phase (Joffe 1969) and that the wish for a penis may then be on a par with the wish for other objects that she does not possess. It is in the phallic-narcissistic phase itself that specific penis envy occurs and may well denote a rivalry with boys, castration wishes, and a general dissatisfaction with her body. But the observable lack of well-being and lowered self-esteem may include other elements deriving from prephallic phases, such as early oral deprivation, inadequate mothering, sibling rivalry, and feelings of feminine inadequacy compared with mother. Both prephallic and phallic-narcissistic feelings of envy, with their concomitant lowering of self-esteem, may interfere with the development of feminine sexual identification.

Deutsch (1944) emphasizes that feelings of envy are the prerogative of every child, particularly so in relation to a new sibling, and that the "anatomic difference becomes significant only in that phase of the girl's development in which her genitals (that is to say, her clitoris) assume functional importance" (p. 236). Moreover, she carefully distinguishes between the "primary genital trauma" and "penis envy," viewing the former as representing an awareness of genital inadequacy and deficiency which becomes generalized. She writes:

> In the psychologic material gathered from the analyses of adult women, particularly neurotic ones, we find repeated expressions of the lack of an organ, feelings of inferiority, etc. According to my present view, the assumption that these complaints result from the lack of a penis is one-sided. Their real origin is the fact that during a period of biologic development in which the inadequacy of an organ leads to a constitutionally predetermined transformation of the active tendencies into passive ones, no ready organ exists for the latter—in other words, the little girl continues to be organless in a functional sense. Her genital trauma, with its numerous consequent manifestations, lies between the Scylla of having no penis and the Charybdis of lacking the responsiveness of the vagina. [p. 230]

Examination of our clinical material and the literature suggests that the development of sexual drive activity and fantasies during the phallic-narcissistic and oedipal phases is less well understood in girls than in boys, and is a subject which deserves further study. We may, however, offer some comments on the observable changes in the girl's relationships during these two phases. It is commonly accepted that for the girl normal development involves dealing with her penis envy by substituting for the missing penis her whole body and its appearance as a source of narcissistic-exhibitionistic gratification. The wish to be admired for her attractive, feminine appearance then becomes part of her positive oedipal approach to father. We have found it necessary, however, to distinguish between this form of feminine exhibitionism as a sign of a wish to be loved on an oedipal level and other forms which are signs of fixation to the phallic-narcissistic phase, or even to earlier preoedipal phases.

Margareta, for example, a nursery school child not in treatment, occasioned much discussion among the staff as to her status in phallic-narcissistic and oedipal development. She was a pretty, dainty, beautifully dressed child, who appeared feminine and self-satisfied. She knew well how to make an entrance and become the center of attention, and soon became known as "the little princess." She had an apparently flirtatious relationship with her father, which was occasionally extended to male observers in the nursery school. When she began nursery school at age 3, it seemed reasonable to suppose that she was entering the oedipal phase. But during her two years in the nursery school it became increasingly apparent that her relationships were superficial; she approached adults briefly in order to be admired, and retreated again once this aim had been achieved. If at times she became more involved, it was only to reveal clearly (at home as well as in school) the obstinate behavior more appropriate to the relationships of a toddler in the anal phase. Throughout the two years, she remained aloof from the other children, never making any lasting friendship. Margareta had a younger brother, of whom she had at one time been overtly and intensely envious. This overt envy had subsequently disappeared. The superficiality and lack of development in Margareta's relationships eventually led the staff to conclude that her feminine exhibitionism was not a sign of true oedipal development, but was rather a defense against intense, unresolved penis envy, which had apparently prevented her from moving satisfactorily into the oedipal phase. Since low self-esteem and feelings of deprivation in girls often become organized around penis envy, the prephallic determinants in Margareta's personality must also be taken into account.

Fixation in the phallic-narcissistic phase is more easily ascertainable in girls who do not show Margareta's deceptively feminine development. Alice, for example, was a 3-year-old who did not appear at all feminine to the nursery school staff and observers. She had an older brother who was favored by the mother because of his more amenable and compliant behavior. Alice was preoccupied with "being big," and her conversation made it clear that she equated this with being a boy. She was intensely competitive with boys and interested only in activities and possessions which had some phallic significance. All her relationships, however, remained on the level of a negativistic toddler in the anal-sadistic phase. There were no signs of feminine attitudes toward her father and other male objects. Alice's difficulties were so marked that the nursery school staff soon concluded from the observations of her that although she was clearly in the phallic phase of drive development, she was quite unable, because of her conflicts, to make the move to oedipal relationships. This conclusion was confirmed when Alice entered analytic treatment.

In contrast to these two girls, Jane (whose infantile sexual theories were mentioned earlier) gradually brought material which was unmistakably oedipal in content, in that the triad of oedipal relationships predominated. For instance, after some months of treatment, Jane frequently cast her mother at home in the role either of a witch or a bad wolf, who had then to be appeased and placated with sweets. Then, in an analytic session, Jane brought the following sequence of fantasy material: while looking out of the window, she maintained, as she often did, that the therapist lived at another Clinic house across the road, that Dr. A. (who had conducted the diagnostic interviews with her in that house) was the therapist's "father" (i.e., husband). Jane next remarked upon a log in the garden opposite and fantasied that a daddy bear and a baby bear were sitting on it together, only hastily to amend this to include the mother bear as well. Two days later Jane instructed her therapist to be father, changing this to Santa Claus, who was to bring her presents while she slept. There had obviously been allied material during this time, and it was thus considered appropriate to interpret to Jane that she wanted her father to give her a very special present, a baby. Some four months later, Jane spontaneously asked the therapist whether she remembered her story of the daddy and baby bears sitting on the log together. This question came within the context of Jane having shared the parents' bedroom on a holiday and having been very much aware of parental intercourse. When the therapist, at one point, put it to Jane that when she grew up, she too could have a "daddy" all to herself and play such "love games" with him, Jane first looked extremely pleased, but then soberly remarked that it was a very long time to wait.

In Jane's material we see some of the paradoxes that the girl has to negotiate in the oedipal relationship. She continues to be dependent on her mother to meet her basic needs, and she wishes too to preserve a positive identificatory relationship with her, and yet she also has to face her ambivalence toward her mother and her envy of her, as well as the pressures of her sexual fantasies toward father. It is therefore hardly surprising that many psychoanalysts, including ourselves, have found it so difficult to disentangle the different wishes, fantasies, and affects that make up adult female sexuality.

Effects of Fixation at the Phallic-Narcissistic Level on Later Development

In the treatment of adolescents and adults who have a strong fixation at the phallic-narcissistic level, we often find that they have failed to consolidate their oedipal relationships in childhood, with the consequence that their later relationships are deficient in truly oedipal characteristics.

The role of phallic-narcissistic fixation in the disturbances of adolescence and adulthood requires a separate study; on the basis of the cases examined so far, we briefly mention a few points. It was often possible to reconstruct that regression from a brief and imperfectly resolved oedipal level of relationships to the phallic-narcissistic level had occurred in childhood. Regression had at that time served as an adaptive attempt to cope with such problems as loss of self-esteem following the object's rejection of oedipal overtures, doubts about the oedipal object's acceptance of the patient's femininity or masculinity, and continuing difficulties in establishing a firm sexual identity due to conflicts. Regression to the phallic-narcissistic level was also used to cope with discrepancies between the ideal and the real self-representations; such discrepancies often had roots in prephallic levels, but were heightened by disappointments and conflicts at the phallic-narcissistic and oedipal levels. While as adults these patients were often able to have heterosexual intercourse (thus indicating the relative intactness of their drive development), their relationships to their objects were frequently characterized by interactions on a phallic-narcissistic level; for example, an inability to achieve a reciprocal relationship in which the object's real qualities and characteristics are recognized and valued, and in which the needs and demands of the object are accepted; a tendency to use the object solely as a source of admiration or condemnation, as a substitute for internalized approval or sanctions; an emphasis on exhibitionistic and voyeuristic behavior in relation to the object; an incessantly phallic-competitive interaction with the object. Indeed, we were struck, as we examined the level of object relationships of these patients, how many of them could also be described as *hysterical characters*, and we would further suggest that in the hysteric the phallic-narcissistic level rather than the oedipal one is the nodal point of the regressive behavior. Most of what is often described as oral-demanding behavior in hysterics is perhaps better understood as a manifestation of phallic-narcissistic demands for admiration and narcissistic supplies from the object.

The cases we have referred to, both child and adult, demonstrate that development may be held up in the phallic phase, not so much with regard to drive development but more so in the appropriate relatedness to self and objects, so that the normal move into oedipal relationships does not adequately take place. This does not imply that fixation and conflict are found only at this level. Indeed, all these cases had major conflicts on prephallic levels which were at least partially responsible for their difficulties in the phallic-narcissistic and oedipal phases, and this also applies to other cases we have studied. We have concentrated particularly on phallic material in these cases because they show in exaggerated form the normal processes of phallic phase development in regard to both drive development and object relationships.

Summary

We have differentiated between the phallic-narcissistic and oedipal phases of development. While both are under the dominant drive organization, they differ radically with regard to relationships to self and objects and drive and ego manifestations.

Within the phallic-narcissistic phase we have specifically examined the building up of the body self-representations, the processes of identification and the acquisition of a sexual identity, the contributions made by the scotophilic and exhibitionistic component wishes, and the differences between phallic and oedipal manifestations in these processes in boys and girls. Pseudo-oedipal relationships, that is, phallic-narcissistic relationships, have been differentiated from oedipal relationships proper, with regard to the child's mode of relating to self and objects.

References

Brunswick, R.M. (1940). The preoedipal phase of the libido development. In *The Psychoanalytic Reader*, ed. R. Fliess, pp. 261–283. London: Hogarth, 1950.

Burgner, M., and Edgcumbe, R. (1972). Some problems in the conceptualization of early object relationships: Part II. *Psychoanalytic Study of the Child* 27:315–333. New Haven, CT: Yale University Press.

Deutsch, H. (1930). The significance of masochism in the mental life of women. In *The Psychoanalytic Reader*, ed. R. Fliess, pp. 223–236. London: Hogarth, 1950.

———— (1944). *The Psychology of Women*. New York: Grune & Stratton.

Edgcumbe, R., and Burgner, M. (1972). Some problems in the conceptualization of early object relationships: Part I. *This Annual* 27:283–314.

Erikson, E. H. (1950). *Childhood and Society*. New York: Norton.

———— (1956). The problem of ego identity. *Journal of the American Psychoanalytical Association* 4:56–121.

Freud, S. (1897). Letter 71. In Extracts from the Fliess papers. *Standard Edition* 1:388–391.

———— (1905). Three essays on the theory of sexuality. *Standard Edition* 7:125–243.

———— (1909). Analysis of a phobia in a five-year-old boy. *Standard Edition* 10:3–149.

———— (1923). The infantile genital organization. *Standard Edition* 19:141–145.

———— (1924). The dissolution of the Oedipus complex. *Standard Edition* 19:173–179.

———— (1925). Some psychical consequences of the anatomical distinction between the sexes. *Standard Edition* 19:243–258.

———— (1931). Female sexuality. *Standard Edition* 21:225–243.

Hoffer, W. (1950). Development of the body ego. *Psychoanalytic Study of the Child* 5:18–23. New York: International Universities Press.

Joffe, W. G. (1969). A critical review of the status of the envy concept. *International Journal of Psycho-Analysis* 50:533–545.

Joffe, W. G., and Sandler, J. (1967). Some conceptual problems involved in the consideration of disorders of narcissism. *Journal of Child Psychotherapy* 2:56–66.

Lampl-de-Groot, J. (1928). The evolution of the Oedipus complex in women. In *The Psychoanalytic Reader*, ed. R. Fliess, pp. 207–222. London: Hogarth, 1950.

———— (1952). Re-evaluation of the role of the Oedipus complex. *International Journal of Psychoanalysis* 33:335–342.

Mahler, M. S. (1958). In panel: Problems of identity. Reporter: D. Rubinfine. *Journal of the American Psychoanalytic Association* 6:131–142.

Sandler, J., Holder, A., and Meers D. (1963). The ego ideal and the ideal self. *Psychoanalytic Study of the Child* 18:139–158. New York: International Universities Press.

Sandler, J., and Rosenblatt, B. (1962). The concept of the representational world. *Psychoanalytic Study of the Child* 17:128–145. New York: International Universities Press.

5

Narcissism and Oedipal Development

Phyllis Beren

A colleague shared with me a conversation she had overheard between her 6-year-old son Tom and his 14-year-old cousin. Her son asked: "How old do you want to be when you marry?" The cousin replied: "40." The cousin then asked how old Tom wanted to be when he married and Tom said: "20." "Oh," said the cousin, "that's young!" "No," Tom replied: "I want to have a long time with my second wife."

Tom knew that his father had been married before and that his own mother was his father's second wife. In his mind you quickly got the first wife out of the way and preferred the second wife.

Changes in social mores and our heightened interest in gender raise many questions concerning our traditional views of the oedipal phase and its unfolding during the course of the life cycle. Today a much greater number of children grow up in one-parent homes as well as in nontraditional ones, including homes with same-sex parents. In treating adolescents it becomes clear that their views about gender identity and gender roles are quite different from those encountered in the past. One striking example is their openly expressed comfort with bisexual feelings and practices.

Considering the enormous social and cultural changes that have occurred, it would seem that the nature of the oedipal phase and its resolution might look somewhat different today than it did to Freud. Today any discussion of these themes would have to consider our changing theories on sex and gender since Freud. It would seem very difficult to discuss the oedipal dilemma without examining, for example, our current views regarding sexual object choice. Birksted-Breen (1996) has noted how Freud's position has been seen by some as ascribing biological destiny to man and woman—"anatomy is destiny." This would imply that the normal oedipal resolution culminates in a heterosexual object choice. Others have understood Freud to uphold the revolutionary belief that, psychologically speaking, we are not born man or woman and that masculinity and femininity are constructed over a period of time and are relatively independent of biological sex. According to Birksted-Breen, this opposition is there not because Freud was inconsistent or changed his mind, but because it is at the heart of the matter (p. 122).

This opposition certainly mirrors the social and cultural changes we see today in regard to sex, gender roles, and object choice. Within the context of these external changes, children and adolescents are still struggling with powerful conflicts vis-à-vis their parents, conflicts that induced Freud to make the oedipal phase the cornerstone of his theory. With the more open freedom to choose one's sexual orientation and partner, we are in a better position to investigate the nature of the Oedipus complex in all its complexities. Schuker (1996) has begun to do just this kind of investigation in presenting clinical material on three lesbian patients. She asks what factors allow erotic object choice to serve conflict resolution in some patients, and what other factors might be involved in object choice itself (p. 495). Her patient G. was involved in a full oedipal drama, while her patient K.'s homosexual relations functioned to repair narcissistic losses. Her conclusion is that: "It seems clear that no specific pathology or unitary conflict provides an explanation for etiology or dynamics for all lesbians. It seems unlikely that a single developmental path exists for object choice" (p. 496). The same might be said for heterosexual object choice, since we are very well aware from our clinical experience that a heterosexual object choice is no guarantee that the oedipal challenge has been successfully met.

In addition to social transformations and our increased interest in gender studies, some of the challenge to the central importance of the Oedipus complex has resulted from the increased attention to preoedipal determinants in the etiology of pathology (Simon 1991). Perhaps partly in reaction to the greater emphasis on preoedipal pathology, there has been a resurgence of interest in Oedipus and oedipal conflict. Today, not only is Oedipus's motivation in question, but we also stress the parent's active role as well as the intergenerational influences that play a part in the unfolding of the oedipal drama (Blos 1984, Hamilton 1993, Loewald 1979, Ross 1982, and Shengold 1989). In this same context, the denial of parental sexuality and its consequences for the reworking of the oedipal struggle has been emphasized by a number of authors (Britton 1989, Steiner 1985, and Chasseguet-Smirgel 1985). Furthermore, recent analysis of the Oedipus myth views it as an anomaly compared with other Greek myths where matricide, not patricide, is at the heart of the myth in its typical form (Goux 1993).

Continuing the tradition of viewing the oedipal phase and subsequent conflicts from this enlarged perspective, I hope to demonstrate how specific narcissistic issues and vulnerabilities distort the oedipal phase of the young child, obscure it in adolescence and have lasting effects on its resolution in later adulthood. By examining the oedipal phase and its relation to the evolving narcissistic concerns of the child, I hope to shed light on questions that have been raised concerning the differentiation between preoedipal and oedipal development and pathology. One may envision the development of the personality as a fugue in which one or more themes are sounded together and gradually built up into a complex form having distinct stages of development and culminating in a marked climax. Focusing on the unresolved issues of narcissism in the child will hopefully enhance our understanding of the oedipal climax.

A good starting point is Loewald 's paper (1979), "The Waning of the Oedipus Complex," in which he argues that we struggle with oedipal conflicts that repeatedly require some forms of mastery throughout the life cycle. Thus there is no definitive destruction of the Oedipus complex as Freud had envisioned. According to Loewald, mastering this complex includes assuming responsibility for one's own life and its conduct, which in psychic reality is tantamount to the murder of the parents.

Also important is Loewald's opposition of the term parricide to patricide, which in a patriarchal society connotes the murder of the father and is the prototype of the crime of parricide. "Parricide, strictly, is the murder of a parent or near relative; it includes the murder of one who represents or symbolizes a parent, mother or father, and even the serious betrayal of an entity or group standing for parental authority. It is a parental authority that is murdered; by that, whatever is sacred about the bond between child and parent is violated" (1979, p. 755).

Loewald also stresses aspects of self-responsibility. "It involves appropriating or owning up to one's needs and impulses as one's own, impulses and desires we appear to have been born with or that seem to have taken shape in interaction with parents during infancy. Such appropriation—notice that I use the same word as when I spoke of appropriating parental authority— such appropriation, in the course of which we begin to develop a sense of self-identity, means to experience ourselves as agents, notwithstanding the fact that we were born without our informed consent and did not pick our parents" (1979, p. 761). Further: "Responsibility to oneself in the sense of being responsive to one's urgings in the manner I described involves facing and bearing the guilt for those acts we consider criminal. Prototypical, in oedipal context, are parricide and incest" (p. 761). According to Loewald then, guilt is not a troublesome affect that one might hope to eliminate, but one of the driving forces in the organization of the self. Parricide is symbolically carried out and atoned for by severance of oedipal object ties, or aspects of them, and by the establishment of new love relations, as in adolescence. It is in the ability to mourn for the fantasied destruction of our parents that we accept the inevitability of our particular sexual identity and our place in the world. Loewald is describing the intensity of feelings that have to exist toward the parents, derived from sufficient separation, autonomy, and sense of self, in order to deal with the conflicts inherent in the oedipal situation.

To have the capacity to fully experience the oedipal drama, as originally outlined by Freud and elaborated by Loewald and others, presupposes that the child has attained an organized sense of self. This implies that the child experiences feelings of separateness, autonomy, and effectance, has gained phase-adequate mastery over sexual and aggressive impulses, and has developed certain superego precursors, including the capacity for empathy. This also presupposes that the parents have related as reliable, affirming caretakers who have encouraged and taken pride in the child's developing autonomy, sexuality, and developing identity. When narcissistic issues predominate, these children are instead preoccupied with using narcissistic defenses to deal with fears of separation, of loss of autonomy, effectance and control; they are confused about whether they are really loved for themselves, and they dread the loss of admiration and love. Such children are overly sensitive to rejections and often quite obsessed with winning and losing; they may also experience serious gender and sexual confusion. Lack of trust in their parents and themselves, and lack of confidence in their own autonomy and gender identity, makes it difficult for them to engage in a true oedipal struggle.

In adolescents these narcissistic strands are often observed in confused identifications and compromised superego functioning. For example, the greater comfort and ease with bisexuality among teenagers today has to do not only with our more liberated sexual attitudes and mores, but perhaps also with significant unresolved narcissistic problems. One adolescent girl who liked and was attracted to boys became very despondent after being rejected by her boyfriend. Her long-standing insecurity about her own sexual attractiveness became heightened. Her discomfort with her own body, coupled with longings for her mother's love and approval, drew her to girls who took a sexual interest in her. One did not here sense that the predominant issue was an oedipal fear of retaliation or a negative oedipal desire to be her mother's lover. Rather, it seemed that she needed to have her body valued and affirmed by her mother, to feel more identified with mother's body and her mother before she could comfortably compete for either girls or boys.

This very attractive mother had always been critical of her daughter's looks and figure. Normally, as a child this girl would have been helped to feel that her femininity was valued and admired by both parents. But this did not occur, and the upsurge of sexual impulses at adolescence brought a resurgence of specific longing for this unmet need. We have long been aware that adolescents have a tremendous need to feel accepted and affirmed. With greater freedom of choice, including sexual choice, adolescents will be particularly susceptible to anyone who will make them feel loved and feel better about themselves. Such choices will not be based on a loosening of incestuous object ties or a trying-on of roles, but rather on repair of a narcissistic defect.

Case of a Child

I will now turn to three clinical examples that consider the narcissistic contributions to oedipal development and the outcome of the oedipal conflict in a child, an adolescent, and an adult.

I met Sam for the first time when he was 4½. His parents expressed total frustration and anger at what they saw as his extreme oppositional behavior, which took the form of constant temper tantrums and refusal to do anything they asked of him. It appeared that the parents had expectations of him that went beyond his young years, and at the age of 2, when his sister was born, Sam understandably regressed while the parents more than ever wanted him to be the mature older brother. The parents themselves appeared rushed and preoccupied, trying desperately to fit their children somewhere into their very busy schedule, and Sam's mother felt clearly overwhelmed. It appeared that as the parents attempted to hurry Sam along, he stubbornly held back.

Sam's very early history indicated a child with special sensitivities, a low threshold for external stimulation, and difficulty with transitions. Under the best of circumstances these kinds of special sensitivities challenge the hoped-for "good fit" between mother and infant, and in Sam's case this "good fit" was seriously compromised by the mother's immense anxiety and her own conflicts. Sam was seen for less than a year in therapy and guidance with the parents. When Sam became more manageable for the parents, they withdrew from treatment.

They returned to consult with me again when Sam was 6, and I saw him until he was 8½. Some of the earlier problems remained, although Sam had shown some marked improvement. This time they were concerned about his entry into first grade, because of his tendency not to listen and his poor relations with other children, whom he either provoked or felt provoked by. In addition, his mother was distressed about his angry and abusive behavior towards his younger sister with whom the mother was very identified. It appeared that Sam's main preoccupation was to feel in control, and to this end he tried to coerce the other person to do as he wished. When he felt threatened, he had little capacity to empathize, and had little sense of how others were affected by his verbal and physical outbursts. On the other hand, Sam was a very intelligent and sensitive child who could be caring and insightful when he didn't feel threatened. I sensed there were times when he wanted very much to please and to be liked and respected by his parents and peers. When he didn't feel a positive response to these yearnings, he became belligerent and depressed.

Sam's mother, an anxious woman, felt overwhelmed by both her children's and husband's needs, and she chose more often than not to capitulate to her husband's desires, thus leaving Sam feeling very rejected. Sam's father was an exceptionally controlling, volatile man whose behavior could become quite irrational and who held peculiar child-rearing ideas. In his relationship to Sam he would alternate between unreasonable expectations, sadistic behavior, and infantilization. He seemed incapable of seeing Sam as a separate person and expected Sam to be a clone of him and thus do whatever he wanted. He had almost no empathy for Sam as a little boy, and his overall attitude towards him was strikingly similar to what Ross (1982) described in those fathers who harbor unconscious envy, resentment, and aggression towards their sons. Similarly, while his mother did not approve of her husband's behavior towards Sam and could see how damaging it was to Sam's self-esteem, she had great difficulty intervening on his behalf and protecting him. I sensed that Sam very much wanted to please both parents but the cost was a total loss of his sense of self. It seemed as if the only way to feel he had an effect on his parents was by his oppositional and aggressive behavior, which at least reminded them of his presence.

Sam entered the oedipal phase of development with significant narcissistic vulnerabilities, which included insecurities about his parents' affection, low-ered self-esteem, a tendency to easily feel threatened and injured, difficulty managing his impulses, and accompanying affects. He handled these painful feelings by resorting to earlier anal-sadistic attempts at control of the other person. The major challenge of the oedipal period is to integrate the loving and rivalrous feelings towards the father so as to establish a positive identifi-cation with him and in this process relinquish the oedipal wishes toward his mother. This more secure identification leads to further ego and superego integration and paves the way for the child to engage in tasks more appropri-ate to latency age.

Sam was not free to fully engage himself in school and with peers because, not having either parent on his side, he was still caught up with feeling hurt and rejected. The father's sadistic behavior made it very difficult for Sam to identify with him in a positive manner, and his mother's inability to protect him left him feeling betrayed. Although the feeling of betrayal is inevitable in the context of the fantasies associated with the Oedipus complex, in Sam's situation the mother's actual behavior of not protecting Sam from his father's irrational demands led to a different kind of betrayal. Instead of "my mother belongs to my father," it meant "my mother does not love me." This in turn produced great rage at the mother and, ultimately, feelings of worthlessness.

However, despite his disappointment in both parents, Sam still sought their approval. He did try to please his mother by doing well in school, and often eagerly showed her his work. However, since she was unable to sustain the attention he needed, he would respond by acting up in school. He would try to gain his father's approval by initially complying with the father's numerous demands, but, since these demands invariably turned out to be unrealistic and posed a direct threat to his autonomy, the end result was a no-win struggle. And again, this struggle for control was more in character with the wish for his father to recognize him as a separate person and love him than with the oedipal wish proper—to compete with the father and win mother.

Blos (1984) proposes a differentiation between the son–father relationship of the dyadic and of the triadic period. The father of the dyadic period is a facilitator who, in conjunction with the mother, activates the individuation process and finally becomes for his son a savior from the beckoning regression and the threatening re-engulfment during the rapprochement subphase. The dyadic father belongs to the post-differentiation, pre-ambivalent, idealizing stage of early object relations. Jealousy is noticeable and so is the quest for total possession. However, the son's turn to the father is not yet affected or burdened by sexual jealousy and patricidal conflict. These emotional discordances belong to the father of the oedipal era.

It was in relationship to his sister that I received a clearer impression of how Sam's identifications were unfolding and their implication for the nature of his particular oedipal resolution. Because of the demands put upon him to be more grown-up before he felt ready, he retaliated by becoming especially resentful and rageful toward his younger sister, bossing her at every turn. This not only signified his inability to share but also was a very direct identification with how the father treated both him and his mother, an identification with the aggressor. He was unable to compete with the father in any normative manner, so instead Sam's competition was expressed with a vengeance primarily toward his sister and, to a lesser extent, toward his peers and toward me. He always had to win, even if it meant not playing by the rules, frequently changing the rules, or, at times, outright cheating. In a true oedipal competition there is a powerful desire to win, but in this phase the superego has matured so that cheating becomes less acceptable, or at least poses a conflict. From his narcissistic vantage point, feeling powerless to win, Sam found it very painful to lose and thus no matter what game we played he managed by any means available to make himself the winner. With his sister he reenacted the sadomasochistic relationship that he experienced with his father and that he witnessed between his parents. Furthermore, his rage at her was also the split-off rage he could not express toward his mother, in a sense protecting the fragile relationship he did have with his mother.

The narcissistic elements that prevailed were his need to get his own way, his need to win at all costs, and the sadomasochistic relationship with his sister that looked as if it could easily become the prototype for all his subsequent relationships. Also striking was his need to care for himself in ways that his parents could not be counted on to do. This precocious ego development, while outwardly a strength, covered up his dependency, his inner fears, and his desperate longings, a not uncommon characteristic of those who often function at a very high level but who are narcissistically vulnerable and can be quite overwhelmed emotionally. Feeling desperately alone in sadness and hurt leads to a strengthening of narcissistic defenses and an accompanying retreat into more grandiose narcissistic fantasies. This set of events makes it far more difficult to proceed to a genuine oedipal position, one that is dependent on developing internalization and positive identification with both parents—and on the parents' maturity, in turn, in dealing with the child's oedipal striving.

Case of an Adolescent

Seth entered treatment at the age of 13, depressed and unable to attend school. He seemed very unhappy, was overweight, and his overall appearance conveyed a lack of care. An only child, he had lost his mother in a car accident when he was 11 years old and was now living alone with his father. Seth was clearly highly intelligent, talented, articulate, and seemed more adult-like than adolescent. What was most striking was his denial of any feelings in the face of his apparently difficult situation. Seth described living a very isolated existence with no friends, but maintained that he liked being alone. He told me that while he had been very close to his mother he did not think much about her or her death, and in relation to his father he felt indifferent at best. The same impervious attitude emerged in his lack of concern about the consequences of not attending school, while at the same time he maintained that he wanted to be successful later in life. He was unable to explain why he was being truant, other than to offer rationalizations about school being boring and feeling picked on by some of the kids. As he became comfortable in later sessions, more emerged as to the possible reason for his truancy. It appeared that as he entered adolescence, with its accompanying physical changes and resurgence of powerful sexual feelings, Seth's confusion about his sense of self was exacerbated. Seth confessed that he felt himself sexually attracted to boys rather than girls but maintained that this didn't bother him except insofar as how others would see him. His attitude in revealing this was matter-of-fact and he had little else to say about it. Despite his denial, I felt that the emergence of these sexual impulses and fantasies had aroused considerable anxiety, and that it was another precipitating factor in his withdrawal from peers and finally from school.

Initially, I learned little about Seth's history other than that he had been very close to his mother and remembered spending a great deal of time at home with her while his father worked late. Like his father, he was not particularly interested in sports, and preferred to have lengthy conversations with his mother, who seemed happy to have him as company, companion, and confidant. He described his mother as a very sweet person who seemed to have a lot of insecurities about herself that she shared with him. In listening to Seth, I sensed that she had not encouraged appropriate developmental separation from her, and in fact she seemed to have discouraged latency-age activities. It seemed that they were both content to have each other as an audience.

The first year of treatment was stormy, as Seth continued to act out and deny the severity of his situation. What became clearly apparent was the delayed mourning for his mother. As he became more involved in treatment, memories of his mother were slowly recovered and a mourning process began that played an important part in his five-year therapy. His early relationship to his mother was evident in the transference and in my countertransference. As Seth's life became less chaotic, he appeared eager for his sessions, spoke freely, and enjoyed filling me in on what happened since we last saw each other. He had a keen intelligence, a good sense of humor, and an insightful and interesting way of observing people and situations. He was in fact a great story teller; I found myself looking forward to our sessions, and he seemed pleased to be provided with an appreciative audience. Often it felt as if both Seth and I were quite content to remain in this mutual gazing and feeding relationship and it reminded me of what Seth had told me about his relationship with his mother. At those times, in the comfort of the therapeutic environment, it was as if he had recovered the early mother. At the same time, while I had the distinct impression that Seth was curious about me and my life (it emerged primarily as an interest in my profession), he did not want me to say much, and if I did interject he seemed to show only a polite intellectual interest. His isolation of affect and his distancing were quite dramatic, especially in contrast to those rarer moments when I was able to interpret how he might miss his mother or feel abandoned by her when he would become visibly sad. Predictably, because of Seth's propensity to isolate and deny feelings, he instead acted on them. Subtly provocative, with little concern or affect, he would inform me of how he had engaged in rebellious or self-destructive behavior, and I found myself driven into enactments in which I assumed an authority position, demanding that he see reality. A father transference was at play: on the one hand, there was the desire for me to be the authority, while on the other hand he needed to disparage that authority by dismissing what I said and proving me wrong with elaborate arguments. From a very early age, Seth remembered hating his father and being very angry at him. His attitude appeared quite dramatic, since in the reality of his early relations with his father there seemed little justification for such strong rejecting feelings. Seth's father was a somewhat withdrawn, passive man but a concerned parent who cared a great deal about Seth. Seth's memory was that on the surface his parents seemed to have a good relationship. He felt that his mother had often treated his father as if he were another child who needed taking care of and to be told what to do. Seth was very disparaging and dismissive of him and felt that his father was not someone he could look up to, although in reality the father, while immature in ways, was clearly intelligent and very competent and successful at his work. Thus the question as to why Seth was so rejecting of his father was at first not easily answered. But what was clear was that, having reached adolescence, his inability to identify positively with his father had immense implications for his oedipal development and his sense of himself in the present and future.

Seth's confusion about his basic sense of self was most evident as his depression slowly lifted, and he resumed attending school and began showing an interest in having friends. What came into focus were his enormous narcissistic needs, such as his need for constant affirmation and admiration from teachers and peers. His moods dramatically fluctuated between grandiosity and insecurity so that when he was the center of attention he would feel very high and, conversely, when he felt ignored he would become depressed and isolate himself further, maintaining that he didn't really need anyone. This need for attention drove him to exhibitionistic, provocative, and at times outrageous behavior. His anger, which for the most part was disavowed, was expressed either passive-aggressively or via provocations. Unable to sustain a stable sense of self, he had difficulty maintaining an objective view of himself, and his sense of time, volition, and reality were compromised, affecting his ability to plan ahead. On one level he appeared to have good values, and there were times when he exhibited concern and empathy for a relative or friend. However there was another side that could emerge that would be cold, cruel, unfeeling, and hurtful. There was a shallow quality and a sadomasochistic component to many of his relationships, and he himself wondered whether he had ever truly loved anyone. His attitude of disregard toward his father was seen in relation to other authority figures with whom he was either quietly rebellious or openly provocative. I often had the sense that he considered himself "above the law." His strong exhibitionistic impulses were at times expressed in outrageous antics where he would use his intelligence, wit, and talent to challenge the established order of things.

It appeared that Seth's oedipal development had been significantly affected by a disturbance in his early relationship to his mother and a failure to establish a triadic position. As a result, he was left struggling with a preponderance of narcissistic issues, and it appeared that a narcissistic character structure was already in place. Mollon (1993), in his discussion of narcissistic disturbance, notes the parents' role in the child's inability to move from the dyadic to the triadic position, and the consequences for the child's ability to establish an authentic oedipal position. "The entry into the oedipal position can be seen to involve a radical restructuring of the self. As the relationship between father and mother (the primal scene) is recognized, the child must experience a profound separation from mother, which at the same time allows him or her his or her own place as the child of two parents who have come together in intercourse, i.e., as the product of the primal scene" (p. 110). Lacan (1957) has also shown that entry into the oedipal position may be associated with entry into the symbolic order, the father being seen as a representative of the outside world, the "law" and the social order. Thus, when a separation from the mother has not taken place, the child remains in a dyadic and/or narcissistic position with the mother.

In Seth's case, it would appear, both from reconstruction and from the nature of the transference, that his mother had often used him as a narcissistic part-object. However, a prerequisite for an authentic oedipal experience is to have a whole-object relationship with the mother or primary caretaker. This whole-object relationship includes, among other things, the capacity for ambivalence: the capacity to learn that early splitting and projections of the good and bad attributes of the object actually reside in the same person, allowing the mother to be loved as a whole person. This whole-object relationship permits differentiation and separation from the mother to take place and paves the way for a whole-object relationship with the father, which includes loving him as well. Simultaneously, the capacity for a whole-object relationship establishes a sense of self vis-à-vis the object. In a true oedipal situation you have established a sense of self and you are in rivalry with one person you love for the other person you love.

Now despite what might have appeared on the surface as oedipal anger towards his father, there was little indication that Seth was actually in rivalry with his father for his mother. There was no doubt that her death and his inability to mourn had played a part in his wish to reunite with the mother of the early years, but there was sufficient evidence to suggest that problems in the area of separation-individuation had existed prior to her death. Mother's subtle denigration of the father by treating him as another child and offering the illusion that Seth was the preferred child was a form of seduction that encouraged Seth's grandiosity and sense of entitlement. This interfered with the process of identifying with his father and contributed to the blurring of generational boundaries.

While Seth identified with his mother's denigration of his father, he was also angry and disappointed in his father for not protecting him from his mother's seduction and not being the kind of man he could look up to as an ego ideal. In the boy's separation from the dyadic mother, the importance of the father's role to counter the threat of regression and engulfment by the mother has been well documented (Abelin 1971, Greenson 1968). Seth's father seemed unable to fulfill that role and left Seth bound to his mother and unable to attain a stable differentiated sense of self.

The parents' attitude toward one another, one which de-emphasized their own sexual union, also contributed to the fantasy that Seth was his mother's favorite and that the parents did not have a relationship apart from him. Britton (1989) notes how the final relinquishment of oedipal objects is evaded and an illusional oedipal configuration is formed as a defensive organization to deny the psychic reality of the parental relationship.

> The acknowledgement by the child of the parents' relationship with each other unites his psychic world, limiting it to one world shared with his two parents in which different object relationships can exist. The closure of the oedipal triangle by the recognition of the link joining the parents provides a limiting boundary for the internal world. It creates what I call a 'triangular space'—i.e., a space bounded by the three persons of the Oedipal situation and all their potential relationships. It includes, therefore, the possibility of being a participant in a relationship and observed by a third person as well as being an observer of a relationship between two people. [p. 84]

While consciously believing that his mother preferred him to his "sibling" father, the sense of self that Seth built on this fantasy was very fragile, because his insecurities, feelings of unattractiveness, and need for constant admiration suggested he was never sure that he was truly admired and loved for himself despite his mother's attentions. This was evident when he became infatuated with boys his own age whom, in contrast to himself, he described in idealized terms, emphasizing their physical attractiveness, coolness, and popularity. They seemed to represent a narcissistic object choice, as if a union with such a person would make Seth perfect and he might love them the way he wanted his mother to love him. Only later did Seth come to experience some anger at his mother for abandoning him. For the most part the anger at his mother was split off and experienced consciously towards the father. This split-off anger was also seen in his fantasies and behavior toward girls, whom he wished both to rescue and to violently attack. In the transference I experienced his anger when he seemed to go out of his way to engage in self-destructive behavior in order to rob me of the possibility of having any effect on him or any meaning to him.

Case of an Adult

Mia was a strikingly attractive woman with a beautiful figure who always dressed in the height of fashion. At a relatively early age she had reached the heights of a highly competitive profession, was married, and had a young child. On the surface Mia presented with difficulties that could easily be mistaken for oedipal pathology, but which on closer scrutiny showed intense narcissistic concerns that left her in a constant and lifelong state of self-doubt and insecurity. She complained of anxiety and uncertainty about every decision she made, fearing she would not do or say the right thing. She spent much time worrying about how others saw her and constantly fearing that someone else might seem smarter, nicer, a better mother, and so on. She knew she was a perfectionist and felt that anything less was demeaning. Given her successful work achievements, her suitable family life, and her meaningful friendships, there was little support in reality for her feelings of low self-esteem, doubt, and insecurity. On the contrary, seen from the outside, Mia and her life seemed enviable from every vantage point. But she constantly repeated a sad lament that went something like this: "If only my father were alive he would tell me what to do and tell me that everything will be alright." Her father had died three years earlier and Mia continued to think about him every day. She totally dismissed her mother, saying she played no role in her life—her father was the only one that mattered. She described her parents as having a terrible marriage with constant fighting and she felt her father clearly preferred her to the angry and very difficult mother. While Mia felt she loved her husband and could feel pleasure and great pride in her child, she was nevertheless most attached to her family of origin, which occupied her dreams and waking thoughts.

A typical dilemma that would preoccupy Mia's thoughts is seen in the following episode. For many months she had been ruminating about whether or not to ask her mother for a very special particular keepsake that her father had given her mother. She very much wanted this piece of jewelry, saying her mother never wore it and that she had always liked it. Yet she was afraid to ask her mother, not so much because her mother would say no, but because she didn't like to have to ask for anything. Asking made her feel greedy and bad, and having to ask for something was not the same as if the person just knew your desires and satisfied them. She also felt that it was more appropriate for her to have this keepsake because her parents did not really care for one another and it was she who truly loved her father.

Hearing such a dilemma, one could easily conjecture that Mia had many unresolved oedipal issues, as in fact she did. But what she was describing was not a true oedipal conflict. And in truth, in an earlier treatment many oedipal interpretations had been made that had little effect on the inner pain that she experienced. We came to understand that the most important reason she wanted this keepsake so much was because in her mind it bore magical properties. If she wore it, her father would be with her, guiding and advising her, and she would be safe.

We also came to understand the dismissive attitude toward her mother who she initially insisted had no influence on her life. In a true oedipal triangle, her mother would have been the loved, hated, and feared rival. Consciously, she was not aware of any such feelings. What she felt toward her mother was annoyance and frustration. We gradually learned that these feelings were based on the fact that her mother had been preoccupied, phobic, and depressed. Slowly Mia recovered memories of herself as a child, frequently crying. She recalled how her own wishes were disregarded and her feelings minimized or ignored. She came to associate any needy feelings with being bad. As is typical in such situations, she developed precocious ego functions while inwardly feeling dependent and deprived of a close union with her mother. Very early she turned to her father for substitute mothering. While he could also be self-centered, he was generally kinder to her and could offer her more definite opinions and rational views than her phobic mother. Mia spent her life doing what she thought he expected in order to gain his love and approval, and consequently she never developed a very secure sense of self. All her accomplishments and successes felt hollow and unreal, and all that she had attained felt tenuous and might disappear in a puff of smoke. This was what underlay her fragile sense of self and her narcissistic vulnerability to any criticism or imagined slight. She needed a great deal of attention and affirmation from the other in order to maintain even a precarious state of well-being. Her magical thinking and superstitions persisted in her adult belief that only her father could make things right with the world.

Summary

In the above three examples of an oedipal-age child, an adolescent, and an adult, I have tried to show how the predominance of narcissistic concerns interferes with the establishment of a secure sense of self, or what Winnicott (1960) referred to as "continuity of being," which I see as essential in meeting the challenges posed by the Oedipus complex. The Oedipus complex includes crucial encounters with realities such as differentiation and separation between mother and child, the differences between the sexes, the difference between child and adult, and the beginnings of acceptance of one's own and others' limitations. The resolution of the Oedipus complex—and here I agree with Loewald (1979) that one contends with its resolution throughout life—includes owning responsibility for one's impulses, tolerating the guilt for one's actions, and ultimately having the ability to mourn.

It has been noted that the capacity for adaptation to reality is revealed in the degree to which the child is able to tolerate the deprivations resulting from the oedipal situation. The capacity to tolerate such deprivation depends on the consolidation of a sense of self growing from the child's secure attachment to the caretakers, a security based on mutually regulatory, satisfying, and reliable interactions with mature parents.

Hamilton (1993) makes the point that the experience of continuity can only grow out of a relationship that can tolerate change. But the narcissistic relationship between parent and child in the cases I have described ultimately denied the possibility of tolerating change and thereby stultified growth. In the end, for a child to have an authentic oedipal experience, he must bring to it not only the achieved preoedipal prerequisites, but he must go through it with parents who are mature enough to allow him to experience it and who also allow themselves to experience it together with him.

References

Abelin, E. L. (1971). The role of the father in the separation-individuation process. In *Separation-Individuation*, ed. J. B. McDevitt and C. F. Settlage, pp. 229–253. New York: International Universities Press.

Birksted-Breen, D. (1996). Unconscious representation of femininity. *Journal of the American Psychoanalytic Association* 44 (Suppl.):119–133.

Blos, P. (1984). Son and father. *Journal of the American Psychoanalytic Association* 32:301–325.

Britton, R. (1989). The missing link: parental sexuality in the Oedipus complex. In *The Oedipus Complex Today*, ed. J. Steiner, pp. 83–101. London: Karnac.

Chasseguet-Smirgel, J. (1985). *Creativity and Perversion*. London: Free Association.

Goux, J. (1993). *Oedipus, Philosopher*. Stanford, CA: Stanford University Press.

Greenson, R. (1968). Disidentifying from mother: its special importance for the boy. *International Journal of Psycho-Analysis* 49:370–374.

Hamilton, V. (1993). *Narcissus and Oedipus*. London: Karnac.

Lacan, J. (1957). On a question preliminary to any possible treatment of psychosis. In *Écrits*. London: Tavistock, 1977.

Loewald, H. (1979). The waning of the Oedipus complex. *Journal of the American Psychoanalytic Association* 27:173–182.

Mollon P. (1993). *The Fragile Self*. London: Whurr.

Ross, J. M. (1982). Oedipus revisited: Laius and the "Laius Complex." *Psychoanalytic Study of the Child* 37:169–201. New Haven, CT: Yale University Press.

Schuker, E. (1996). Toward further analytic understanding of lesbian patients. *Journal of the American Psychoanalytic Association* 44 (Suppl.):485–511.

Shengold, L. (1989). The parent as sphinx. In *Soul Murder*. New York: Fawcett Columbine.

Simon, B. (1991). Is the Oedipus complex still the cornerstone of psychoanalysis? Three obstacles to answering the question. *Journal of the American Psychoanalytic Association* 39:641–669.

Steiner, J. (1985). Turning a blind eye: the cover up for Oedipus. *International Review of Psycho-Analysis* 12:161–173.

Winnicott, D. W. (1960). The theory of the parent–infant relationship. In *The Maturational Processes and the Facilitating Environment*, pp. 37–56. New York: International Universities Press.

6

Adolescent Narcissism

Marsha H. Levy-Warren

Adolescence is a period of great transformation. Child-size bodies transform into adult-like bodies, concrete thinking capacities shift into abstract ones, and dependent children come to feel like comparatively autonomous young adults. One of the significant changes of the time is a shift in the sources for healthy narcissism. Where children focus intently on their caregivers for the looks, smiles, and physical affection that leave them with a sense of basic goodness, well-being and pride, the cornerstones of healthy narcissism, adolescents ultimately must be able to look to themselves. To change from focusing primarily outward to focusing primarily within to achieve a sense of healthy narcissism is a difficult and complex task. It takes the whole of adolescence to complete.

Adolescence is not a homogeneous period. It divides into three major subphases: early, middle, and late. In each, females generally begin the subphase two years before their male counterparts, a situation that arises because girls generally begin puberty (the beginning of adolescence) two years earlier than boys. These subphases roughly correspond to the ages of 10 to 14, 15 to 18, and 19 to 22 (though, at times, it is more accurate to place the end of adolescence as late as 25).

In each subphase of adolescence, there is a change in the sources of healthy narcissism. Among early adolescents, there is a shift in focus that takes them away from concentrating on the love and attention of significant caregivers and toward a focus on the adolescents themselves, important adults outside the family, and peers who become special to the adolescents. Middle adolescence brings with it a shift to an even greater focus on the self and to those seen as similar, especially in the peer group. Late adolescents derive a sense of basic goodness, well-being, and pride from being the kinds of people they aspire to be, both in terms of what they do and how they are in the world.

Early adolescence, which is initiated by the vast changes of puberty, is the time when those who are emerging from childhood loosen their dependencies upon caregivers. The once idealized adults who took care of them are now seen in a more realistic light (while other adults and peers are often temporarily overvalued). This shifting of admiration and attention affords early adolescents an opportunity to readjust their views of themselves and their caregivers. A growth in their cognitive capacities contributes to their ability to see both themselves and those around them more accurately. Not relying as much on the love and appreciation of their caregivers, however, leaves early adolescents with fewer consistent sources of self-esteem. They feel more emotionally labile and less certain about who they are.

Even their bodies are lost to them as consistent sources of pride, for their bodies are in a state of constant flux during early adolescence. For girls, there are the fat deposits forming that ultimately become hips and breasts, signs that the girl's body is becoming the young woman's body—but also signs that are rarely welcome in this world that overstresses thinness. For boys, there are the dramatic growth spurts that often leave them feeling relatively gawky and/or uncoordinated. These bodily changes stabilize as adolescence progresses, but it takes some years, and there is instability in the sense of the bodily self during this time.

Adolescents in the beginning of this phase tend to be more critical of their caregivers than they had been in the past. Where once the authority of the adults was relatively unquestioned, now the questions abound. The result is not just that the adults in these early adolescents' lives feel challenged, but also that the adolescents themselves feel a sense of loss. The admiration that these adolescents had felt as children toward their parents, for example, the sense of power that the parents once had in their lives, is now lost. A hug, a smile, a look of appreciation from a parent—each so meaningful in a child's life—no longer have the same impact for these same individuals when they become adolescents. This is the form that the narcissistic shift of early adolescence takes: it primarily is experienced as a loss.

It is the loss of the power of the parents (and other significant adults in their lives) to serve as a source of a sense of basic goodness, well-being, and pride that moves early adolescents out of the home and into the social world, in a search for this lost sense of narcissistic satisfaction. The power that parents and others once held for them is now taken into themselves and others in their social world. The significant adults in their lives are often aware of this shift of power and authority. The parents feel that their young adolescents' attention is elsewhere. The early adolescents are more involved with their friends, other adults in their lives, and themselves than they are in garnering the love and attention of their parents. The result is that their relationships with their parents are more erratic than they had been in the past.

Middle adolescence brings with it an intensification of self-focus, a diminution in focus on the adult world, and a preoccupation with the world of peers. All of these serve to aid in the adolescent individuation process. Where the shift in narcissism in early adolescence primarily supports the separation process that is initiated by puberty, the narcissistic shift of middle adolescence permits a degree of self-focus and comparison with same-aged peers that fleshes out the emerging sense of self that is critical to middle adolescent development.

In this context, separation is the growing awareness of Self and Other, the complex development of a sense of me and not-me. Individuation refers to the growing awareness of self, as reflected in the differentiation of self and object representations. Adolescence is a period of tremendous growth in both separation and individuation.

Middle adolescents are more affiliative than early adolescents. They seek out groups that they feel represent specific aspects of Self. This aids them in shoring up their growing awareness of themselves as individuals. They gravitate toward athletic teams, drama groups, literary publications, and others who just appreciate the same kind of music. In each instance, self- and object representations are modified, made to be more aligned with a current sense of who they are.

Where early adolescents look back and compare themselves with how they were then and now, middle adolescents are fully focused in the present. To the adults around them, their actions often seem to be taken without any awareness of the potential consequences. Indeed, adolescents of this age may first take actions, then consider the meaning of these actions. They are on a quest for meaning; they constantly seek self-knowledge through their actions, words, and thoughts. They are quite preoccupied with who they are, who they are becoming, and how they are perceived by their peers. Where once their parents' views were the most highly valued, they are more likely to turn to their friends at this time. This particularly applies to matters of everyday dress, social interactions, and social endeavors. Their values and ethical beliefs remain more rooted in those of their parents.

Looking within to establish moral and ethical values is a development of late adolescence. In this last subphase, adolescents become focused on who they aspire to be. Their pride, well-being, and sense of basic goodness ultimately correspond to the degree to which they act in accordance with their wished-for self. This wished-for self is the ego ideal. It matures in late adolescence, particularly, into a set of self-representations that correspond to a realistic view of what is possible for the adolescent. Adolescents' cognitive ability to perceive the world with more complexity is utilized in the evolution of their ego ideals.

The ego ideals of children are very oriented toward what their parents wish them to be. During the adolescent separation and individuation processes, ego ideals are re-formed to correspond to what the adolescents come to realize about their *own* wishes for themselves—in all spheres. They are especially concerned with what kinds of people they want to be and in what manner they want to pursue their goals. When they feel that they have acted in accordance with their ego ideals, they feel good about themselves, and there is narcissistic satisfaction. When they act in ways that do not correspond to their ego ideal aspirations, they feel ashamed of themselves, and there is narcissistic injury.

During this subphase, although adolescents rely primarily upon themselves for their narcissistic supplies, they also respond to those in their lives that they have designated as important to them. The admiration or appreciation of respected teachers, loved parents, or valued friends can leave adolescents of this age with a sense of pride or well-being. They do not rely on others for this sense of pride or well-being, however; they simply enjoy it when it is offered. The distinction is one that is reflected in the difference between need and want: where children need their parents and others to offer them love and appreciation in order to feel a basic sense of goodness, late adolescents may want or enjoy such attention, but not require it.

Adolescents, therefore, need to turn their attention to themselves in order to make the changes necessary for their developmental journeys. Without extensive self-focus, of the type that often leaves those around them feeling estranged, provoked, or ignored, important development steps may not be taken. Adolescents must come to rely on their own perceptions, feelings, thoughts, and reactions. They need to have confidence in these self-experiences in order to function in an adequately autonomous fashion. Without this confidence, they will require others to supply them with their views, thoughts, beliefs, and feelings, and ultimately, with their sources of self-esteem.

Healthy narcissistic development during adolescence requires self-focus. Where the circumstances of an adolescent's life make such self-focus difficult, narcissistic development may be impaired. The case that follows offers an illustration of such an impairment.

The Case of Kevin

A turning away from the family and toward the world of peers is critical to middle adolescent development. An adolescent of this age who is preoccupied with issues in his family is likely to find such an outward move difficult to negotiate. Kevin is an example of someone with this kind of stumbling block in his middle adolescent development.[1] Though he came into treatment chronologically at the age of a middle adolescent, and (physically) looking like a middle adolescent, he still regarded himself as much younger and was still primarily struggling with the issues of early adolescence.

What is presented here is a twice-weekly treatment that took place over a period of twenty-seven months. First, there will be a brief description of Kevin's history, and then of the treatment process. The discussion will focus on how his treatment permitted Kevin to continue in his interrupted narcissistic development. This enabled him to move from early into middle adolescence, and thus, to feel more rooted in his appropriate developmental subphase.

The Treatment

Kevin began treatment at the age of 17. At first glance, he was a tall, thin, muscular, square-chinned, dark-haired, handsome young man. Upon further study, his averted glance, slumping shoulders, and general air of nervousness made him seem somewhat boyish and timid.

A court ordered Kevin to be in psychotherapy. A couple of months before, he and a friend had broken into a department store. They tripped off an alarm

---

1. This case was first discussed in Chapter 9 of *The Adolescent Journey* (Levy-Warren 1996).

system and were caught on the way out. When I asked him if he knew what this incident was about for him, that is, why he might have done it, or what it meant for him to have done it, Kevin first said he "really didn't know." A few moments later, he continued by saying: "My friend Billy wanted to do it. He asked me if I was too chicken to do it with him, and, I guess I just kind of wanted to see whether I was or not."

Kevin seemed to look at himself from the outside in; he would take an action, then try to infer what his feelings and motivations were from that action. It was very difficult for him to think ahead, to make a plan, or to know what he was thinking or feeling. He often went along with what others wanted to do. By both his own description and his father's, he felt moody, detached, and depressed much of the time. He rarely applied himself at home or in school. Kevin felt that he was a shell of a person. He had little or no sense of inner drive, feeling, or thought. He looked to those around him whom he admired to supply him with self-definition. He looked to others at exactly the moment that he needed to look to himself.

History

Kevin's parents divorced when he was 3 years old. Their relationship afterward was usually amicable, though, according to Kevin, quarrelsome when it came to making arrangements for him. When they divorced, Kevin moved from New York City to southern Oregon with his mother. He lived there with her until he was 10, at which point he came back to New York to live with his father for two years. He then returned to Oregon, where he lived until he was 17. At 17, he came back to New York City, where he planned to remain until he went to college. Summers and Christmas were always spent with the parent with whom he was not living.

In describing his history, Kevin tended to focus on the relationships in his parents' lives and on his own acts of unexplained violence. His father remarried when Kevin was 5, and divorced when Kevin was 15. His mother began to live with someone when he was 8, whom she then married when he was 16. His father currently had a steady girlfriend.

The acts of violence included breaking into his school when he was 8, getting into numerous fights with boys his age, and kicking his father's second wife in the shins. Kevin reported that his father was more effective in controlling him than his mother, but that neither of them was able to understand the roots of his behavior and help him to stop it. He felt that each of these incidents was followed by his being sent to the other parent's place to live. As he put it:

"They just got sick of me after awhile. I was too much to deal with; and, anyway, they had their own problems."

Kevin described his mother as a loving, overprotective, somewhat childlike person. She taught preschool, which Kevin felt was "the perfect age for her. She could be affectionate and playful, and wouldn't have to deal with any serious behavior problems." He said that when he was growing up, his mother was more concerned with finding a new husband than she was with anything else. She didn't understand him very well back then, but she "definitely didn't understand" him "at all now."

Kevin felt his mother had allowed her boyfriend, now husband, to dominate her and ("even") to dictate to her how she should bring Kevin up. As a child, Kevin had always been frightened of this man. He was subject to bursts of temper, and occasionally "smacked" Kevin "around." To Kevin's knowledge, his stepfather never hit his mother, but he bellowed at her with some frequency, especially when he drank. Kevin often felt enraged at his stepfather, but also felt impotent to take any actions that would protect either him or his mother.

When he was 12, Kevin walked into the living room after school and found his mother and stepfather naked on the couch in an embrace. He felt embarrassed and frightened. Despite the fact that it was obviously quite upsetting to Kevin, the incident was never discussed. At the point that he entered treatment, Kevin had vowed never to talk to his stepfather again. He noted that it would be quite awhile before he talked to his mother, either.

Kevin's father sounded like a perennial adolescent. He loved fast cars, sports, dating different women, and talking to his son about "scoring." He was multi-talented, according to his idealizing son. He could "sing, play the piano and guitar, hit a mean tennis ball, and charm the pants off anyone he bumped into." He and Kevin were pals. Kevin described his father as his idol; he "was always on top of things."

Kevin had two best friends, one on each coast. The one on the West Coast, Billy, was "bad," into drinking, troublemaking, and doing poorly in school. He tried to get away with whatever he could at all times. He came from a family that was "more messed up" than Kevin's. The friend in New York, John, was a more serious student, less into getting into trouble, and from a family that Kevin admired for its stability and "family feeling." Family feeling was noticeably lacking in Kevin's life.

Kevin felt that his own persona changed when he went from one coast to another, based upon who his best friend was and with whom he was living. He believed that living with his father and being around John would ensure better school performance and less getting into trouble. He also felt that his father treated him as if he were older and more responsible, and that made him act more responsibly.

Treatment Process: Beginning Phase

My first contact was a telephone call from Kevin's father, who set up an appointment for him after telling me about the department store incident, how Kevin had always gotten into scrapes with the boys at school, and how he had lived a bicoastal life. Neither Kevin nor his father thought it necessary for me to meet with anyone but Kevin.

Although Kevin first seemed rather shy, he took quickly to the treatment situation. Within the first few sessions, he began to talk easily and openly about his fears and concerns.

"Life is hairy," he noted. "I'm 17 and I feel like a little kid a lot of the time. I sure as hell—sorry—don't feel ready to be 18, 19. You know, go to college. I don't know where things went wrong with me, but they did."

When I inquired about what he felt was wrong with him, he responded that he had no mind of his own, and that he was "lazy" and "stubborn." He knew he hated "being forced" to do anything, and that it was a matter of pride not to give in when someone tried to force him to do something. He said that this attitude had created serious problems for him in school.

In school, he said that he could only do well if he liked the teacher. He also said that he couldn't talk to girls. He was most successful athletically, but only in team sports. He said that it was easiest for him to make real efforts when it was for the team; individual performance sports were "not his thing."

Individual performance was something Kevin knew was a problem for him. Early on, he told me he could not even lift weights unless someone was in the room with him. This led to our talking about what he needed other people for and what he did not need them for, and how his feelings changed when others were in the room. It became clear that he was easily embarrassed, and that he all too quickly came to the conclusion that he was being perceived as "showing off" in situations of individual performance.

Kevin showed real interest in looking at himself in treatment. He said that he was not used to being with an adult who paid such attention to him. It was hard for him to believe that I did not have a personal agenda.

Raising the issue of adults with personal agendas gave Kevin the opportunity to talk about what the major adults in his life were like, both in the present and in the past. He acknowledged feeling loved by his mother, but noted that he felt it was a kind of generalized love: "She only loved me because I was her kid. She never seemed to get very involved in who I was or what I was doing. As long as I didn't flunk out of school or act fresh with her boyfriend, everything was okay. As soon as I stepped out of line in some way, she would cry and plead with me to behave."

We came to frame these experiences as being about Kevin's feeling both too important and too unimportant. He felt too important because he "made" his mother cry so easily (and so frequently); too unimportant because she seemed so uninterested in who he really was. His "importance" led him to want to tone down his presence, which we saw as one of the reasons individual performance was such a struggle for him. His "unimportance" was a view of himself that he came to see he shared with his mother. Until beginning treatment, he placed very little value on knowing himself.

The degree to which he relied on others to help him in establishing what to do was a connected and prominent issue in this first phase of treatment. He realized that he had never valued his own feelings, thoughts, and attitudes enough to pay much attention to them. The fact that I was paying attention and seemed genuinely interested in him felt like something new to Kevin. When I pointed out that we might suffer the same problem, in that, once again, perhaps he was following someone else's (that is, my) lead in looking at himself, he responded: "Yeah, I thought of that. But this is different. I can use this to figure out what I really do think and feel, then I can make up my mind about things. And, anyway, you don't tell me what to do."

The last part of Kevin's statement was a particularly telling one. He was seeing something about our working process that he had not acknowledged before. In general, he had (up until this time, which was about three or four months into treatment) often asked me what I thought he should do about one situation or another, usually related to a school problem (for example, a late homework assignment) or minor disagreement with his father (such as a household chore he disliked). My consistent response was to press him about *his* thoughts on the subject, with the explanation that it did not make sense for me to become still another person who would tell him how to lead his life, and that I thought he was quite capable of figuring this one out on his own.

"That's what you always say," was Kevin's smiling response.

"That's what I really think," was mine, also said with a smile.

This was a typical kind of interchange in the first year that Kevin and I worked together. There was a good deal of warmth and humor between us. After the first few months of treatment, Kevin began to think that his father, also, had a personal agenda. His first descriptions of his father were practically blemishless: his father could do anything, knew everything, and was (almost) always right. The sole source of conflict between them, from Kevin's point of view, was the unequal distribution of household chores that his father demanded. Since he "was the breadwinner," his father required that Kevin both cook *and* clean up. This struck Kevin as unfair and, in his most critical moments, manipulative.

"He's the father, I'm the kid. It's ridiculous. I'm not supposed to take up all the slack. I'm not his wife or something. He's jerking me around, just because he doesn't want to do this stuff."

These were the first hints of what became Kevin's growing dissatisfaction with his formerly idealized father. He began to see more and more of his father's self-involvement. Even the nature of his interest in Kevin's life came into question: "So, big deal . . . he comes to all my games. I think he gets off on it. He likes having a son he can brag is on varsity teams. He sure never makes me feel good about playing. He acts like he's my personal coach or something, always telling me what I did wrong. Like he knows it all. I *have* a coach. *He* tells me how I played. I don't need my father to do it, too."

His father's attitude toward girls bothered Kevin as well: "He's always bugging me. He pushed me toward some girl in a restaurant the other day, whispering 'hot stuff' in my ear. I was *so* pissed, and *so* embarrassed. I could have killed him for that."

"What happened?" I asked.

"Nothin'. Absolutely nothin'. I didn't say anything to her—and, I gotta admit. She *was* cute. And I didn't have the balls to say anything to him, either."

"Takes 'balls'? What happens if you *do* say something to him?"

"I never do. I'm sure he knows I'm pissed. He doesn't care. He just gets a kick out of it or something. Or he really thinks I *should* go after her."

This was a significant point in Kevin's treatment. He began to talk about his father's attitude toward women, his feeling of being both pushed and upstaged by his father when it came to girls, and his own shyness and timidity when he felt drawn to a girl. He also started to address the tremendous difficulty he had confronting his father. His talking about not having "the balls" to say anything to his father opened up the issue of how he felt about being male, and a young man (as opposed to a boy).

These were difficult sessions for Kevin. He felt embarrassed, even mortified at times, about his wanting to remain a boy, rather than entering the world of men. He saw how his reluctance to be the young man he actually appeared to be was connected to his wanting to hang onto having a strong father who could protect him, and how this interfered with his capacity to confront his father directly. He saw that the world of men and women together was a world he felt afraid to enter.

After about eight or nine months, the first phase of this treatment drew to a close. What had been an easygoing, open treatment relationship became more strained as Kevin started seeing his mother in somewhat more understanding and accepting ways, his father in more critical ways, and our work as somewhat more painful than he originally either imagined or experienced it to be. The subject of the relationship between his changed and changing feelings about his parents and his current difficulties with his peers began the next phase of treatment.

Treatment Process: Middle Phase

During the next year (plus) of his treatment, Kevin shifted the way he looked at the world; it went from outside in to inside out. He looked carefully at his own role in the way events in his life had happened and continued to occur. He talked much less about his parents and much more about himself and his relationships in school, both with his peers, his teachers, and his coaches. The primary context in which his parents came up was when he was looking for the origins of his own traits.

The relationship between Kevin and me also shifted. It remained strong, but there was considerably more tension. He sometimes questioned the point of coming for treatment (though he never missed a session and was regularly on time), and said at times that he "hoped that this was going to do something for him" or he'd "really be pissed off." My tendency was to respond to him directly and frankly: that is, to talk to him about how and why treatment could and did help, and to point out that he had already seen how he had changed since he began talking with me and felt good about the changes he had made. I would then address what some of the other reasons might be for his raising these questions now, such as the nature of his difficulty in dealing with what we had been discussing most recently, like his fear of embarrassment.

This phase of treatment was ushered in, in some respects, by the beginning of a new school year. In his first phase of treatment, Kevin had started in a new school. It was a private school in New York City, and more rigorous than his previous (public) school in Oregon. The school required that he repeat tenth grade. Kevin was embarrassed by this in some respects, but relieved in others.

He did not want his schoolmates to know that he was 17 (when they were 16), but was (with me) openly relieved at the prospect of having a chance to do his tenth-grade year again. He had gotten mediocre grades in what he regarded as a "second-rate" school in Oregon, and wanted to see if he could do better in a better school. Initially, he said that if he were surrounded by kids who cared about school, he would, too (an example of what we came to call his "outside in" approach to life).

He did, in fact, get better grades in school (he had a B average, as compared to a C the year before), but was well aware that some of his classes had been repeat classes from the previous year, which made the classwork easier. He also was aware that eleventh grade was a pivotal year for high school students, in terms of college plans, and that his new "inside out" approach to life was moving him in the direction of confronting his own real thoughts and feelings about the future.

His peers were quite caught up in thinking about college applications, and the best high school classes to take for college preparation. Kevin felt highly ambivalent about going to college. He knew that this set him apart from his schoolmates and wondered why he felt the way he did. We began to make connections between his wish to remain a boy and his anger at and disappointment in his parents and their "personal agendas." He realized that he felt robbed of a stable childhood, having been shuttled back and forth between the two coasts. He came to see that he shied away from competing with his father in any way, which eliminated many areas in which he could be exercising his capabilities. Perhaps most importantly, he began to see how the many ways he had sabotaged himself were ways of (passively) expressing the anger and disappointment he felt toward his parents, particularly his father. He felt that it was his father who wanted him to go to college; Kevin did not know whether he had ever decided for himself whether or not he wanted to go. He only saw it as something that he was going to do because his father wanted him to do it, or he was not going to do it because his father wanted him to do it.

"How did I make him this important? It's like my whole life revolves around him, rather than me."

Kevin began to scrutinize himself. Although he became far more self-conscious, at times, as a result, he also seemed to become stronger and more self-possessed at others. He was beginning to get a sense of knowing himself. His separation and individuation processes were in motion.

"I can't stand these zits. What are they from? I never used to have them. At least I don't think I did. But I never even looked, so how would I know? You know, otherwise, I think I look okay. I like this haircut. And I've been lifting every morning and I definitely can see the difference."

It wasn't only Kevin who was looking at Kevin. He also began to notice that others, especially girls, were looking at him. He was self-conscious, but intrigued, by the prospect that they might be interested in him: "I know Susie was looking at me. You know, not just looking, but checking me out. And she's cute, you know? I mean, I could get into that, you know?"

"Kevin, that's a lot of 'you knows' all in one paragraph. Something going on here about what you do or don't know about girls, boy–girl stuff, that kind of thing?" I asked.

"That's a tough one. I know and I don't know. I know I'm supposed to be cool and all that, but, the truth is, I think I have some hang-ups about all this stuff. My father is such a stud—at least, that's what he makes himself out to be. But, lots of women dig him, so maybe he is. But what does that have to do with me? I don't know. All I know is, when I like a girl, I can't talk to her. I feel like I'm tongue-tied. Maybe it's one of those things where I'm comparing myself to my father. He's such a talker. But, I don't think that's all that's going on. I think . . . I can't believe I'm even saying this to you. But if I don't tell you, who the hell am I going to tell? I think I'm really scared shitless to have sex." (Kevin looked down at the floor.)

"So, you think that talking to someone you like immediately gets connected to having sex?"

"Well, you know, one thing leads to another and all that."

"Got any idea what you're scared *of* in having sex?"

Kevin fell silent. I waited a few minutes, then asked: "Can you say what just crossed your mind?"

Kevin clearly felt awkward and uncomfortable. He looked as if he were about to cry and was trying to fight it off.

"I know this is right out of the books or something, but I thought about that time when I walked in on my mother and Pete (his mother's second husband). I know I told you they were holding each other, but I really think they were having sex. I try to block out the whole thing, but that's what I thought about when you asked whatever you asked me before. What did you ask, anyway?"

"I asked if you had any idea what you were scared *of* in having sex."

"Guess something's going on with that thing with my mother and Pete. I know I was completely freaked out at the time. I mean, I didn't think my mother ever had sex with him. I was only 12 for Chrissakes. I didn't want to know about it, I sure as hell didn't want to see them at it. It disgusted me completely. It still does, in fact. He's such an asshole."

"Are you disgusted when you think of sex, altogether?"

"Well, I know I've got this thing about which girls will do it and which won't. I don't want to think that a girl I'd like would do it—which I know is screwed up. A guy my age is supposed to want to have sex, right?"

The many issues for Kevin about what he wanted, and whether it was acceptable for him to have wants, sexual and otherwise, became the major topic of his treatment at this time. Discussions ranged from sex, to scholastic and athletic accomplishments, to relationships with friends, to dating girls. Kevin was extremely engaged in treatment. He often bounded in and right away began with comments like this:

"I'm 5 feet, 8 inches, 128 pounds, I want to be 6 feet, 150 pounds. That's my ideal. I've been working my ass off in cross-country. Coach says I've peeled a full 20 seconds off in the last two months. He's totally impressed. He's not the only one. I think it's going to my head. I almost got myself to say something to Jessica today. Do you believe it? *Jessica*. She is *so* gorgeous. Hey—do you think this means something? I've been having this same daydream over and over again. I'm in Madison Square Garden. It's the last few seconds of the game. We're down by one. I steal the ball and haul it down from midcourt, go up for the layup . . . and I score. The clock goes off. The crowd goes wild. I love it."

Kevin felt better and better about himself. His improved self-esteem developed in concert with an increasing awareness of his thoughts, feelings, and fantasies. As a consequence, he was building up his courage to ask out a girl; someone he thought was quiet and pretty and "who seemed kind and thoughtful." He said he thought that he had seen her looking at him, and this was boosting his resolve. The day he managed to talk with her for the first time, he was exuberant.

"I did it! Do you believe it? I actually talked to Stacey for a good ten minutes after school today. We walked out together. I waited with her for the bus. Maybe I'll call her tonight. What a trip!"

His pride filled the room.

Stacey was the first of several girls he talked to, dated, and with whom he had some sexual contact. There was one girl in particular, Margaret, to whom he became very attached. This opened up a whole other set of issues for Kevin about commitment and closeness.

"I dunno, Doc. This Margaret thing, it isn't like all the others. She's really something else. She's different. She thinks about things. And her life has been tough. She's also gorgeous, ya know. She's 5 feet 8 inches, thin. She's really got a great body. Her skin is the color of coffee. Her mother's black, her father's a WASP, like my father. Though he doesn't treat her mother too well. A little like my mother's deal. Though he screws around . . . I don't think Pete does that. And she's an incredible athlete. She's beautiful to watch. She does hurdles better than any guy I've ever seen. She's got grace, real grace. And she works really hard in school. She wants to do as well as she can. Not like me, kind of getting by, barely using what I've got. Even afraid to know what I've got and what I don't. Makes me think about what's important . . . where I'm going. All that stuff. Plus, she's not as into sex as some of the other girls. It's gotta mean something."

Kevin was troubled by his relationship with Margaret. He realized that he was afraid of getting hurt, or of hurting her. He seemed to have the conviction that male–female relationships inevitably led to someone getting hurt.

"Look. My mother got hurt by my father, and sure got hurt by Pete. My father never stays in any relationship very long, so he's probably afraid of getting hurt."

"So, is that it?" I asked. "Don't you think it's possible that there are other ways that people can be in relationships?"

"I don't know. Maybe. Takes work, I guess. You've got to look out for the other person *and* yourself, I guess."

"So, what do you think? Does that seem like something that's possible for *you*?" (I persisted, knowing it challenged some of Kevin's preconceptions.)

"I don't know. Gotta think about it." And he became quiet.

I waited. I knew that these were very complicated issues for Kevin. For him even to imagine being different from both of his parents pressed his sense of separateness, as well as his capacity to be individuated. It seemed important at that moment to do so, but it clearly posed a risk for him.

The session that day ended before Kevin had responded. Then, for the first time, he arrived quite late (fifteen minutes) to his next appointment.

"Sorry I'm late," he said as he walked in. (I didn't say anything.) "You mad or what? I couldn't help it. I had to talk to my computer teacher after school."

"Hey. I didn't say a thing!?"

"Well, I know you shrinks. Everything's gotta mean something. So you probably think I came late because of what we were talking about last time.

But that was no big deal. In fact, I've been thinking that I really don't need this any more. I'm fine. I mean, why *do* I have to come, anyway? The court only required six months. It's definitely been way more than that. And I'm okay. I'm fine."

"It's a good thing I didn't say anything. I can't imagine what you would have said if I had! This is all on the basis of what you figured I was thinking."

Kevin was silent. He looked angry for a moment, then broke out in a big grin. "Got you, didn't I? Thought I was outta here, right?"

"Actually, what I thought was that I probably said something last time that really rocked your boat . . . and I wasn't sure it was so smart of me to do it."

"I don't know what happened. I know I was upset, and that hasn't happened in a long time. I was kind of pissed, kind of sad. I thought about not coming today. Then I couldn't figure why I felt that way. It bothered me that I didn't understand the whole thing."

"We touched on some sensitive stuff, you know? For you to really think about being your own person, different from your mother *and* your father. Someone who is as he wants to be, not as he thinks other people want or expect him to be. It's new. Different."

"Maybe I'm not ready for this," he said, looking down in front of him.

"Maybe," I responded. "But I kind of thought you were at least ready to think about it."

"Yeah, maybe."

The next few weeks were difficult ones. Kevin was more open about his ambivalence about independence, but it left him feeling somewhat more embarrassed than he had in quite some time. Outside the treatment, he was feeling very good. His relationship with Margaret was strong, and he was doing reasonably well in school—scholastically, athletically, and socially. He also was getting along with both his father and mother.

"Look" he said to me during this time. "This is the only place I don't feel good. So why am I coming, anyway? If it wasn't for this, I'd be batting 1000."

"That's a tough one, Kevin," I responded. "I figure that the reason it's hard to come here is that there are some things that you actually have to deal with that you feel are best dealt with here. And they're not easy things. You know, they're things like figuring out exactly who you are, independent of your parents and friends. Who you want to be. What you want to do with yourself come next year. These things will be around for you to deal with whether you come here or not."

"Yeah, yeah, okay. I know. But I *am* doing all right."
"You're not going to get any argument from me about that."

And so it went. The push–pull character of the treatment remained, as Kevin continued to try to sort out what kind of person he was and wanted to be. His spirits, while he was in the consulting room, were up and down. Outside treatment, he stayed on a relatively even keel. Then, one day, toward the end of his junior year of high school, Kevin came in and said: "I'm not going to college. I'm just not ready. I don't care what anybody else thinks, either. Including you. Or my father."

"Something happen?" I asked in a gentle, but matter-of-fact tone of voice.

"I slept through my final this morning. I can't believe it. I can't believe that I still have to screw everything up. What good is all this therapy or anything else? I'm just too screwed up to get anything right. My father was so furious at me. He really screamed. Said that I was just a loser. I'd never come to anything. He was sick and tired of paying for me coming here when it didn't do anything, anyway. Made me feel like shit. But he's right. I *am* a loser. And I never will come to anything. I might as well just give it up. Forget school. Forget this. Let him save his goddamned money." He got up and started pacing around the room.

"What good *is* this? Why *did* I sleep through the thing? I certainly *thought* I set the clock right. But I put it on 'PM' instead of 'AM.' I was so tired, by the time I went to bed, that I couldn't see straight. I just can't believe this. And I was ready for the thing. I studied my ass off for it."

"Which one was this?" I asked.

"Chemistry."

"You were going into this final with about a B, right?"

"Yeah."

"So, certainly, Mr. T. (teacher) knows you're serious about the class."

"True. I mean, I went from a C- to a B. He knows I've been working really hard in there."

"He knows you're not a loser."

"Maybe if I go talk to him and tell him what happened, he'll still give me a chance to take it."

"You never know unless you give it a shot."

Kevin *did* go in the next morning and talk to the teacher. The teacher asked him if he had heard anything about the exam (he hadn't), and then permitted Kevin to take it on the spot. Kevin was enormously relieved, and pleased that he had gone in to speak with Mr. T. He actually ended up doing better in school at the end of his junior year than he had ever done before. He was on the honor roll, having achieved a B, B+ average. His father's "knew you could do it" fell on somewhat deaf ears.

"He's full of it. You know what he said to me? He said that he was just trying to get me off my ass by yelling at me the way he did the day I slept through the Chem final. Do you believe that? He's always got a quick answer. I felt bad enough that day without his telling me I'd never come to anything."

That summer brought a hiatus in the treatment. With some trepidation, Kevin went off to Oregon for two and a half months. He planned both to have a job and to fulfill the two hundred hours of community service that had been the other requirement of his court proceeding from the department store break-in incident of the year before.

"So, Doc, ya think I'll be okay?" he asked at the end of our last session before the break.

"This is going to be one of those typical answers, Kevin, because it isn't *really* up to me, you know? So . . . what do *you* think?"

"I could just be a smart ass about this. But, what the hell. I think I'll be okay. Even without you. *And* Margaret. Even *with* Billy around. But, hey, will ya miss me, or what?"

"I don't know, Kevin. At the risk of being a repetitive bore . . . what do *you* think?" I asked (with a smile).

"Yeah, you'll miss me. I know you like me. I can tell these things."

"Psychic?" I responded.

"Nah. I just pay attention now. Must have learned something from someone."

Treatment Process: Final Phase

When Kevin returned after the summer break, he was in good spirits. At one point, he had confronted Pete about mistreating his mother; at another, he had told Billy that he thought Billy had to "get himself together or he'd ruin his life." He had fulfilled his community service obligation, and made enough money in his job to get the stereo he had his heart set on buying.

"It was cool. I feel okay about the whole thing. I mean, I really missed Margaret . . . but I handled it. I talked to her almost every night. My mother's gonna freak out over the phone bill. But I even told her ahead of time, *and* I gave her some money for it. And, hey, I almost wrote *you* a letter. Okay, I never got it together. But I thought about it. Hope you had a good summer. Did you?"

"Yes. Thanks for asking. I *did* think about you. And I certainly wondered how things were going for you. I'm glad all went well."

"Well, you know, as well you could expect. Pete is still an asshole. Billy is still immature. But my mother was good. I felt like it was the first time I had really talked to her in a long time. She's all right, my mother. And she definitely loves me. Nothing wrong with that. She was really proud of me for making honor roll." (His face flushed.)

"Sounds like you were really able to be yourself out there," I responded.

"Guess so."

The summer in Oregon worked out better for Kevin than he had imagined was possible. Being back in New York, however, meant that he was expected to go full steam ahead in the college application process. This was not easy for him. He remained unsure about whether he even wanted to go to college.

"I really don't know what the big deal is. I don't mean I'll never go. I just don't feel like going now."

"What would you do instead?" I asked.

"I'll get a job or something. I don't know. What's the difference?" he responded (with some irritation in his voice).

"This subject really seems to bother you. What's up, do you know?" I asked.

"I'm just not like other kids, that's all. Even Margaret doesn't get it. Maybe, especially. She can't wait to go. I'm just not into it."

Kevin *did* know more than he was saying. One of the unmentioned problems was that Kevin was unsure about whether he could get into a college that he wanted to attend. His grades had improved dramatically, but his scores on standardized tests ranged from average to below average. Things changed dramatically in December of his senior year: "The track coach [from a midwestern college he was interested in] was in town today. He told my coach he was impressed with me. Can you believe that? He said my scores were okay enough to get in there, with track and my grades. Maybe I better get those applications out. I can't believe it, but I actually have a chance to get in, after all."

"So, all this time, you think you've been worried about getting in?" I asked, with a smile.

"You knew that, didn't you?" he said, with a big grin.

"Thought it was possible. But, why do you think you didn't bring it up?" I asked.

"Do I have to bring up everything? It was bad enough bombing the tests in the first place." (Kevin looked uncomfortable.)

"Well, we've got to deal with the facts, you know? We all are who we are, and all that." (I said this seriously, as I looked directly at him.)

"Maybe there are things I don't want to face about myself." (He looked pensive.)

I waited a few minutes, then asked: "Something in particular you have in mind?"

Kevin looked at me with his jaw set. He seemed sad, but determined to let me know what he had in mind.

"There was this party out in Oregon. I got really smashed. I don't even remember what I drank, how much. But I *do* know that there was this girl at the party who was all over me. She was, you know, kind of a slut type. Anyway, I woke up with her. We were both naked. I don't even know *what* happened. I mean, I guess I assume we did it. But I don't know for sure. Here, Margaret and I have been talking and talking about it—and *not* done it, because we both acknowledge it means something to us. And I go out there and just have sex with this girl. At least, I assume I did. And without using anything, as far as I know. Man, the whole thing is just lousy. And I feel lousy about it. I haven't told Margaret. I feel like I did something that she would never forgive me for. I don't even forgive myself for it. It's like I'm still a different person when I go out there. And then I felt bad that I didn't even tell you. You made that comment about really being myself out there, and I just couldn't tell you. I *was* mostly myself." (He fell silent.)

"You think, maybe, this is you, too? That you're not all one way or another? That you like to party *and* you like to be serious, for example?"

"I don't know. Maybe. I never really thought about it that way," he replied in a low voice. "I think I'm still hung up on being the good boy or the bad boy, and all that stuff."

The next few weeks were hard ones in Kevin's treatment. He came late a number of times, and he missed a session altogether for the first time. The message he left was telling: "Hey, Doc. I'm not gonna make it there today. I've got something to do with my friends that can't wait. I'll see ya next week."

Kevin's attention was shifting again. He no longer seemed to need to be the "good boy" in his treatment that he had been all along. For the first time in the two years he had been in treatment, for instance, he was making a clear statement that his activities with his friends took precedence. He was also struggling with how much more to let both of us know about who he actually was. He was beginning to seem like the 19-year-old he had just become. I was not surprised when he came in and said: "I don't want to hurt your feelings or anything, but I'm thinking that I've had enough of this therapy thing. I feel okay. It was fine being away over the summer. Obviously, I've been getting along in the last few weeks coming here a lot less. And I don't like having to think about coming, when I've got other things I want to do. You know, with my friends. With Margaret. Whaddya think?" he asked, somewhat nervously.

"I'm glad you brought it up," I responded. "I certainly noticed that you were busier with your friends and Margaret than you used to be, and that you seemed to feel less like coming here. But, what's this about hurting my feelings?"

"Well, I don't want you to feel insulted or anything if I am not into this anymore."

"That would almost make it seem like I had one of those personal agendas we used to talk about. Strange as it may seem, I think it's great if you feel like this is something that's not as useful for you anymore."

"So, you think I'll be okay without it?" Kevin was grinning, but seemed genuine in asking the question.

"What's 'okay?'" I asked.

"Well, you know, I won't flip out or anything," he responded.

"To be honest, I never thought of you as someone who had flipped out in the first place," I said.

"Yeah, I guess that's true. But I *am* used to coming here. And you're okay . . . if I stop, can I give you a call or something if I want to come in or talk to you?" he asked, somewhat anxiously.

"What do *you* think? Of course!" I said.

"Well, I don't know. I figured you'd say it was okay, but I wasn't 100 percent."

"Sounds like you've been thinking about this for awhile," I noted.

"Yeah, definitely."

"So, what did you have in mind for when we'd end?" I asked.

"Well, like today, I guess."

"This is one of those things that it might be good to live with for a bit before we make a final decision. What do you think about a few more visits, so we can sum up things and think some about the future?" I asked.

He agreed. We planned to meet for two more weeks, four more visits. As it turned out, Kevin only came to two of the appointments. The first one, he came late; the next two, he missed altogether. He came on time to the last appointment.

The sheer emotional intensity of the ending process was hard for Kevin to tolerate, which he acknowledged in our last session. He said that he would miss me, that he sometimes felt that he didn't know what he had gotten out of coming, but that he had the feeling it was more than he could understand at this point in his life.

"So, I guess this is it," he said, somewhat sadly, as the session came to a close.

"Guess so," I responded (feeling filled with emotion myself, keenly aware of how much I would miss him).

"So, thanks. I'll be in touch," he said as he extended his hand for a handshake.

"Take care," I responded, as we shook hands.

"Yeah, you, too," he said softly, as he left the room.

I never heard from Kevin again. I did get a note from his father with the last check, saying that he had gotten into the two colleges to which he had managed to send applications (his way of putting it), and that he would most likely be going to one of them.

Discussion

When Kevin began treatment, his physiological development was that of a middle adolescent, but his psychological development was that of an early adolescent. He knew he was no longer in childhood, but he had never given up the strong desire to be there. He did not want to be his age or at his point in life.

Kevin had an abundance of anger toward and disappointment with his parents that he had been unable to confront. This was particularly the case in relation to his father. In maintaining the idealized version of his father that he initially presented in treatment, he was fending off both the de-idealization process and the shift in the sources of narcissistic satisfaction that are so necessary to early adolescent development.

Underlying the anger and disappointment (especially toward his father, but certainly toward both parents) was a storehouse of unconscious guilt. This guilt led him to get involved in situations that resulted in his getting in trouble. The anger and disappointment (about which he was not initially conscious) motivated the guilt, which he attenuated through taking actions that led him to be punished. This is, for example, what drove him to break into the department store.

His strongly fending off awareness of these negative feelings about his parents made Kevin's aggression relatively unavailable to him to utilize in other ways. He tended to express aggression passively, and so he was unable to excel in school or sports and taking the initiative in social relationships was quite difficult.

His attachment and attention were so strongly caught up in his parents and their lives that he had little energy available for the pursuit of his own friendships, girlfriends, or overall sexual and/or narcissistic development. Ritvo (1971) emphasizes the vital importance of the intimate sexual and emotional relationships that adolescents seek in the external world in their emergence from what he terms "the narcissistic retreat" (p. 252). Kevin's preoccupation with his family initially kept him from the pursuit of such relationships.

Kevin also had focused very little on what kind of man he wanted to be, or even what it meant to him to be male. His father dominated his image of manhood. In order for Kevin to identify with his father as a man, he needed to see his father in life-sized terms. His father's grandiosity and Kevin's childlike attachment to his father made the de-idealization and identificatory processes so necessary at this time in Kevin's development hard to negotiate.

When an overidealization of parents is maintained into early adolescence, adolescents often are bolstered in their urges to look more carefully and realistically at themselves and those who were important to them in childhood by their friends. This comparison between himself and his friends, so typical and so necessary for early adolescence, had been absent in Kevin's life.

The first phase of treatment primarily focused on these early adolescent issues. We talked about who his parents actually were and had been, when and how he had difficulty pursuing people or experiences that he was interested in, and what it had been like shuttling back and forth between the two coasts. Kevin began to get a sense of the ways in which he had found his childhood troubling, including his parents' "personal agendas," and how, in his mind's eye, their lives had come to take precedence over his own. This aided him in putting his childhood behind him and becoming more focused on his own needs and wants in the present.

The experience of focusing attention on and receiving appreciation from those who are most important to children is the bedrock of healthy narcissistic development. This kind of individualized awareness was notably absent in Kevin's life until he came for treatment. He was very struck and moved by my consistent attention to and interest in *his* feelings, thoughts, and fantasies. He was unaccustomed to having an adult dealing with him in this manner, and very appreciative of it. It aided him both in attending to and valuing his inner life. While he entered treatment with virtually an exclusive focus on what others around him thought, he was able in the context of treatment to begin to think about what *he* observed, thought, and felt.

By the end of the first phase of treatment, he was squarely involved in the middle adolescent developmental process. His attention was on himself and his friends, more than on his parents and their lives. He was thinking about his own sexuality, including the difficulties in thinking about himself as a man and as a sexual person. He began to enjoy his own body and capacities in a way and to a degree that had not been available to him before.

In this context, regressive, dependent feelings became more troublesome for Kevin. He resented his reliance on his parents, and my role in his life came into question. His need for me and/or treatment became a problematic issue. His peers were talking about going off to college, while Kevin was struggling with whether he could manage to define his life for himself. He simply did not feel he had enough faith in himself to consider going to college.

Much of the second phase of treatment involved the shift from his looking at everyone around him to define who he was, to his looking within and at himself to define who he was. It was in this phase that he became, psychologically, the middle adolescent that he was physiologically.

At this time, there was dramatic growth in Kevin's narcissistic development. This was illustrated by his Madison Square Garden fantasy, awareness of girls' looking at him, and interest in his own appearance and performance. Where the first phase of treatment was dominated by Kevin's talking about his parents and childhood, the second phase brought with it a focus on Kevin's inner life and social life. The sources for his feelings of narcissistic well-being had shifted. There was also a change from a predominant focus on separation issues to a predominant focus on individuation issues. These are critical characteristics of the move from early to middle adolescence.

As a middle adolescent, Kevin felt more solidly rooted in the social world (rather than the world of his family). His relationship with Margaret was especially important in this context, for it made him far more aware of how *he* wanted to be in a relationship and how that differed from the ways his parents had been in their relationships. This focus on his experience of the world rather than the experience of those who had been so important in childhood reflected a change in his narcissistic development. This was also the time when issues about sexuality, so crucial for middle adolescents to examine, surfaced in Kevin's treatment.

In the final phase of treatment, though still a middle adolescent in most ways, Kevin demonstrated the first hints of late adolescent development. He brought up issues related to commitment, for instance, in his relationship with Margaret. Adatto (1991) describes the difference between the intimate relationships of late adolescence and those of the earlier subphases. He notes that the focus shifts from detaching from the old important relationships to the forming of new and more permanent ones. The way Kevin began to think about his relationship with Margaret showed that his form of relationship was moving into that of late adolescence.

Kevin also showed empathy and mature understanding of both Margaret and his mother. At moments, he showed that he had a real sense of how I felt and thought about him. He had clearly begun to define a sense of who he wanted to be, which permitted him to develop a mature ego ideal.

This treatment served to aid Kevin in his journey through the adolescent process. Developmentally speaking, when he ended, he was solidly his age. He would go off to college just beginning his late adolescent development, as would be the case for most of his peers. He had regained his footing, and was, therefore, back on the path that he had lost in the early stages of his adolescence.

He seemed to have arrived at adolescence unprepared for the vast transformations that are part of this developmental period. He simply did not have sufficient energy available to undergo these changes. The degree of self-involvement and preoccupation in both of his parents during Kevin's early years precluded their attending to him in the ways and with the intensity that he needed for adequate narcissistic development to occur.

Kevin first shifted his focus from his parents to me. Where once he had looked to them for the awareness and appreciation of him that lead to a sense of narcissistic satisfaction, he now looked toward his treatment. He then was able, through an identification with the attention that both of us focused upon him during his treatment, to look more carefully, objectively, and constantly at himself. This permitted him to observe his parents more realistically, which freed up his energy and attention so that he could be more involved with himself and his peers.

At first, his attention was turned outward, toward his parents, at precisely the moment when he most needed to turn his attention inward. His focus was on staying at home, when what he needed was to proceed out into the world. Thus, the main thrust of the psychotherapy was to support his capacity to look inside, thereby facilitating narcissistic development. He ended treatment with his pride, well-being, and basic goodness largely deriving from within.

References

Adatto, C. P. (1991). Late adolescence to early adulthood. In *The Course of Life, vol. IV, Adolescence*, ed. S. Greenspan and G. Pollock, pp. 357–375. Madison, CT: International Universities Press.

Levy-Warren, M. H. (1996). *The Adolescent Journey: Development, Identity Formation, and Psychotherapy*. Northvale, NJ: Jason Aronson.

Ritvo, S. (1971). Late adolescence: developmental and clinical considerations. *Psychoanalytic Study of the Child* 26:241–263. New York: Quadrangle Books.

II

Assessment and Differential Diagnosis

7

Self Pathology in Children

Agi Bene

In this presentation, I would like to concentrate not so much on a specific narcissistic disorder as on the question of self pathology: the way we assess it initially at the diagnostic stage, how we perceive its manifestations in the clinical setting and, finally, how we handle it in the sessions.

I hope it will be borne in mind that I am highlighting only *one* group of atypical pathology and will focus on one aspect of the disturbance which is in the self, neglecting the discussion of conflictual and other aspects of the pathology. Equally, I will emphasize *one* "initiator" of this disorder, and that is the environmental one. I do acknowledge, of course, that the manner in which a particular constitution reacts to a particular set of external circumstances is important. Nevertheless, in the two cases which I use to illustrate self pathology it is a hazardous task to evaluate the importance of the constitutional givens. Personally, I would question whether they had a significant impact. I would like to differentiate, also, between predominantly narcissistic and borderline pathology and, if possible, separate narcissistic disturbances from the imprecise diagnostic group labelled "atypical."

Returning to the question of self pathology, I follow Hartmann (1964) in understanding narcissism as an emotionally significant investment of the self rather than the ego. The self is seen not as a mental structure in the sense that id, ego, and superego are. In this context, the self refers to a specific group of human experiences, to the *content* of the mental apparatus. The self, in my usage, always refers to self experience and thus includes elements of experience of which we may be quite unconscious. The sum total of conscious and unconscious sensing of oneself is responsible for the quality of the *sense of self*. It is responsible for the cohesiveness of the self, for its continuity over time, and for the way in which the essential sense of continuity and sameness in the midst of developmental changes is retained. I use the term "self-esteem" simply as referring to a value put on oneself.

I would follow Kohut's (1971) view of the pathology of narcissistic disorders, i.e., that such disorders imply psychological problems centered on an insufficiently consolidated self, but where the self nevertheless has attained a certain cohesiveness. In this, one can see an essential difference between borderline and narcissistic pathology. Borderline and psychotic patients can be said to lack a cohesive self. It is important, in this context, to understand the meaning of *self-object* since the correct recognition of the existence of the self-object plays a central part in understanding and interpretation during the first phases of treatment. The self-object is an object used in the service of the self in a very special way. Self-objects are objects which are experienced as part of the self. People who relate predominantly by way of a self-object may nevertheless have the capacity for self and object differentiation and for firmly differentiated self-object representations. They have comparative well-defined self and object boundaries, which is another feature differentiating them from borderline or psychotic patients.

In narcissistic disorders the object is frequently and primarily experienced (or felt) as a part of the self, unlike Anna Freud's need-satisfying object (1966) which is placed *outside* the self, though it is used in the service of the self. The recognition and understanding of this phenomenon are important to the way in which one interprets the treatment relationship. Its manifestations have to be differentiated from transference proper, which is based on being able to *feel* different from the object and yet have the capacity to fantasize about it.

I would like to describe briefly some differences in the way the idea of the *grandiose or omnipotent self* is understood by various authors, since such differences have important repercussions on how one comprehends and interprets the grandiose self in treatment. Kernberg (1975) considers narcissism expressed in the grandiosity of self as a pathological phenomenon. According to him, it reflects a pathological condensation of some aspects of the *real self* (i.e., the very specificity and specialness of the child), of the *ideal self* (including fantasies of power, beauty, wealth, etc.), and of the *ideal object* (e.g., fantasies about parents who are ever-giving, ever-loving, and accepting). This usage follows Jacobson's views (1964). Kernberg—along with Kleinian analysts—sees this grandiose (or omnipotent) self mainly as a defense against a re-emergence of intense early oral envy and oral rage. In Kohut's thinking, there is a continuity of paths between normal and pathological narcissism. Pathological narcissism finds expression in the grandiose self as either a regression to, or an arrest at, an early mode of being. This does not, of course, exclude the possibility that patients will use the grandiose self in a defensive way as well. I would see the defense as being mobilized not only against rage and envy but primarily against the reality-based perception of the inadequate, helpless stage of the self.

The emphasis which the analyst puts on the role of inborn envy or rage, or, conversely, on the failure of the environment in the child's early development, or on constitutional factors, influences the view which he takes in regard to the etiology of the disturbance. Again, the way we think about the cause of the disturbance influences the way we understand and interpret the clinical material. If, for instance, grandiosity and the grandiose self are seen primarily as a defense against oral rage and envy, the systematic clinical interpretation of this will be crucial to the analysis. If grandiosity (or omnipotence) is seen, besides its defensive significance, as an outcome of fixation or regression to an early stage of self development, caused by a failure in the child's holding environment, then (I think) there will be more emphasis in the analysis on reconstructive work: the interpretation of defenses will be directed more at the rejection of unacceptable aspects of the self, toward the defenses mobilized against painful experiences such as feelings of shame, humiliation, and rage, and toward feelings of impotence. Interpretations are certainly not primarily and exclusively directed at oral rage and envy expressed, for instance, in the patient's aggressive wish to denigrate his analyst, or directed at the defense of splitting. These are important theoretical differences which have an influence on both the assessment and the treatment of this disorder.

Diagnostic and Clinical Observations of John and Spencer

Relevant Features as they Emerged at the Diagnostic Stage

Reason for Referral

John was 5½ years old and Spencer 6½ years old when first referred for treatment. The main reason for both the referrals was the threat of expulsion from school. Both boys showed bizarre behavior and struck the teachers by their oddness. Both were hyperactive and restless and flew into quick tempers whenever they met frustrations. They both seemed to withdraw into their own world and were isolated from others. When they were relating to the outside world, their behavior was uncontrolled, aggressive, and bizarre. John bewildered his teachers by making extraordinary noises and strange grimaces, and pretended to climb up the walls. In an attempt to contain him, his teachers had to resort to tying him to his desk. Both boys were of superior intelligence. At the diagnostic stage, John's IQ was found to be 155 and Spencer's 133. Despite their high intelligence, the boys' interest was invested almost entirely in their grandiose fantasy world, at the expense of outside interests, and they related to people on the basis of these fantasies. What I found of particular interest was that both boys were referred for treatment by their schools, though their restless, withdrawn, bizarre, and disturbing behavior was evident in their home life as well.

Developmental History

Both boys' developmental history, according to their parents' accounts, strikes one as precocious but also as uneven. Both were big babies (within the normal range) and were "ravenous feeders." John was feeding on a two-hourly basis up to the age of 4 months and then was weaned to the cup at 5 months. He was able to say "Dada" and "Mama" at 5 months and was standing at 8 months. He used the pot until the age of 4½ and was wetting his bed up till that age. However, during a family holiday in Majorca he stopped bedwetting.

Spencer impressed everyone with his phenomenal strength. He had six to seven bottles a day, which needed to be increased rapidly. He sat at 2 months and crawled at 5 months and walked at 9 months. Father thought they had given birth to a genius. Spencer spoke four words at 1 year and then stopped until he was 4 years old. During his nonspeaking period there was no question about his ability to comprehend what was said or about letting others know his wishes. The impression was that he need not bother to express his wishes in words. Perhaps it was some inattention on his mother's part which forced him to utter his first sentence at the age of 4 years when he said: "Will you please switch on the television, Mother." On the other hand, he toilet-trained himself at the age of 2, learning how to do it from his mother by observing *her* in the bathroom.

Other events in the two boys' lives which might have had great significance were the following:

At around 7 months, *John's* mother partly handed the care of her infant over to her parents and husband while she was involved in Weight-Watching activities, and during this time she suffered what was called "a marked personality change." At 2, John had severe measles as well as an accident when he fell off a table. He was treated in a hospital casualty department where "he had to be tied to the table" (similar to the event which occurred later at school). *Spencer* spent his first 18 months to 2 years of life almost alone with his mother. Father lived away from home with his own parents. Spencer's parents, in fact, married only shortly before his birth. Spencer also had an accident when 2 years old which necessitated stitches, administered without an anaesthetic. From that time onward, according to the parents, Spencer went off his food and suffered a "personality change." At about this time his younger brother was born.

To understand the psychological situation somewhat better, I would like to comment briefly on *parental handling and needs* which might have affected the children's development. These comments are separated from the factual events in the boys' lives described above, since they are speculative to some extent and open to critical appraisal. Nevertheless, I want to stress that although the boys had a particularly good endowment it was, in my view, within the range of normality. I suggest that their uniqueness predominantly originated in the way they were perceived and handled almost from birth onward.

For the first two years of John's life the family lived in the maternal grandparents' home, where John must have been considerably restricted because of the much-valued objects in the house. Taking off his shoes at the diagnostic interview so as not to dirty the room, and complaining about a plant being in his way, might be indications of his having had to comply, to an unusual degree, with his inanimate environment. On the other hand, he was also the apple of the eye of the four adoring adults in the home. Mention has already been made of the mother's withdrawal from him at the time when John was 7 months old, leaving his care to the husband (often away on business) and to her parents, and of her becoming, from a strikingly over-weight woman, a much slimmer and perhaps also a much younger-looking one. I often wondered whether the mother's personality change uncon-sciously expressed her wish to recreate the past, to be not only the young daughter to her parents but also the sister to her much admired, brilliant, and wayward brother. In this respect, John represented this gifted, much loved, unusual, violent brother, now restored to the grandparents.

In the case of Spencer, he was given an extraordinary and special name at birth. This could indicate unusual expectations of him. The first 18 months to 2 years of Spencer's life were shared in an exclusive way with the mother. They shared a double bed. Later, to protect him from feeling left out, the mother pushed a divan near the parental double bed. When John was 6½, his mother left the home for a few weeks because of a marital rift. It was Spencer whom she took with her, leaving the two younger children behind. While the father considered Spencer a genius (somewhat similar to the way he saw himself) the mother thought of him as a special friend. The diagnostician, who interviewed the mother, remarked that it was evident that the mother really meant *boy*-friend, and that it was a great narcissistic hurt for her that Spencer needed treatment. The diagnostician also thought that by referring Spencer for treatment, the mother was referring herself as well, frequently mentioning similarities between herself and her son.

Reviewing briefly both the factual events in the boys' lives and some of the parental (environmental) handling and expectations, what strikes me is that both boys seem to have been allowed and encouraged to assert a kind of omnipotent control over their environment. However, at the same time they had to endure an unusual degree of helplessness and imposition. I consider this factor important in the causation of their disturbance.

Recapitulation of the Contradictory Environmental Influences

During the first two years, John was very much the center of attention of four adults, who thought him brilliant and extraordinary, and must have indulged his sense of omnipotence, and the feeling that he must be the cleverest person in the world. This, in fact, was the way John later related both to his peers and to adults. On the other hand, since physically he lived in a rather precious adult environment he had to be more considerate with regard to his physical surroundings than is normally the case. John may have experienced this as a powerful controlling force over him. More important, though less concrete: what intruded in his natural development of self-feelings was his mother's unconscious need to see her son not for what he really was but rather for what she needed him to be (i.e., her brilliant, uncontrollable brother). This, once again, may have increased John's omnipotence as regards his abilities and uniqueness but could also have led to a feeling of helplessness via-à-vis the mother's withdrawal. Additionally, the intrusion of *her* image of John created a false or unreal feeling of being special and must have affected his values and sense of his self (or personality).

In the case of Spencer, the unusual closeness with his mother, both physical and later emotional, is well documented. The striking closeness, and the mother's overinvestment in Spencer—needing and using him in some ways instead of the father—emerged in the diagnostic picture. In fact, she considered the father as also quite extraordinary. These parental feelings must have fostered feelings of omnipotence and specialness in Spencer. This is well reflected in—among other things—Spencer's not having to bother to talk till the age of 4. Additionally, the father's identification with or projection of his own specialness onto his son must have increased Spencer's grandiosity. On the other hand, the boy must have been unusually *un*prepared for the arrival of his father (when Spencer was about 18 months old his father broke a leg, and stayed unexpectedly all day at the maternal home) and, later, the arrival of his siblings. Both boys were exposed to a painful, unexpected traumatic hospital experience at the age of 2, increasing and probably reinforcing a sense of helplessness which intrusions of parental pathology had already caused.

The intrusion of parental needs was different in the two cases, and one could hypothesize that the different kinds of maternal need, or parental expectation, which are imposed on the child's self, must create different types of narcissistic disturbance. Nevertheless the basic similarity of these intrusions is that they greatly interfered with the gradual relinquishing of the child's natural omnipotence. The parents did not offer age-appropriate gratifications and frustrations. Instead, they imposed—to an unusual degree—aspects of their own selves onto their children as well as hope of fulfillment of their own unconscious needs. This did not permit the boys the gradual development of self-feelings which would ultimately lead to the establishment of a more autonomous self. By this I mean, as pointed out previously, a specific group of human experiences which includes unconscious elements. The boys' difficulties in allowing the object to *feel different* from their own selves is well demonstrated in the nature of their treatment relationship. The striking unevenness in their self-feelings, both omnipotent and helpless, expressed in their fantasy life as well as in their relationships, is characteristic of narcissistic disturbances.

Some Material from the Analyses

Treatment Relationship

One of the relevant and basic characteristics of both boys' treatment relationship was their wish to make their therapists part of and participants in their sometimes gruesome and always omnipotent fantasy existence. There was a comparative lack of tension and anxiety when the therapist complied with these wishes, and a sense of outrage, anxiety, fury, and disappointment when the therapist attempted to interpret the defensive nature of their fantasy preoccupations or the content of their fantasies.

John's therapist first described John's relationship to him as "a pressing need to engage him as someone who would help him put himself together and contain his mess." This need, his therapist felt, overrode any threat that he might represent as a potentially attacking or dismissing person. Various permutations of John's fantasies of being a "superman" served the purpose of mastering anxiety about great helplessness, but also gave him intense sadistic gratification in possessing such grandiose power. In all of this, the therapist felt "curiously incidental, needed as a sharing and admiring object, but nevertheless aware of John's underlying fear of dependency on him. The anxiety was not due only to his dependent needs, but to his fear that his omnipotent powers will destroy the therapist." The therapist felt he was never or rarely acknowledged as a separate person in his own right. Another aspect of the treatment relationship was the unconditional expectation that the therapist would attend to his demands for attention and admiration and sustain his grandiose self-perception.

Spencer's therapist described his relationship to her by saying that she was "an adjunct," always part of a "we," who had to do exactly what Spencer said. She existed, but not as an independent thinking being. If she attempted to step out of this unity, Spencer would go into a panic or rage. It was as though he said, "You and I do exactly the same: we are exactly the same." She described Spencer's state of panic as bordering on a state of disintegration at the time of separations (in particular during the first years of treatment). This was seen on the occasion when Spencer almost "went to pieces" when his therapist had to leave the room for a brief period of time. Looked at from the object-libidinal angle, one could say that the object was wanted in order to continually satisfy his needs as in the past, when Spencer was supplied continually with bottles and with his mother's presence. But this was not the way it was experienced by his therapist. Looking at it from the point of view of self pathology or the development of the self, one might say that when the object was missing—mainly as far as rejecting his grandiosity and specialness is concerned—the self felt incomplete and confused. Both boys' existence was dominated by the interlocking of the omnipotent fantasy object and the helpless counterpart. In both cases, it was not a question of the therapist accommodating to a specific aspect of the child's fantasy, as seen so frequently in the treatment of neurotic cases. Rather, the therapist became—if he or she permitted it—an integral part of this fantasy experience, and its disruption caused outbursts of rage and frustration in the boys. This is, in my view, the kind of self-object relating which is very characteristic of people whose *predominant* disturbance is in the realm of narcissism. Nevertheless, it is important to note that this relating is based on the capacity to differentiate between self and object representation and on having established relatively secure ego boundaries. (One could place this level of relating in the second and third subphase of Mahler's [1975] separation and individuation phase.) Spencer was able to function and say: *you* and *I* should do exactly the same. When John was separated from his therapist he wanted him, via the phone, to become part of the experience of listening together to the television program by putting the phone on top of the television set. In this way he disregarded the reality of his therapist's physical absence. The predominant wish was for both to be part of the same experience. The borderline psychotic case (like, for instance, my former patient Mark) cannot share and make the therapist part of his experience because he merges with the therapist. Mark indicated this in his facial expression, posture, and words, which frequently became similar to mine. He could not share the experience of a television show with me, or require me to be either the participant or admiring audience. He *was* the television show himself. Or, he could not make me a participant or audience in his enactments of his Dorian Gray fantasies, but he became Dorian Gray himself, thus demonstrating the lack of established self and object boundaries. Children like John and Spencer, whose disturbance is predominantly in the narcissistic sphere, need the object to *feel and experience* as they do, as if they were denying (disregarding) the existence of the other person's independent needs and feelings, but they do not become or did not have to be the same as the object. John and Spencer needed the therapists to be unconditionally available to them and to accept them and reflect their omnipotence. Both neurotic and borderline children have these features present to some extent in their way of relating. It is taken for granted that all children seen in treatment have narcissistic problems, mainly expressed in problems of self-esteem. Nevertheless, the almost exclusive way of relating in the manner described above seems typical of children whose disturbance is predominantly in the self. The *way* John and Spencer experienced themselves in their inordinately destructive omnipotent fantasies (which were often also the defensive expression of their opposite feeling state), became abundantly clear from their continuous fantasy enactments. One of the essential differences between the borderline child and the children whose pathology is centered on the self is that the ego functions—in particular the capacity for reality testing and secondary process functioning (thinking)—is often impaired in the borderline child, while in the predominantly narcissistically disturbed child this *capacity* remains intact, although one can often observe secondary interference in the secondary processes.

Technical Points

I would like to make a few comments on the *question of technique*. With regard to the treatment relationship, children who were unable to differentiate their selves in a *feeling* way from the intrusion of their close early environment have specific problems concerning their feelings about their own selves. These children will establish a different kind of treatment relationship and treatment alliance from that of the neurotic or borderline child. In my view (and following what Kohut and others have described in relation to the treatment of adult narcissistic patients), early interpretations of what I would call object-libidinal aspects are inappropriate. Such interpretations require a sense of separateness which I think John and Spencer had. I believe these early interpretations might be experienced as a repetition of early intrusions by their parents into their separate functioning. Some of our cases show—and, not altogether unexpectedly, even provoke—a re-experiencing in the treatment of these intrusions. Sometimes, as therapists, our remarks are directed toward ascertaining to what extent the child is able to differentiate, for instance, between fantasy and reality (something which these children usually are capable of). This serves to reassure us that they are not borderline or psychotic children. While *we* feel reassured, *they* feel disappointed, raging and revengeful at not being understood and at being let down by the therapist's failure to participate in their omnipotent world. Incidentally, affects of rage, revenge, disappointment, and shame (not guilt) are the most typical affective expressions. I believe one should permit, tolerate, and be a part of the child's grandiose and often destructive fantasies, without attempting to interpret them until the child learns to trust himself with his therapist. Gradually and hopefully, some benign, tolerant aspect of the therapist will be internalized by the child. Interpretations with regard to the defensive, instinctual, and genetic nature of their fantasies can then proceed, and we can hope that they will be able to relinquish at least to some extent the omnipotent views held about their own selves and those of their objects. It goes without saying that these phases of treatment—the predominantly sharing one and the predominantly interpretative one—overlap, and it is rather a question of emphasis than of either/or.

Finally, I would like to address myself to the following question. Why are there so few children in treatment at the Clinic in whom the nucleus of their pathology is in the realm of narcissism; or, as I would now prefer to say, in a specific developmental failure of the self? I will leave metapsychological considerations aside for the moment and make a few comments in logically reverse order, that is, I will first concern myself with the analytical process and then consider questions relating to the diagnostic assessment.

The Analytical Process

As far as I can see at present, there may be two main reasons why the predominantly narcissistic pathology is insufficiently recognized in the analytical treatment. Firstly, by pursuing the object-libidinal kind of interpretation alone, we do not allow the establishment of what is called a narcissistic type of treatment-relationship, and hence this kind of pathology is not allowed full expression and recognition. With hindsight I recall some of my own cases where this probably happened. Another reason might well be that mothers (or parents), because of their particular involvement and intrusiveness with their child, cannot tolerate the treatment, and prematurely interrupt it.

Some Questions Regarding Diagnosis

I wonder whether it would be useful and possible to pinpoint a predominantly narcissistic pathology at the diagnostic stage.

In both the cases discussed, the diagnostician indicated the presence of an atypical development. In John's case, the diagnostician spoke of "permanent drive regressions to previously established fixation points, with conflicts of a neurotic type." He also pointed out that John's behavior may have been due to mishandling, and further suggested that "there may be evidence of early deprivation which has distorted development and has produced an atypical quality in John." Certainly all these assumptions were confirmed in John's treatment, but I wonder whether one could be more precise? As regards Spencer, his diagnostician was "uncertain" whether the arrest in his development was partial, whether it involved the whole of his personality, whether the disturbance should be regarded as psychotic in nature, or reflecting an atypical personality development. She drew attention to the continuing impingement of the parental psychopathology.

While the assessment of "atypical" is obviously accurate and does draw attention to the non-neurotic aspect of the child's psychopathology, I think we would agree that "atypical" remains a much used but rather unsatisfactory and vague diagnostic label.

The Diagnostic Profile

Indications of the presence of a narcissistic disturbance are, of course, contained in the Profile under the section "Assessment of Development; Drive Development: Libido—Regarding Libido Distribution; Cathexis of Self," as well as under "Cathexis of Objects." In fact, both boys' Profiles indicate a disturbance in the self, Dr. T. speaks of John's "confused sense of self." Dr. H. says: "By providing Spencer with everything, the parents did not help Spencer to bear frustration, and there was little incentive for him to communicate his needs or begin to establish a separate identity in the first two years." Dr. H. adds: "I find it very difficult in this case to make any retrospective formulation of self cathexis in terms of primary and secondary narcissistic supplies, or to have much idea of the aggressive or libidinal quality of the mother's early cathexis of her baby." There follows a description of the cathexis of objects and the level of libidinal development which the boy had reached.

I find the distinction between primary and secondary "narcissistic supplies" not helpful. Besides, the description of the quantitative balance between cathexis of self and cathexis of objects, it may be useful also to find a place in the Profile for the assessment on the development of the self. In this context—as I have mentioned before—the self refers to the content of the mental apparatus, both to the conscious and unconscious self-experiences. If one could view narcissistic disturbances as psychological problems centering on an insufficiently consolidated self (Kohut 1971), they could perhaps be accommodated under "Self or Personality Development" (in the section on assessment of development). This could have two advantages. It would reduce the group of "atypical" cases or those of "atypical development," and give more diagnostic precision to this group of "bizarre" children. Secondly, it would alert us to the specific therapeutic measures which, in my view, this kind of narcissistic pathology requires.

My aim has been to draw attention to a group of children, usually described as "bizarre" or "atypical," who are different from the borderline child, mainly because of their relatively intact ego functioning and greater cohesion of self.

Different from the "ordinary" neurotic child whose disturbance is based predominantly on conflict, the children I have discussed withdraw into their omnipotent and bizarre world at the expense of reality. In this respect they remind one of the borderline child. The presence of the occasional "loud" unresolved aspect of their oedipal situation, and conflicts on all libidinal levels, demonstrate the presence of the neurotic side of their disorder. Nevertheless, I think the special focus of their illness is the establishment and the development of the self. I think this is the feature which distinguishes them from the neurotic or borderline child, and this needs greater attention. It would be helpful to be alerted to the signs which present themselves already at the diagnostic stage, and perhaps find a specific place for the disturbance of the self in the Profile. With some modifications in our technique, we could— besides helping these children to come to terms with the conflictual side of their disturbance—also assist them in facilitating the development of their primitive grandiose self into a more age-appropriate one, and help them to see the world and the people in it in a less omnipotent and less frightening way.

References

Freud, A. (1962). Assessment of childhood disturbances. *Psychoanalytic Study of the Child* 17:149–158. New York: International Universities Press.
———— (1966). *Normality and Pathology in Childhood*. London: Hogarth.
Hartmann, H. (1964). *Essays in Ego Psychology*. London: Hogarth and the Institute of Psycho-Analysis.
Jacobson, E. (1964). *The Self and the Object World*. New York: International Universities Press.
Kernberg, O. (1975). *Borderline Conditions and Pathological Narcissism*. New York: Jason Aronson.
Kohut, H. (1971). *The Analysis of the Self*. London: Hogarth.
Mahler, M., Pine, F., and Bergman, A. (1975). *The Psychological Birth of the Human Infant*. New York: Basic Books.

8

Attention Deficit Disorder and Its Relationship to Narcissistic Pathology

Andrew Morrel

Psychoanalysis stands in uneasy relation to neurobiology and its continuing research into the etiology of psychological disorders. From the beginning, Freud ceded primacy to organic factors and defined the scope of psychoanalysis as covering that which could not be explained biologically. While this view left psychoanalysis plenty of ground to explore at the end of the last century, it is a far more precarious position now. With enormously increased knowledge about neurochemistry and brain anatomy, and with greatly improved techniques for their study, there is growing acceptance of a perspective which maintains that all "mental disorders" can be best understood neurobiologically and that the treatment of these disorders is primarily a psychopharmacological matter. From this standpoint, therapy is seen primarily as a supplement to the medical treatment, serving the function of helping people accept the fact of their having a neurobiological disorder and facilitating their adaptation to this objective reality. At best, therapy is seen as helping people undo or change behavioral patterns that they developed in trying to cope with their "illness" prior to the advent of appropriate (medical) treatment. Moreover, therapy is viewed as inherently cognitive/behavioral in nature; psychoanalytically oriented approaches are seen as irrelevant at best and potentially antitherapeutic in the sense that they might lead doctor or patient to eschew "real treatment." I recently had a psychiatrist who is a strong believer in the biological/behavioral paradigm plead with me not to take on the long-term treatment of a boy he was medicating on the grounds that therapy might give this boy the idea that he had valid reasons to be angry (and therefore aggressive) and that this implicit acceptance of his behavior would undermine the attempt to "modify" it.

A central premise of this chapter is that psychoanalytic theory and practice have a unique contribution to make to the understanding of human behavior and motivation and that this contribution ultimately derives from a belief in a dynamic unconscious which contains psychic elements that are denied to consciousness but which powerfully influence conscious thoughts, feelings, and actions. Beyond that, it will be argued here that the contents of this unconscious can be most fruitfully understood as affects (and the self- and object representations that are organized around them) which have been denied access to the central ego or self system. Typically these are affects that were experienced as traumatic in the past and which the individual has not yet learned to tolerate. Since these affects are therefore viewed as dangerous, the person must avoid all thoughts, actions, and, perhaps most importantly, relationships which might precipitate them, thus effectively limiting his or her capacity to live and interact freely in the world. In this view, the goal of treatment is to create a therapeutic environment that is safe enough to allow the patient's heretofore repressed, dissociated, or split-off feelings to begin to emerge (often within the context of the therapeutic relationship) and thereby have the opportunity to be integrated into the broader personality. To the extent that a psychoanalytic treatment succeeds in this endeavor, it offers an invaluable service to the patient, a service that cannot be effectively provided by any other treatment modality.

Thus, the position espoused in this chapter is one that, while mindful and respectful of the advances of neurobiology, affirms the value of psychoanalysis both as a means of understanding people in their full complexity and as a means of helping people to live fuller, more satisfying lives. It assumes that human behavior is so multidetermined that the premise "everything is biological" is accepted as a truism—there are obviously changes in the brain and/or body for every human thought, feeling, or act—without this truth in any way contradicting the analytic belief in the "psychic determination" of various mental states and disorders. Neurobiology is not the enemy of psychoanalysis; reductionism is. The task of the mental health practitioner is to be conversant with as many explanatory systems as possible, and the modes of treatment they lead to, yet to maintain the ability to approach each new patient in a state of "not knowing" and to allow the data of observation and interaction to determine one's formulation of the case. Above all, what is essential to understand is that the complexity of humanity makes it fundamentally unthinkable that any one approach to a problem could obviate the need to consider alternate perspectives.

Recent Shifts in the Criteria for ADD

It is in the context of the ascendance of the biological/behavioral world view that the recent proliferation of attention deficit disorder (ADD) diagnoses can be best understood. ADD is not a new diagnosis; it has been around for a long time and its validity is well established. However, what has happened over the last few years is that the definition of what constitutes ADD has been quietly but systematically expanded to include a wider and wider range of behaviors. This loss of specificity has both threatened to obscure the otherwise valuable use of the "classic" diagnosis and created a potentially dangerous situation where diagnosis impedes rather than facilitates a clearer understanding of the clinical presentations it presumes to describe.

Up until quite recently, the criteria for ADD were relatively clear cut. Diagnosis was behaviorally based and was contingent on marked disturbances in the areas of activity level, impulsivity, and/or distractibility. The symptomatic behaviors typically manifested themselves from very early on in development, and were noted across a wide range of situations. They were particularly problematic in group situations, causing the youngster much suffering, and filling his daily life, particularly once he began school, with conflict and unhappiness. The introduction of medication in these cases often effected an immediate and dramatic change. Simply by making the child more able to sit in class and attend to the work, his functional learning capacity was greatly enhanced and his relationships with teachers and peers became less adversarial. These changes often had a salutary impact on the child's self-esteem, thus setting in motion a positive ripple effect that led to improvement in all areas of the child's life.

Thus, ADD in its original definition was one of the few diagnoses in the realm of childhood disorders where a specific intervention (medication) led to dramatic change in a very short period of time. Given this fact, it is entirely understandable that clinicians, when faced with an otherwise difficult or "messy" case, would be inclined to expand the parameters of the diagnosis in order to justify the use of a medication that offered the best hope of a "cure" that might otherwise be a long time in coming. From this perspective, it was just one small step to the position of using the medication as a diagnostic tool, that is, medicating all ambiguous cases and "working backwards" diagnostically by stating that children who respond positively (even on a short-term basis) to a drug which has effectively treated ADD can themselves be diagnosed as ADD.

These approaches have led to several problematic changes in how ADD is conceptualized. As suggested above, the valuable specificity of the "classic" presentation has been sacrificed in order to make way for the formulation of milder and/or more subtle presentations of the hypothesized disorder. These newer cases are typically diagnosed much later in the child's life, and the retrospective evidence for early manifestations or precursors of the disorder tend to be ambiguous at best. Similarly, the criterion that these target symptoms manifest themselves across a wide range of contexts has also been lost, and it is no longer unusual for a child to be diagnosed as ADD on the basis of a delimited difficulty in a single aspect of his life, most typically relative to school or schoolwork. Essentially what has occurred is that the criterion has shifted from significant and pervasive deviance from the norm in activity level, impulsivity, and distractibility (usually at least two of the three) to observable deviance from a hypothesized optimal level of functioning in any of the three areas in any of the several contexts of the child's life.

One particularly troubling aspect of this expanded definition of ADD is the way it has been used to obscure or invalidate psychodynamic approaches to this and other childhood disorders. Without in any way denying either the enormous value of a correct ADD diagnosis (and the corresponding psychopharmacological treatment) or the relevance of neurobiology to the field of child pathology as a whole, it is still possible to object to a theoretical position which reduces the quality of the child's relationships and her affect development to mere epiphenomena. Since all human actions have neurobiological correlates, it is theoretically possible to "translate" all subjective phenomena (thoughts, feelings, wishes, beliefs) into neurobiological events, thereby implicitly or explicitly denying their unique, idiosyncratic meaning in a specific person's life. However, the act of attributing children's difficulties in living to "hard wiring" rather than to psychological development in all its complexity gives them a message about who they are and "what they're made of" that is neither value-free nor necessarily wholesome in terms of its impact on the child's future development.

Behavior-Based Definitions of ADD

Though the behaviors currently viewed as evidence of an attention deficit disorder are too diverse to be easily enumerated, they can be broadly sorted into two functional categories: disorders of independent functioning and disorders of classroom behavior. Disorders of independent functioning are most often noted in relation to school assignments and include such difficulties as "settling down" to homework, completing assignments or handing them in on time, and poor quality of work relative to perceived intelligence. Vulnerabilities in planning and organizational skills are often used as evidence for the diagnosis, so that symptoms such as inefficient study habits, erratic note-taking ability, "sloppy" or poorly organized written work, and poor time management (especially in relation to preparing for tests and long-term projects) are frequently noted as well. When problems of independent functioning are reported in out-of-school contexts, they typically cover much of what used to be subsumed under the heading of "oppositional behavior," for example, not keeping one's room clean, ignoring or not correctly following parental instructions, all sorts of dawdling (getting out of the house in the morning, getting ready for bed), and all sorts of forgetting (of chores, of time, and of parental edicts in general).

Disorders of classroom behavior are of particular import because the majority of all ADD referrals result from them. Defined most broadly, these can be said to include any aspect of the child's behavior or self-presentation which results in his not complying with and/or benefiting from the teacher's preferred way of running the class. Perhaps the most common variant is simple disruptiveness, as marked by such behaviors as calling out in class, getting out of one's seat, interacting with peers when the lesson plan prohibits it, or acting in a way that distracts others from the work at hand. Difficulty with "transitions" is a related and frequently noted complaint and typically means that the child is likely to manifest disruptive (or noncompliant) behavior whenever a shift in expectations occurs, for example, settling down upon entering a classroom, staying attentive when the teacher moves to a different lesson or subject, negotiating the halls between classes, and generally demonstrating "self-control" in those unstructured breaks that periodically dot the daily school schedule. Finally, classroom disorders also include "quieter" symptoms which are related to the child's ability to take in the presented material, and tend to overlap considerably with the disorders of independent functioning just elaborated. Children manifesting these behaviors are often described as "daydreamy" or "spacey," meaning that they sit quietly at their desks, in nondisruptive fashion, but do not appear to be listening to the lesson being presented. They may be doodling, staring out the window, or simply looking vacant. Among the functional problems they are likely to manifest are failing to copy material off the board in the time allotted, not following classroom discussions, taking inadequate notes, and forgetting to bring books or assignments home.

While all these behaviors are found with greater frequency in ADD youngsters, the problem with using them as prima facie evidence of ADD is that they are associated with a range of childhood disorders so broad that it is frankly hard to think of a diagnosable condition where none of these "symptoms" would be present. The biobehavioral model has simultaneously acknowledged and denied this lack of specificity through its emphasis on the construct of "co-morbidity," which has allowed them to justify the fact that attention deficit is being applied to such a wide range of clinical presentations by stating that it simply coexists with a number of other childhood disorders. Yet, what is so troubling about this definition is that its very vagueness makes it virtually impossible to *not* diagnose a co-morbid ADD in any marked disturbance of childhood. In other words, it is certainly true that difficulties in independent functioning and classroom behavior are both widespread and highly relevant to understanding childhood pathology. However, the assumption that these symptoms reflect a primary deficit in the attentional system that somehow causes this wide range of behaviors does not seem justified. Rather it seems closer to the data of observation to say that the attentional system, as it is currently defined, is extremely complex and mediates virtually all interactions between the person and the outside world. Therefore, any pathological entity will have an impact on the attentional system in some fashion and reduce its efficacy. Ultimately, the clinician's goal is not merely to note and label these ubiquitous deficits but rather to develop some deeper understanding about how these *specific* deficits came about in *this* specific individual and what these manifestations can teach us about who this person is and what they need in order to be able to function more effectively in the world.

Ultimately, what the biobehavioral model of ADD ignores is the profound impact that relationships have upon every aspect of child development. Therefore, it is the task of the psychoanalytically oriented clinician to affirm the essential value of understanding the subjective or phenomenological world of the person one is treating and of using empathy and introspection as a means of attaining that understanding. From this perspective, it immediately becomes clear that the behaviors described above as symptomatic of ADD can be understood as the child's adaptation to a complex set of internal and external factors. Specifically, the construct of narcissistic pathology can be fruitfully applied here, if by that term it is suggested that (a) children can be expected to act in ways that will protect their self-esteem, (b) self-esteem is invariably contingent on the quality of one's relationships, and (c) both the range of one's self-esteem-protecting maneuvers and the range of one's possible relationships are determined by those affects one can tolerate and those that must be defended against and avoided.

Though these issues will be addressed in greater detail in the case studies presented below, what can be emphasized now is that the psychoanalytic position is historical, in its belief that understanding how someone came to be exactly who they are over time is a worthwhile endeavor, and relational, in its belief that human behavior, and beyond that human subjectivity, can only be fully understood through a consideration of one's past and present interactions with others. By contrast, the biobehavioral model is largely ahistorical, in its presumption that the factors most relevant to treatment are genetically determined, "hard wired," and present from birth, and is inclined to minimize the value of relationships and their contribution to the patient's presenting problem. Thus, while it is possible to delineate a perspective that incorporates relevant aspects from both models, it would be foolish to deny that they represent threats to each other, and that psychoanalysts, as the threatened "old guard," need to give careful thought to how to productively present their position in a world that is increasingly skeptical of them.

Temperament and Goodness-of-Fit

One way of looking at ADD that gives both biology and psychodynamics their due is to think of it as related both to temperament and to the developmental lines that stem from certain temperamental configurations. Speaking broadly, temperament refers to innate or genetically determined predispositions, especially as regards the organism's response to internal and external stimuli. The three variables that define ADD—activity level, impulsivity, and distractibility—all have their roots in temperament. Activity level refers to a general rate of behavior, while impulsivity reflects the related issue of the organism's predisposition to act in the face of new stimuli and its ability to inhibit responses when the situation demands it. Distractibility refers to the organism's threshold of responsiveness, that is, the point at which incoming stimuli can no longer be ignored and begin demanding a response.

Thus, temperament is offered as a way of viewing the biological bedrock of childhood disorders. However, of equal importance in this understanding is temperament's corollary, "goodness of fit." This refers to the ability of the environment to adapt itself to the child's temperamentally based needs—Winnicott's (1965) facilitating environment—as well as to the child's ability to avail itself of these adaptations. Speaking broadly, the parental role is twofold. On the one hand, it is their job to "shape" their child's predispositions such that temperamental extremes can be modulated over the course of development in a way that allows their child to "fit in" to the world of others (and school par excellence) without undue stress and conflict. On the other hand, they must be accepting of their child's unique configuration of temperamental attributes in a way that allows her to "go on being" (Winnicott 1962) without having to stifle or abandon the developmental course that unfolds naturally given a "good enough" adaptation on the part of the environment.

This temperament/goodness-of-fit model allows for an understanding of the etiology of ADD (and childhood disorders in general) that fully incorporates both biological and dynamic factors. It challenges an understanding of ADD as a discrete disease entity that can be said to be either present or absent. Rather it suggests that each temperamental variable can be placed on a continuum, and that the diagnosis of ADD is contingent on where on those continua a line is drawn separating normal from pathological. Furthermore, it suggests that the way the child's innate temperament is responded to by his parents and broader environment affects where the child falls on the continuum and, thus whether or not he will be diagnosed as ADD. Two related factors need to be considered here. One is parental influence. It seems fair to say that certain children, by virtue of their configuration of temperamental attributes, can be considered vulnerable, "at risk," or difficult, by which is meant that parents will find it particularly difficult to figure out ways to adapt to their child's needs. In these cases, the parental response plays a central role in determining whether the child ultimately presents as ADD, that is, their response to her "difficultness" can either exacerbate or assuage her innate vulnerability. The other factor is goodness of fit with school and broader cultural institutions. In this regard, the parents function as mediators between the child (and his temperamental needs) and the "outside world." Thus, it not infrequently occurs that a child whose adaptation at home is and always has been considered adequate begins having problems at school because the range of temperamental styles that can be accommodated by that school's specific learning environment matches up poorly with the child's needs. In these cases, ADD can be diagnosed primarily as a result of the child's (or the child–parent family unit's) inability to adapt to the school's valid but ultimately rather arbitrary demands.

This view of ADD as a diagnosis that invariably reflects some combination of biological, relational, and cultural factors can also be fruitfully applied to the area of learning disabilities as well. Though it falls outside the scope of this chapter to consider learning disabilities in all their complexity, because they often co-exist with ADD (either as cause, effect or "co-morbid" condition), it is worth discussing them briefly as well. As someone who has done a considerable amount of psychoeducational testing, I have become increasingly impressed with how contingent the LD diagnosis is on interpersonal and cultural factors. Without denying that most learning disabilities have neuropsychological underpinnings, it can nonetheless be said that parental response to a child's unique patterning of cognitive strengths and weaknesses is of enormous importance as well, especially in determining what the child's attitude and motivational level will be as regards realizing her potential and overcoming her weaknesses. In addition, the child's school is also relevant since her teachers and classmates will all have roles in determining whether her level of cognitive and academic functioning is perceived as reflecting a learning disability.

In adopting this relativistic position, it is freely acknowledged that, when considering severe learning disabilities and the "classic" presentation of ADD, it makes sense to cede primacy to neurobiological phenomena. However, even in those extreme conditions where neurobiology must be given primary attention, interpersonal, familial and cultural factors significantly impact both the presentation and the course of the disorder. In addition, the increased number of referrals to clinicians working with children in recent years appears to be largely a result not of an increase in the severe, clear-cut cases but rather in those ambiguous cases where a model favoring complexity is most necessary. It is these complex cases that we will turn to next.

Case Illustrations

Assuming the essential relevance of neurobiology, relational history, and cultural factors to all childhood disorders, it is in the realm of relationships, and the affects that are inextricably bound up with them, where psychoanalysis has a unique contribution to make. The case studies that follow have been chosen both because they reflect composites of typical presenting problems, and because they illuminate certain dynamics that seem particularly relevant in those cases which are currently most likely to be diagnosed as ADD.

Alan, Age 7

Alan was referred for testing by his first-grade teacher who, after a year of trying to keep Alan "in step" with his thirty other classmates, began to have concerns that his difficulties were related to ADD. This young woman was quite fond of Alan and emphasized both that she thought he was a "workable kid" and that he had managed to acquire all his basic academic skills. Nevertheless, she noted that he was very restless in class and had difficulty sitting still. In addition, there were times when he would become verbally provocative toward both teacher and peers; by contrast, at other times, he seemed dreamy and disengaged. He had difficulty completing assignments and staying focused on his classwork. He was socially rather outcast and typically spent recess and free times alone. Thus, his teacher worried that he was in danger of "underachieving" unless he received some form of treatment.

Alan's parents were seen separately prior to the beginning of testing; though divorced for two years, they were still so prone to arguing that they both felt it best to meet alone. They had separated shortly after the birth of Alan's younger brother and they both acknowledged feeling guilt over the impact their longstanding arguing and marital discord had had on their son. They described him as an active and demanding child who had always needed a lot of attention. In general, their perceptions of their son were quite consistent; in fact, neither felt he had ADD since they each noted his capacity to work for long stretches of time on projects that engaged him. They disagreed only on their attribution of blame for Alan's current difficulties. His father related it to his mother's anxious overprotectiveness, while his mother related it to his father's emotional unavailability.

Alan was, as advertised, a temperamentally active boy, constantly fidgeting and shifting in his seat. However, he thrived in the presence of an adult's undivided attention and this, in conjunction with the structure provided by the formal tests, enabled him to work in a focused and effective way. Alan presented as a sweet and earnest boy, who seemed overtly anxious about his performance and was prone to making self-denigrating statements whenever he experienced any difficulty. Though Alan was thoughtful and articulate beyond his years, he had some minor delays in visual and graphomotor skills which made writing and drawing a struggle for him. He was very aware of these difficulties and they caused him a considerable degree of embarrassment and frustration. He spoke openly about wishing that his parents would reconcile and complained that his mother was too "bossy" and that his father didn't do enough things with him. He found school boring and thought the teachers were mean; he also complained about bullies at school and could not name a classmate whom he considered a friend. He spoke enthusiastically about his hobbies— sports, fishing, and computers—and had shown considerable initiative in learning about them.

Over the course of the testing and the therapy that followed, it became clear that Alan's parents had been so absorbed in their marital conflicts that they had had neither the time nor the patience to respond to Alan's admittedly difficult and active behavior in a constructive way. By reacting with either placating overindulgence or explosive counteraggression, they had inadvertently exacerbated his temperamental vulnerabilities rather than helped him to modulate them. In addition, the lack of adequate interaction with them had kept him from developing the social skills he needed to get along easily with others. This left him feeling like a lonely outsider, both at home and at school, which in turn precipitated painful feelings of hurt and anger. He defended against these intolerable feelings through constant action (often in the form of sport) and absorption in one of his hobbies; in these ways, he provided himself with the care and soothing that were otherwise lacking in his life. School, in its demand that he inhibit activity for long stretches of time and its expectation that he pursue the lesson plan rather than his own intellectual interests, was a torment to him. He thus oscillated between directly expressing his anger and resentment (leading to provocative behavior) and attempting to sup-press these feelings in the interest of being a good boy (leading to his presenting as dreamy and disengaged).

Viewed in terms of narcissistic pathology, Alan can be seen as an example of an "unmirrored" child whose parents were unable to either (a) tone down his temperamental dispositions in a way that prepared him for the broader social arena, or (b) take sufficient interest or pleasure in his abilities in a way that allowed him to develop a sense of proud competence and of belonging in the world. As a result, his self-esteem was poor and, except when pursuing his rather narrow range of interests, he was anxious, restless, distracted, and irritable. Given this understanding of his ADD symptoms, it was recom-mended that the issue of medication be deferred until other interventions were explored. The parents agreed to this, and an individual treatment, with collateral parental meetings, was begun. In addition, Alan was transferred to a school where classes were smaller and there was less exclusive emphasis on grades and achievement. This combination of therapy and school change proved to be adequate to alleviate Alan's presenting symptoms and, though his current school still finds him a "handful" at times, they are confident about their ability to educate him. Similarly, though he remains socially reserved and anxious, therapy has enabled him to establish a small circle of friends and to develop a wider repertoire of interpersonal responses with both peers and adults.

Brian, Age 13

In Brian's case, it was his parents who thought he might have ADD and brought him for testing after a surprisingly poor first-semester report card in seventh grade. Both well-educated professionals, they were familiar with the recent literature and felt that Brian's organizational difficulties and forgetfulness fit well with current definitions of ADD. They said his room was a "disaster area" of strewn books and clothes and his notebook was "a mess." In addition, he frequently forgot to bring books and assignments from school to home and back again; sometimes he would put his completed homework in his notebook, bring it to school and simply forget to hand it in. They were also very concerned about the poor quality of his written work in general. He seemed content with sloppily presented and inadequately "fleshed out" papers; he was also a poor editor and his work reflected an inattention to detail and a lack of fluency in the basic mechanics of writing. Finally, they found him increasingly sullen and secretive, resentful of any parental interest in any aspect of his life. While they knew enough to attribute some of this to his having just turned 13, they worried that these trends presaged a potentially disastrous adolescence.

The school had a different perception of the situation. They were generally less concerned about Brian and more inclined to attribute whatever difficulties he was having to "motivational" factors rather than to attentional ones. Brian had been at the same school since kindergarten and was both well-known and well-liked. Teachers viewed him as charming and articulate, with an almost theatrical style when participating in classroom discussions. He was described as a boy who was sought out by peers, though he did not seem to have any really close friends. While they shared Brian's parents' concerns regarding his written work and falling grades, they thought it was more likely related to Brian's simple unwillingness to put in the time and effort required to do well at a high-achieving private school. One teacher suggested that Brian was "spoiled" by the success his verbal facility had afforded him in the lower grades and was having trouble adjusting to both the competition and the sheer volume of work in the upper school. It was also implied, albeit guardedly, that his current behavior was an expectable adolescent rebellion against his parents' unrealistic expectations for him.

Brian thoroughly disliked being tested. While he was animated and engaging during our pre-testing conversation, and whenever we took a break from the proceedings to talk informally, he became extremely anxious as soon as the shift was made to formal testing and nothing short of ceasing to test him tempered these feelings. He frequently asked how he was doing and would roll his eyes in disgust when given a task he found daunting. He seemed angry both at himself for his difficulties and at the examiner for exposing them. His ability to tolerate frustration was minimal. Though he was usually able to greet each new task with a wary enthusiasm, he got discouraged quickly, often to the point of being on the verge of tears, and, once having reached this state, would abandon the task precipitously, remaining unresponsive to either encouragement or reassurance. Despite these reactions, Brian did not do badly on the cognitive and academic tests administered. However, except for the area of oral language where his skills were very superior, Brian's scores were generally in the average range, a result which took on significance because it placed him below the majority of his classmates and thus became a source of distress and shame.

What the testing clarified psychodynamically was that Brian had a powerful need to feel special or exceptional and so was only comfortable pursuing activities he believed he had a gift for. He experienced having to struggle for success as a burden and a humiliation. In addition, he was unable to tolerate the feelings of weakness, inadequacy, and uncertainty that accompanied his efforts to acquire skills that did not come naturally for him. Written expression fell into this category and, as a result, when the requisite output mode in school shifted from primarily oral to primarily written, Brian became less able to compete with peers and school became more and more associated with anxiety and negative feelings that needed to be avoided. Thus, his organizational difficulties and his proneness toward forgetting, though broadly having their roots in some minor vulnerabilities in his attentional system, were better understood as a function of his unconsciously determined need to avoid tasks that threatened his self-esteem. In addition, it became clear that his difficulties were becoming more prominent because Brian was caught in a vicious circle in which his avoidance was exacerbating the very situation it was designed to manage, thereby increasing the need for this maladaptive defensive maneuver.

This case illustrates how behaviors currently associated with ADD can be reconceptualized as manifestations of narcissistic pathology. Kohut's (1971) notion of a "vertical split" is of particular relevance here. The personality is organized around a grandiose self-representation that incorporates both the child's special skills and the love and admiration that have come to be associated with them. However, coexisting side by side with this self-selfobject-affect configuration is another one that includes a self-representation marked by inadequacy, inferiority, and unworthiness. The corresponding selfobject is typically rejecting, disappointed, or disinterested. The feelings attendant to this state are to be avoided at all costs and the child's actions and modes of relating can usually be understood as maneuvers to keep the grandiose self in ascendance and the devalued self secreted away. When the "real world," in the form of school, makes demands that force the appearance of the devalued self, the psychic equilibrium is disturbed and the child becomes symptomatic, often in ways that are suggestive of ADD. Psychoanalytically oriented treatment of these cases is often difficult and slow, but can lead to essential changes in the child's affect tolerance and the quality of his relationships. However, because of the arduousness of the treatment, these are the types of cases where therapy is always in danger of being abandoned in favor of the quicker-acting treatments, among which medication is the most prominent.

Barbara, Age 11

Barbara was referred for testing toward the end of fifth grade at the suggestion of her mother's therapist, who had become increasingly concerned that Barbara's erratic behavior might have neuropsychological, that is, attentional, underpinnings. The incident which precipitated the referral was one where Barbara had had a severe panic attack owing to her inability to finish a history paper due the next day. Barbara had initially rejected her mother's offer to help her on this assignment. However, at midnight, she stormed out of her room, cursing her mother for abandoning her and cursing herself for her stupidity and incompetence. Only after a frighten-ingly long bout of screaming and crying was the crisis finally resolved by having Barbara's mother write the report on the computer while Barbara dictated it to her.

The history given by Barbara's mother (her father was against her being tested and refused to come in) revealed long-standing concerns about Barbara, both at school and at home. Barbara's schoolwork had always been uneven. Her report cards almost invariably described her as a sweet, bright girl who could do better if only she paid more attention in class or put in more effort at home. Her scores on standardized tests also fluctuated widely from year to year and there was no consistent pattern noted in terms of strengths or weaknesses. Her current teachers emphasized what a "mystery" Barbara was. She could be completely "spaced out" and unable to follow a class discussion one day, yet capable of taking a leadership role in the same class the following day.

The situation at home was even more complicated. Barbara was the youngest of three children in a house where marital discord was chronic and severe. Her two older brothers were close to each other and to their father, but rejecting of mother and sister. Barbara and her mother had a "special relationship" and had always spent much of their time together; however, Barbara also played the role of "peacemaker" in the house, especially when her parents fought. In addition, the mother suffered from a long-standing dysthymia which she felt had affected her emotional availability to her children. She also worried that she had "used" Barbara in the sense of wanting to be close to her as a means of obtaining the emotional support and intimacy lacking in her marriage. She saw much of herself in Barbara and remembered receiving similar school reports.

Testing revealed no significant cognitive or academic deficits, though it did confirm Barbara's tendencies toward erratic performance. More importantly, however, it revealed how attuned to others' feelings Barbara was, and how sensitive she was to how they responded to her. For example, she constantly asked for feedback on how she was doing on the tests and more than once apologized when she thought she'd done badly. She worried about the examiner's state of mind, often asking him if he was bored or upset or needed to take a break. She also spoke movingly about how much she hated it when her parents fought and described her various mechanisms for tuning them out, such as playing her clarinet loudly or sitting in the bathroom with the shower running. In discussing her school problems, she admitted that it was often hard for her to care about her work and that, when she drifted off in class or over her homework, it was usually either because she was worrying about her family or because she was lost in one of the fantasies she'd invented in order to make herself feel better. As regards the work itself, she acknowledged that she had almost invariably done her homework with her mother and that her mother often helped her study and/or do her writing assignments. She said she had reached the point where she felt ashamed of needing her mother's help in this way and wanted to become more independent but she worried both that this would make her mother sad and that she herself would be unable to do the requisite work without some adult assistance.

This is a complex case where many factors contribute to Barbara's ADD-like symptoms. However, what is of greatest relevance to the theme of this chapter is the effect of Barbara's mother's narcissistic use of her on her ability to function independently. Winnicott's (1958a) understanding of the "capacity to be alone" is crucial in cases such as these. If the parent is unable to "let the child be" in their presence so that the child is always reacting to them, then this capacity never gets developed. Similarly, if the child experiences "getting lost" in her work as either abandoning or being abandoned by the parent, then this process is also disrupted. In Barbara's case, this dynamic was complicated by her attunement to and identification with her mother's vulnerability and need. Barbara unconsciously felt it was her duty to keep her mother alive during their separations by keeping her constantly in mind. Thus, her attention was always split between internal and external reality, so that, when her mother's depression or her parents' marital conflicts worsened, she had to allocate more of her psychic resources to preserving her internal landscape and therefore presented as withdrawn, distracted or disengaged.

Carl, Age 16

Carl was diagnosed with ADD by his school drug counselor following Carl's second suspension for smoking marijuana on school grounds. This counselor felt that Carl was "medicating himself" with marijuana as a way of treating an attentional deficit that made him unable to stay focused in classes or to settle down to work when at home. He therefore intervened on Carl's behalf with the principal, who was inclined to expel him, and Carl was allowed to return to school provided that he agree to be tested for ADD and learning disabilities.

Carl had a long history of academic underachievement and was repeating the tenth grade after having failed several classes the previous year. His report card showed he had done very well in the two classes he attended regularly but that his attendance in the other classes was so poor that his teachers had no choice but to fail him. He was perceived by his teachers as a "nice kid," capable of doing good work but having fallen in with a "bad crowd." His parents agreed with this to a point but also expressed concern as to whether the school was innovative and challenging enough to engage their son's interest. In addition, Carl's mother was worried about Carl's level of depression and suspected that it was this, rather than ADD, that he was "treating" through his drug use.

Carl presented initially as a sad and rather passive young man who was surprisingly easy to engage. He thoroughly enjoyed the testing and was able to sustain a high level of motivation and effort. He was also quite open about many aspects of his life and spoke frankly about his feelings of "alienation" from much of modern culture. As regards school, he acknowledged his long-standing aversion to it and admitted that he had great difficulty paying attention to classes he found boring. However, he made it clear that he enjoyed learning and pointed out that, even last year, he had done well in those classes where he liked the teacher and the material. He also emphasized that he was a "big believer" in reading and that he read for pleasure and information rather than for school itself. He did not deny his drug use and, in fact, spoke in a very positive way about the group of kids he got high with, praising them as individuals and talking about how honestly everyone related to each other. The only area of his life where he seemed less than candid was his relationship to his parents. Carl's parents had been divorced since he was 5 and he saw his father, who was remarried and living out-of-state, very infrequently. Whenever this topic was broached, he would look sad and distracted, make some kind of simple statement to the effect that he got on well with both parents, and fall silent; the most he would acknowledge were some "normal teenage" desires, such as a later curfew and more spending money.

Carl's scores on the cognitive tests indicated that he was an intellectually gifted youngster with a wide range of strengths and no significant weaknesses. His academics, though not at the level of his intellectual ability, were nonetheless solidly above average. However, Carl perceived himself as doing poorly on the academic testing, particularly when writing was involved, and expressed frustration and self-contempt in relation to it. Interestingly, even though Carl's overall reading ability was good, his phonic skills were relatively weak, a finding that often indicates early difficulties learning to read. When this was mentioned, Carl noted that he had been placed in a gifted class in first grade but taken out of it when he couldn't keep up with his peers. When it was suggested to him that his dislike of school might date from these early experiences, he agreed this might be so.

Carl's projective testing was full of violent imagery and themes of rage and aggression. Suicidal material was also frankly present. What was striking about Carl's responses was the contrast between his calm, laid-back persona and the passion and intensity of his inner affective world. Many of his stories seemed to be thinly disguised criticisms of his parents for the way they had "let him down" in his times of need; he communicated a view of them as superficial and emotionally out of tune, too absorbed in their own lives to take an interest in his. Seen from this perspective, his use of marijuana was best understood as being in the service of what Winnicott (1935) has referred to as a "wet blanketing" of his affective world. Carl had never had the opportunity to develop a tolerance for angry or aggressive feelings, so that when he experienced them, rather than serving as a signal for appropriate action, they immediately led him into a full-blown rage. Under these conditions, any negative feeling was extremely dangerous, and thus Carl had organized his life to avoid any situation or relationship where these feelings could be evoked.

Carl thus employed what Spotnitz (1976) refers to as the "narcissistic defense." It entails turning one's aggression against the self as a means of protecting and preserving the object who would otherwise be attacked and destroyed. It is typically set in place early in development as a result of the child's experiencing his parents as unable to tolerate or deal constructively with his negative feelings. This parental response confirms the child's fears that these feelings are dangerous and destructive and therefore must be suppressed and/or denied. As a result, the child does not have the opportunity to learn to modulate these feelings or otherwise "filter" them through an accepting adult. Once this dynamic is in place it is a breeding ground for depression and self-destructive behaviors. Because the narcissistic defense frequently interferes with the child's ability to fully realize his intellectual potential, it often leads to "underachievement," which is a construct currently being reconceptualized as ADD.

Cases such as these also raise the issue of what message is given to a teenager who is already using drugs to manage affect when "the authorities" replace his drug of choice with one of their own. In addition, they highlight the extent to

which narcissistic disorders manifest themselves as disorders of affect tolerance, and suggest that addressing this affect pathology within the context of a
"good enough" therapeutic relationship is crucial to treating them.

Clinical vignettes such as these, no matter how carefully selected, can do no
more than allude to the complexity of the subject being covered. One general
theme worth reemphasizing is that in cases where an early history of attentional problems is not present, it is important to think of later-onset ADD
symptoms as defensive maneuvers or what Sullivan (1953) called "security
operations" in the service of maintaining an affective status quo in the child's
established mode of relating to the world. In particular, the use of such
maneuvers as devaluation (of peers, teacher, school, and/or learning), the
manic defense (compulsive attention seeking via humor and a high rate of
behavior), and the flight to fantasy (social withdrawal accompanied by soothing imagined scenarios where the desired self-state is reinstated) are all both
very common and increasingly likely to be viewed as manifestations of ADD.
What makes the construct of narcissistic pathology of special value in organizing these varied operations is the way it focuses attention on the child's
efforts to maintain self-esteem, especially via the avoidance of those feelings
that would threaten it, and the impact that these efforts have upon how the
child manages his or her various relationships.

ADD and Cultural Narcissism

The growing popularity of ADD as a diagnosis is a cultural phenomenon
worth exploring as a function of narcissistic pathology. There is an obvious
appeal to viewing one's child's (or one's own) life difficulties as a correctable,
genetically determined, biochemically based disorder. It eases the feelings of
guilt and responsibility that we as parents feel when our children fail to thrive,
in school or elsewhere, and allows us to feel that we did the best we could in
the face of circumstances beyond our control. In addition, it holds out the
promise that, if only the right medication is found, we can regain the perfect
child we dreamed of having—who could be, have, or do all we could not—in
place of the child we actually have. It also assuages the fear that one's child is
"fated" to suffer from the same flaws and limitations that the parent did.
Finally, it offers the hope that all that is wrong within the family can be
righted without the parents' being forced to reflect too much on how the
family's established mode of interacting, or the emotional tenor of their

relationships, has contributed to their child's being who they are. Three brief vignettes will illustrate some of these issues:

A father brings his son in for an evaluation to see if the boy has ADD. The assessment suggests that, though the boy has some attentional vulnerabilities, he does not meet the criteria for ADD and therefore medication is not recommended. At this point, the father requests a medication consultation for himself, saying that he has many of the problems his son has. Though the father has been quite successful professionally, he reasons that if he has done as well as he has to date in spite of his ADD, then the Ritalin ought to make him a "superman" capable of exceptional achievement.

A 14-year-old boy is brought in for a consultation by his parents to determine whether psychotherapy is indicated. The boy's grades have recently dropped, he is oppositional at home, and hanging out with the wrong crowd. In our initial interview, he presents as intellectually gifted, quite depressed, and clearly in the midst of an adolescent identity crisis during which everything must be questioned. Prior to the beginning of treatment, his parents take him to the chief psychiatrist of a prominent hospital who diagnoses him as "mild attention deficit disorder without hyperactivity" and prescribes Ritalin. The parents feel "this explains a lot" and decide to forego therapy.

A 17-year-old girl is brought in by her parents after obtaining "disappointing" scores on her SATs, making it seem unlikely that she will be accepted at the very selective college she and her parents had always talked about her attending. While the girl feels her scores are "good enough" and privately acknowledges that she fears the work will be too demanding at the chosen school, her parents are hopeful that untimed testing and medication will allow her to raise her scores sufficiently to get accepted.

Again, it must be emphasized that it is appropriate for both parents and clinicians to consider whether a given presenting problem might be best explained neurobiologically. The danger comes in only when this becomes the sole explanatory principle for complex, multidetermined clinical presentations. In related fashion, there is often a contempt for nonbiological (i.e., psychodynamic) approaches among the most ardent advocates of the biobehavioral model that suggests the narcissistic need to be right in an absolute, rather than a relative, way and to deny all uncertainty; for these professionals, it seems to be the feeling of not knowing, with its implications of fallibility and vulnerability, that must be avoided at all costs. Yet tolerating these feelings is ultimately exactly what enables clinicians to listen to their patients in all their uniqueness without needing to foreclose the assessment process with a rush to diagnostic definitiveness.

At the broadest level, the burgeoning use of ADD as a diagnosis reflects a cultural trend that is both generally anti-intellectual and specifically antipsychoanalytic. What is at stake is the role assigned to emotion in the contemporary common-sense theory of behavior and the value attributed to fully experiencing and tolerating all one's feelings, both good and bad. For psychoanalysts, feelings are the core of subjectivity and the royal road to self-knowledge. Therefore, the goal of treatment is to enable people to experience their full range of feelings without needing either to act on them immediately or to deny them via defensive security operations. It is believed that if people can tolerate their feelings, then they can use the information that the feelings provide them in order to make life decisions that are in their enlightened self-interest. Stated another way, only by fully knowing one's feelings can one determine when and to what degree it is appropriate to act on them. Furthermore, since affect is the language of relationship, it is ultimately desirable, even necessary, to be able to experience the full range of feelings in the service of making intimacy and mutuality possible between people. By contrast, in the minds of the more aggressive biobehaviorists, feelings are viewed primarily as potential disruptors of smooth functioning and adaptation to the social grid. The goal is to truncate the range of feelings experienced (with a strong emphasis on "accentuating the positive") and to train people to behave appropriately in spite of or regardless of their feelings in the hope that if new behaviors are established, then feelings will change in accord with them. The emphasis is on result rather than process and on avoidance of interpersonal stress and conflict rather than on "muddling through" to intimacy. Self-knowledge itself, and the introspection and empathy which further it, is minimized in value; what matters is "getting along" with others and not suffering too much internal Sturm und Drang. Medication, in its ability to smooth rough edges and mute strong and upsetting thoughts, feelings, and impulses, is clearly the treatment of choice; analytically oriented therapy can only stir the waters to no immediately observable avail.

America is a "can do" culture and there is much to recommend this point of view. Its clichéd movie belief that "you can be anything you want to be" is a wonderful and inspiring message that has done many people much good, but it is not literally true. We bristle at our limitations and cannot tolerate the fact that to be human is to be subject to the "ineluctable traumas" (McDougall 1980) of life. These are the aspects of human life that cannot be altered, among which are included the trauma of separateness from mother, the trauma of getting to be only one gender, the trauma of aging and death, and the trauma of the very facticity of one's life, by which is meant that one gets a specific, non-negotiable set of attributes (age, height, temperament, body type) which determine the limits of one's possibilities. If narcissistic pathology is defined as the inability to accept these existential traumas and the need to deny feelings and distort perceptions that would force one to confront them, then it seems fair to have concern that the current lust for biological bases for problems in living is related to a cultural form of narcissism.

In the face of this, the essential value of psychoanalysis lies in its commitment to embracing the entirety of the human condition and to celebrating the widest range of human experience and emotion. Without standing in the way of scientific progress that is capable of reducing unnecessary human suffering, it is nevertheless the psychoanalyst's task to acknowledge that "normal human misery" is unavoidable and to help people learn to accept and to tolerate this while simultaneously finding ways to affirm their lives and the meaningfulness of their relationships and their work. At the core, it is the task of psychoanalysis to safeguard the possibility of human freedom in a world full of dictates, constraints, and impingements. If treatment succeeds in enabling people to know their full range of feelings and to make life decisions that are respectful of these feelings without being driven by them, then it has provided an invaluable service. Similarly, if people can live without fear of feelings, confident in their ability to tolerate and learn from even the most powerful and disturbing affects, then they are free to pursue the dreams and desires that arise from the wellspring of their essential subjectivity.

References

Kohut, H. (1971). *The Analysis of the Self*. New York: International Universities Press.
McDougall, J. (1980). *A Plea for a Measure of Abnormality*. New York: International Universities Press.
Spotnitz, H. (1976). *Psychotherapy of Preoedipal Conditions*. New York: Jason Aronson.
Sullivan, H. S. (1953). *The Interpersonal Theory of Psychiatry*. New York: Norton.

Winnicott, D. W. (1935). The manic defence. In *Collected Papers: Through Paediatrics to Psychoanalysis*. London: Tavistock, 1958.

————— (1958a). The capacity to be alone. In *The Maturational Processes and the Facilitating Environment*, pp. 29–36. New York: International Universities Press, 1965.

————— (1958b). *Collected Papers: Through Paediatrics to Psychoanalysis*. London: Tavistock.

————— (1962). Ego integration in child development. In *The Maturational Processes and the Facilitating Environment*, pp. 56–63. New York: International Universities Press, 1965.

————— (1965). *The Maturational Processes and the Facilitating Environment*. New York: International Universities Press.

9

Narcissistic Disorders in Children

Phyllis Beren

In the past two decades a greater understanding of certain pathological conditions in adults has been gained by the elaboration and expansion of the theory of narcissism. These theoretical formulations have influenced our diagnostic assessment and our clinical technique with adult narcissistic disturbances (Bach 1985, Kernberg 1967, 1970, 1975, Kohut 1966, 1968, 1971, 1972, Modell 1976, Reich 1953). In the literature on assessment, diagnosis, and treatment of children, mention has been made of narcissistic defenses (Mahler and Kaplan 1977), but until recently little attention has been paid to the possibility of an already existing narcissistic disorder (Bene 1979, Bleiberg 1984, 1988, Egan and Kernberg 1984).

This chapter looks at some of those children who at first glance seem ideally suited to psychoanalytically oriented treatment but who do not respond in the anticipated manner to our therapeutic interventions. For example, some child cases end in a therapeutic stalemate or fall considerably short of the treatment goal, despite what appears initially to be a relatively benign diagnosis and a good therapeutic prognosis. It sometimes also appears that standard psychoanalytic technique, such as the analysis of defense and interpretation of unconscious conflict, may have little positive effect and instead may make some children only more resistant and defensive or even disorganized. Certain children also present the therapist with unusual countertransference reactions which may take the form of feeling bored, ineffectual, or doubtful about the usefulness of the treatment. These feelings may in turn lead to finding reasons for lessening the frequency of sessions, changing the modality of treatment, or terminating the treatment altogether.

A number of authors have written about the "corrective emotional experience" as a special therapeutic technique for certain developmental disorders (Alpert 1957, Berger and Kennedy 1975, A. Freud 1968, 1976, Weil 1973). When clinicians need to deviate from standard analytic technique by the use of the "corrective emotional experience," they may sometimes be treating children who suffer from a narcissistic disturbance. Likewise, cases in which the reported focus is on the countertransference of the therapist and his or her difficulty in establishing and maintaining a standard analytic atmosphere and working relationship may also indicate a narcissistic disturbance in the child (Bornstein 1948, 1949, Kabcenell 1974, Kay 1978).

I want to illustrate these considerations with the case of Jane, who was 8½ years old when she entered therapy. The main complaint of her parents was that she did not make an effort in school and had difficulty completing her work. At home she had tantrums every day, usually about wanting her mother to buy her something special. The parents found her exceedingly demanding and unreasonable. She had difficulty being alone and occupying her time and instead wanted to be entertained. She often complained that her parents were nicer to her two older sisters than they were to her. Unlike their middle daughter whom the parents described as an easy and wonderful baby, Jane from early on seemed difficult to satisfy and was exceptionally clingy. While Jane had friends and liked to have other children around her, she was disappointed that the popular girls did not choose to socialize with her. One way that Jane seemed to differentiate herself from her sisters and mother was to dress in what she thought to be the fashion of the times: like a punk teenager. She expressed both envy and disparagement of her sisters and felt the parents favored them. Jane did not acknowledge having any problems and viewed her need for treatment as totally her mother's desire. All she would grant is that her mother called her tantrums "the fit of the day." She herself had no idea why she had tantrums. She denied any problems in school, even though her school reports were very poor. She blamed everything on the teachers playing favorites.

For half the duration of her treatment, which lasted four years, Jane continually denied her unhappy and painful feelings or her role in any of the difficulties in school and at home. I have discovered this to be common in children with narcissistic disorders, who tend to have little or no objective self-awareness. Over the course of treatment Jane disliked and resented it if I tried to empathize with what she might feel. For example, when she complained one day how unfair it was that her sister had been given some new furniture for her bedroom and her parents refused to do the same for her, I said that this must make her feel angry and disappointed. Jane screamed at me, "Don't tell me how I feel, no one knows except me." Or she yelled at me that I could not read her mind if I attempted to make some interpretation of her defensive stance. The most benign intervention or interpretation always was rejected or, worse yet, caused her to become very hostile followed by a refusal to talk to me.

This high level of guardedness, denial of problems, and lack of empathy in such children can pose difficulties for the therapist, making it hard to feel that a mutual working relationship has been established. Although many of these children may complain about coming to therapy, they will come dutifully and appear engaged in the session if they are not relating directly to the therapist. In contrast, the classical theory of child analysis suggests that in order for a child to benefit from therapy, he or she must perceive, experience, or acknowledge a problem. For example, in Bornstein's well-known case of Frankie (1949), to be discussed later, the teachers were instructed that once Frankie made a positive attachment to them, they were to inform him that his mother could no longer stay with him in school. When he protested that he could not remain alone, they were asked to tell him that there was someone he could talk to who would help him stay in school. "This pre-analytic phase was designed to create a conflict in the child between his symptom and reality. . . . By our pre-analytic scheme we hoped to produce in him insight into his need for help, without which no psychoanalytic treatment can make any progress" (p. 184). This implies that a child has to have a number of well-developed ego functions, such as a capacity for insight and self-awareness, to benefit from an analytic approach. The ability to admit to problems and perceive one's own part in them presupposes a relatively well-developed sense of self. Narcissistic children's sense of self is usually less developed, more vulnerable, and more dependent on outside approval. It is as if their sense of self is still in the process of formation and more dependent on the admiration of others and their own grandiose fantasies. Such children have a tendency to feel easily injured and, in response to these perceived slights, to react with a good deal of anger. It would be unlikely that such children could easily admit to problems or see the purpose of treatment, since they often externalize their problems. Frequently, the treatment itself may be experienced as a narcissistic injury.

While it is beyond the scope of this chapter to give a detailed account of Jane's therapy, I have chosen to discuss a few aspects which I feel highlight some of the difficulties in the treatment of a narcissistic child. Many of the sessions had a very formulaic quality to them. Jane often came in with a snack which she proceeded to eat, giving it her full attention. While she was eating she read the contents on the package and rationalized that it did not contain too many calories, since she was concerned about how she looked and was in fact considerably overweight. When I said that I knew she was worried about her weight, she denied this. Once the eating ritual ended, she entered the second stage of her therapy session. She walked around the room in what appeared to me to be an aimless fashion, usually doing some strange foot stepping while bouncing her head and snapping her fingers. Because she wanted me to guess and would not say what she was doing, it took me a while to figure out that she was trying to imitate the rock star David Byrne of the Talking Heads. Having guessed correctly, I was rewarded by learning a little more about her. Her desire and pleasure in having me guess contained a deeper meaning which she was unwilling to analyze or understand and which felt to me as if it were one more example of her controlling behavior. What she did confess was her desire to be a rock star. She clearly wanted to have an audience and she wanted to use our sessions for me to be her audience and to admire her imitations and give her my undivided attention. She had no interest in interacting with me. She was content to have me watch her eat and then perform. I might add that it is this type of demand on the therapist that may engender countertransference feelings of being bored and exploited. It is also the behavior of a much younger child who wishes the mother to admire everything she does. Another example of this need for an admiring audience was her bringing her recorder to play in sessions. In reality she was not very accomplished because she spent very little time practicing. One had the clear sense that she believed she could be whoever she wanted to be just by wishing it. Thus she could eat all the cake and candy she wanted and still be thin and beautiful. She could be a teenager like her middle sister, and she could be a star. This was a further indication of her poorly developed sense of self, her shaky identifications, and the omnipotence of her thought. Thus she could also disregard reality by insisting that she was doing fine in school when in fact she was not. This disregard for reality by children who otherwise might appear normal in their reality testing and judgment is not unusual in children with narcissistic disorders. Sometimes parents will complain that these children lie or make up stories. In Jane's case her near total denial of her poor school functioning was a narcissistic defense she used because she could not tolerate admitting she was not good at something.

Another example of how her reality testing and judgment became compromised in the service of maintaining a kind of grandiose self was in her total disregard for the rules of the game. In contrast to the usual strict adherence to rules by latency-aged children, Jane seemed unaffected by them. Thus in playing checkers or some other board game, Jane made up the rules as she went along. When I tried to understand how she came to play this way, she insisted that it was how she played with her friends. When I tried gently to suggest that perhaps some children played one way and other children another, she told me I was wrong and that her way was right. Her manner of playing was so difficult to follow and was so controlling that it made me feel confused and manipulated. It was as if there was no way to play with her other than to allow myself to be used as an extension.

There were, however, moments when I intuitively sensed Jane to be more amenable to hearing what I said about her near failing in school or the fights with her mother and sisters. I had come to learn that she was better able to tolerate my interventions if I used some humor or made a joke. Thus, I would preface my intervention with, "Jane, you know that the only reason I am saying this is because it's my job. That's what therapists are supposed to do, to talk about the things nobody wants to talk about—but what can I do, it's my job; and if I didn't do that, I would be out of a job." This was often received with a big smile. She then allowed me to say, "I know how you hate it when I suggest you might feel a certain way about something, because your mother is always telling you how she thinks you feel and that makes you so angry." Jane could respond to this and say, "You bet!" and give me examples of fights where her mother insisted on seeing things her own way. Over time she came to be less guarded with me as she came to feel that I was her ally. The issue of how she played checkers was approached again. I asked her who taught her how to play and she responded that her uncle had. Again I used humor. I said, "Jane, I have some very bad news for you that will make you very upset because you will think I'm a terrible person for what I'm going to say about your uncle." Her eyes opened wide and I went on to say, "Your uncle all these years has taught you the wrong way to play checkers. I know you like your uncle and how hard this must be for you." She responded by smiling and went on to ask me how others played. In this way I managed to get around her feeling narcissistically injured by having to admit that she did not know something. It was alright if someone else was ignorant, but not she.

It might be questioned what in this interchange made it possible for her to react differently. First, I should note that she in fact had certain problems with other children. She could only be friends with those girls whom she could boss and manipulate. She desperately wanted to be accepted by the more popular girls, but they rejected her because in many ways she was immature. It would have been very difficult for her to find many children who would play board games the way she did. She would also have had a hard time admitting that she did not know how to play. Thus I gave her an opportunity to turn to me for some assistance without having to lose face. I had learned that a precondition for her hearing what I said was for me to devalue myself in some fashion so that I did not appear smarter than she. Earlier in the treatment she had frequently played a teacher who gave me tests for mental retardation. The need for me to be the retarded, devalued child was enacted with her rather than interpreted. As unconfrontive as this was, it must have taken us almost two years to arrive at this point. Later in the treatment I was able to analyze the transference from the standpoint that she needed to devalue me as she did her mother as well as her father and sisters. Further, her need to have me devalued was also interpreted as a reflection of how she felt about herself. At the time that she was able both to hear and accept my interpretation, her struggle with her mother lessened and she began to relate in a more satisfying manner with her father.

It is not uncommon for narcissistic children to take a very long time to gain some trust. Because the work is so slow and the play so repetitive and often controlling, the session may appear to move slowly and both child and therapist may at times feel bored and restless.

When the narcissistic child complains of being bored, it is often an expression of dissociated feelings of emptiness and oral longing or of repressed anger. Boredom leads them constantly to search for external stimulation or gratification, expressed in demanding requests for new toys, new clothes, or other diversions. The narcissistic child often expects the therapist to admire her new clothes, new possessions, or her performance, and not to intrude herself in any manner.

The narcissistic child's level of object relationship is different from that of a neurotic child. The narcissistic child's self and object constancy and self–other representations are not as fully developed, and the child often does not view the therapist as a person in her own right. The therapist's reaction to the child's aloofness and apparent lack of emotional connection may be to feel used rather than useful, so that an induced countertransference ensues. This may take the form of boredom, restlessness, or discouragement, and may reflect her own hopelessness and repressed anger at her inability to connect with the child as well as an induced response to the child's provocations. When a child's play and behavior in treatment are excessively controlling, the child may also be showing the therapist that she herself feels controlled, powerless, and helpless. This controlling behavior also reflects the child's disbelief in the give-and-take of a relationship and her conviction that she can rely only on herself to get what she feels she needs. The therapist who does not understand this motivation may instead try to work in a more confronting manner or bring herself forcefully into the transference, but this often results in the child becoming more defensive, angry, or withdrawn.

I believe that the roots of this disorder lie in the early relationship with the mother and in particular in the inherent contradictions of the anal rapprochement subphase as described by Mahler et al. (1975). While the child is becoming increasingly more independent, she is at the same time also demanding the mother's constant involvement. As the child becomes more aware of her separateness from mother and exercises this, there is still an attempt to coerce the mother into functioning as a dual unit. The child can no longer maintain her delusion of parental omnipotence and gradually realizes that her love objects are separate individuals with their own personal interests. She must gradually and painfully give up the delusion of her own grandeur, often by way of dramatic fights with mother, which Mahler calls the "rapprochement crisis." It is also in the anal rapprochement stage that objective self-awareness begins to develop and that the affect of shame becomes associated with anality and later with phallic strivings as the drives come into conflict with parental demands and prohibitions.

In the course of this developmental stage there are especially difficult demands on the parents to be emotionally present for the child, while at the same time setting limits and maintaining empathy with the child's struggles. The parents of narcissistic children usually have great difficulty responding to them in a comforting, supportive, or appropriate manner based on the child's developmental needs. The Furmans (1984, also Chapter 4, this volume) describe a group of parents who for various reasons, perhaps their own depression or self-preoccupation, either turn away from their children at important times or are there but not emotionally present. They give the example of a mother who could not hear what her child was saying unless the child forced the mother to look at him. They contrast this kind of dysfunction with the more usual parental functioning of uninterrupted investment as, for example, when a mother who is in the other room suddenly shouts, "What are you doing in there?" because it is unusually quiet.

This quality of intermittent decathexis by the parent has been striking in parents of both the narcissistic children and adults that I have seen. One adult patient described how at a very young age he would climb out the window of his home at night to be gone for hours playing with the neighborhood boys who were much older. His parents had no knowledge of this routine activity. This patient as a child was very precocious and grew up preoccupied with an elaborate fantasy of how he could survive alone in the world if it came to that. As an adult going on a camping trip he felt obliged to take every kind of imaginable provision for every possible occurrence, even if it was the shortest of trips.

One day Jane asked me what I thought of the dress she was wearing. I felt this direct question indicated an important change in our relationship. Carefully considering her question, I responded that the dress was quite nice but that I had liked the one she wore the other day even better. I had by this time been taught by her not to ask her why she was asking or to tell me more about her question. Jane said a heartfelt "Thank you!" and I asked her why she was thanking me. She replied that I had given her a truthful answer. And why was that so important to her, I inquired, secretly excited that we actually had a dialogue. She went on to describe an example of a common interaction with her mother. "If I was going to school that morning and was walking out of the house nude and I asked my mother what she thought of how I was dressed, my mother would say, 'That's nice dear.'" She went on to explain that her mother let her wear anything she wanted and always said it was wonderful. This was in fact true, since I had also heard it from the mother. Furthermore, in the early part of the treatment Jane was always dressed in an odd way, all the while insisting that she was in the height of fashion. This changed during the course of her treatment.

I noted how puzzling that must be to Jane, since it appeared from what she was telling me that her mother was not paying attention, and that her comments that everything looked terrific must be experienced by Jane as insincere. I was then able to connect this to how demanding and clingy Jane would become with her mother as if this were the only way she could be sure of her mother's attention. Jane demonstrated that she had some understanding of her mother's failures. She told me that the maternal grandmother had been exceedingly intrusive with the mother, never giving her any choice in anything, so that Jane's mother was determined to let her own children make up their own minds and to be approving of them. Jane and I together were able to understand how her mother felt she was doing something that would be beneficial to her children, yet it had had the effect of making her feel that her mother did not really care. In addition, it had left Jane feeling very unsure of herself since, like all children her age, she needed a mother's opinion. Jane gradually was able to accept that many of her defenses were in the service of making herself feel more secure when in fact underneath she felt so very insecure. It was to this end that she often insisted that whatever she did was the right thing even when in reality it was not. I should add that Jane's mother was practically incapable of talking about any of her daughters without comparing them not only to one another but also to herself at that age. It was strikingly obvious that the mother could not see these children in their own right, and consequently Jane's way of orienting herself in the world was primarily through imitation rather than through identification. Eventually, Jane came to feel more understanding and less critical of her mother and herself, which resulted in significant improvement in all areas of her life.

A case that appears to demonstrate some of these issues is Bornstein's (1949) Frankie. It has justly become a teaching classic in the use of defense analysis with children. Furthermore, this case has an important place in the history of psychoanalysis because, seventeen years after its publication, it was the focus for a discussion of obsessional neurosis at the International Congress (A. Freud 1966). Ritvo (1966) analyzed Frankie as an adult and presented a report of this later analysis, offering a unique opportunity to correlate child and adult analyses. This case is of special interest because at that conference the issue of Frankie's diagnosis was still in question. The question then centered on whether his diagnosis changed from a phobic neurosis to an obsessional neurosis. More recently, Pine (1990) again took up this question and emphasized the defect in Frankie's capacity to bind anxiety.

Frankie was 5½ when he entered analysis. He suffered from a number of phobias, the primary one being his inability to remain in school without his mother. His separation anxiety had existed for more than two years. In addition, he had severe insomnia, refused to use a bathroom outside the home, and retained urine for hours. While he could not move from his mother's side, he was at the same time rejecting of her. He was very jealous of his younger sister and treated both sister and mother in a very demanding and bossy manner. During the course of his analysis other fears emerged, including a fear of elevators and of imaginary wolves that stood guard under his bed at night. His compensatory fantasies and defenses took the form of grandiose and omnipotent behavior and thinking. His behavior in the latter part of his analysis was so out of control that the analyst finally resorted to threatening him with hospitalization.

Greenson, one of the discussants at the conference, noted that, "if so skilful and experienced a therapist had to resort to so un-analytic a manoeuvre, we might well be dealing with a problem beyond the realm of neurosis" (1966, p. 149). Greenson as well as Winnicott emphasized the preoedipal pathology and in particular the pathology in the sphere of his object relations. Greenson stressed Frankie's desire for female identification as a way of being at one with his mother. Winnicott emphasized Frankie's experience of his mother as being held by "a split-off maternal function" (p. 143).

To my mind Frankie shows many typical features of a child suffering from a narcissistic disorder. Although his phobias might be thought of as neurotic, symptoms alone are not reliable indications of a diagnosis. His problems of severe separation anxiety and fears of abandonment seem to suggest a deeper disturbance. A disorder of narcissism may be inferred from his disturbed self-esteem regulation as evidenced by his need for admiration and attention, much like Jane's. He is obliged to devalue his mother and sister and at times inappropriately to idealize his nurse. His grandiosity and sense of omnipotence and uniqueness were expressed in his fantasies of being an all-knowing God and later in his King Boo-Boo fantasy. His play and his behavior had a provocative and controlling quality characterized by his insistence on being the boss and demanding that others do just as he wished. His object relations were predominantly dyadic in nature and strongly suggested a need for a self-object. The grandiose fantasies were an attempt to compensate for a shaky sense of self and feelings of vulnerability. Frankie's wish to be chased, caught, and lifted can be understood as an attempt to get close to his mother and to be touched and held by her in a nurturant way he had never fully experienced. The sadomasochistic quality of this behavior suggested the confusion between nurturance and sexuality typically seen in problems of unresolved separation-individuation. It is as if not having the security of nurturance and the consequent internalizations necessary to negotiate the tumultuous anal rapprochement crisis leads to an unclarity and confusion in each successive phase of psychosexual development.

Frankie did not respond to interpretations in the way we would expect of a neurotic child, even though the material suggests that these interpretations were accurate. Instead, the interpretations seemed to have a disorganizing effect. Bornstein was working within a framework in which she viewed

Frankie as neurotic and the core conflict as oedipal in nature. While Frankie was certainly also struggling with oedipal issues, what seems most prominent in retrospect were his narcissistic vulnerabilities.

Discussion

Because the initial evaluation of a child very much influences the subsequent treatment approach, I will enumerate a set of characteristics potentially discernible at the evaluation stage that might alert us to the possibility of a narcissistic disorder. These characteristics include:

1. A disturbance in regulation of self-esteem. Overvaluation of the self may be observed behaviorally as a need for constant admiration, attention, and/or self-aggrandizement, or a need to devalue others. Grandiosity may be expressed in a sense of entitlement or uniqueness, or in other ways such as excessive daydreaming in which the child sees himself as a hero, or in play with others where he insists on being the leader and makes others do exactly as he wishes. Another typical overcompensation may be seen in pathological lying, used to maintain the child's grandiosity.

Undervaluation of the self may be observed in the tendency to feel easily injured and to experience mental pain through feelings of inferiority, worthlessness, and shame or guilt (Joffe and Sandler 1967), or in a reactive need inappropriately to idealize others. It is not unusual for these children to have hypochondriacal preoccupations and extreme castration anxiety as evidenced by their fears of cuts and bruises, of hurting themselves at sports, or fears of death.

2. A compelling need for the self-object, that is, an object used in the service of the self in a very special way and experienced as part of the self. This may be observed in children who require a mirroring, exclusively dyadic relationship in order to maintain an ideal state of self. "In narcissistic disorders the object is frequently and primarily experienced (or felt) as part of the self; unlike Anna Freud's need satisfying object (1966) which is placed outside of the self, though it is used in the service of the self" (Bene 1979, p. 210).

3. A lack of self-awareness which leads to both a lack of empathy for the needs and feelings of others and a lack of empathy and perspective on themselves. This lack of self-awareness may be most easily observed in their problematic and precarious friendships. The capacity for successful peer relationships means that the child can indulge in teasing and sadistic behavior and accept it without feeling unduly injured or criticized. The narcissistic

child does not have this flexibility. As a result, one often hears complaints from such children that they are being "teased," "picked on," or "talked about." Since the narcissistic child is still using the other largely as an extension of herself, she does not seem to have the capacity for more give-and-take in relationships. Thus, the peer relationships also replicate certain aspects of the transference.

4. Precocious ego development. This can be observed in the extreme unevenness of development, where certain capacities and functions may be highly matured or overdeveloped while others lag behind. This uneven development usually dovetails with the parents' inability to see the child as a whole in a developmentally appropriate way, and with their overemphasis on certain of the child's functions that fit in with their own narcissistic needs.

For example, the parents may give a good deal of praise and encouragement for independence, at the expense of emotional and physical closeness. Thus the child discovers that the parents will not accept his dependence, and learns early on to take care of himself. Or the parent may overvalue one particular ego function such as speech, so that speech becomes overvalued and used for defensive purposes rather than for communicative or thought-clarifying purposes (Newman et al. 1973). What happens to these children is that they tend to use intellectualization and become emotionally removed and aloof. Another outcome may be the child who functions emotionally and physically as a little parent in the family, that is, when there is an extreme form of role reversal in the parent–child relationship (Buckholz and Haynes 1983).

Observing and evaluating these characteristics in the child may help us in formulating a diagnosis and a treatment plan. Diagnosing a child as neurotic dictates an approach that will predominantly analyze transference and resistance and interpret the libidinal and aggressive conflicts. Utilizing this same approach with a narcissistic child may often lead to an impasse and be experienced as futile by the therapist. Here the major narcissistic determinants in such cases suggest a therapeutic orientation that would create more of a "holding environment" and focus on eventually establishing a mutuality in the object relationship. In such cases the child's low self-esteem, narcissistic vulnerability, and incapacity to view herself objectively must be addressed as an essential prerequisite before most interpretations of unconscious material, conflict, or transference become possible.

How a child relates to the therapist and how she experiences the treatment process as a whole are very important indicators of the child's personality and overall psychosocial development. Understanding that we are dealing with a narcissistic disorder should make a major difference in our expectations of how the case will unfold and also in our treatment technique. Finally, having this understanding may allow us to react in a more analytic way should we find ourselves constantly feeling frustrated or ineffectual when treating a child patient.

References

Alpert, A. (1957). A special therapeutic technique for certain developmental disorders in pre-latency children. *American Journal of Orthopsychiatry* 27:256–270.

Bach, S. (1985). *Narcissistic States and the Therapeutic Process*. New York: Jason Aronson.

Bene, A. (1979). The question of narcissistic personality disorders. *Bulletin of the Hampstead Clinic* 2:209–218.

Berger, M., and Kennedy, H. (1975). Pseudobackwardness in children. *Psychoanalytic Study of the Child* 30:279–396. New Haven, CT: Yale University Press.

Bleiberg, E. (1984). The question of narcissistic personality disorders in children. *Bulletin of the Menninger Clinic* 48:501–518.

——— (1988). Developmental pathogenesis of narcissistic disorders in children. *Bulletin of the Menninger Clinic* 52:3–15.

Bornstein, B. (1948). Emotional barriers in the understanding and treatment of young children. *American Journal of Orthopsychiatry* 18:691–697.

——— (1949). The analysis of a phobic child. *Psychoanalytic Study of the Child* 3/4:181–227. New York: International Universities Press.

Buckholz, E., and Haynes, R. (1983). Sometimes I feel like a motherless child. In *Dynamic Psychotherapy*, vol. 1, pp. 99–107. New York: Brunner/Mazel.

Egan, J., and Kernberg, P. (1984). Pathological narcissism in childhood. *Journal of the American Psychoanalytic Association* 32:39–63.

Freud, A. (1966). Obsessional neurosis. *International Journal of Psychoanalysis* 47:116–122.

——— (1968). Indications and contraindications for child analysis. *Psychoanalytic Study of the Child* 23:37–46. New York: International Universities Press.

——— (1976). Changes in psychoanalytic practice and experience. *International Journal of Psycho-Analysis* 57:257–260.

Furman, R. A., and Furman, E. (1984). Intermittent decathexis. *International Journal of Psycho-Analysis* 65:423–434.

Greenson, R. R. (1966). Comment on Dr. Ritvo's paper. *International Journal of Psycho-Analysis* 47:149–151.

Joffe, W. G., and Sandler, J. (1967). Some conceptual problems involved in the consideration of disorders of narcissism. *Journal of Child Psychotherapy* 2:56–66.

Kabcenell, R. (1974). On countertransference. *Psychoanalytic Study of the Child* 29:27–35. New Haven, CT: Yale University Press.

Kay, P. (1978). Gifts, gratifications, and frustration in child analysis. In *Child Analysis and Therapy*, ed. J. Glenn, pp. 309–354. New York: Jason Aronson.

Kernberg, O. F. (1967). Borderline personality organization. *Journal of the American Psychoanalytic Association* 15:641–685.

——— (1970). A psychoanalytic classification of character pathology. *Journal of the American Psychoanalytic Association* 18:800–822.

——— (1975). *Borderline Conditions and Pathological Narcissism*. New York: Jason Aronson.

Kohut, H. (1966). Forms and transformations of narcissism. *Journal of the American Psychoanalytic Association* 14:243–272.

——— (1968). The psychoanalytic treatment of narcissistic personality disorders. *Psychoanalytic Study of the Child* 23:86–113. New York: International Universities Press.

——— (1971). *The Analysis of the Self*. New York: International Universities Press.

——— (1972). Thoughts on narcissism and narcissistic rage. *Psychoanalytic Study of the Child* 27:360–400. New Haven, CT: Yale University Press.

Mahler, M. S., and Kaplan, L. (1977). Developmental aspects in the assessment of narcissistic and so-called borderline personalities. In *Borderline Personality Disorders*, ed. P. Hartocollis, pp. 71–85. New York: International Universities Press.

Mahler, M., Pine, F., and Bergman, A. (1975). *The Psychological Birth of the Human Infant*. New York: Basic Books.

Modell, A. (1976). The holding environment and the therapeutic action of psychoanalysis. *Journal of the American Psychoanalytic Association* 24:285–307.

Newman, C. J., Dember, C. F., and Krug, O. (1973). "He can but he won't." *Psychoanalytic Study of the Child* 28:83–129. New Haven, CT: Yale University Press.

Pine, F. (1990). *Drive, Ego, Object and Self*. New York: Basic Books.

Reich, A. (1953). Narcissistic object choice in women. *Journal of the American Psychoanalytic Association* 1:22–44.

Ritvo, S. (1966). Correlation of a childhood and adult neurosis. *International Journal of Psycho-Analysis* 47:130–131.

Weil, A. (1973). Ego strengthening prior to analysis. *Psychoanalytic Study of the Child* 28:287–301. New Haven, CT: Yale University Press.

Winnicott, D. W. (1966). Comment on obsessional neurosis and Frankie. *International Journal of Psycho-Analysis* 47:143–144.

III

*Clinical Challenges:
Enactments,
Countertransference,
and Narcissistic Defenses*

10

Narcissistic Pathology and Play in Psychotherapeutic Work with a Seven-Year-Old Boy

Corliss Parker

In Bulfinch's narration of the myth of Narcissus, a proud, exquisitely handsome youth fails to respond to Echo and other lovely nymphs who desire him. Humiliated and heartbroken, Echo languishes and dies. To punish Narcissus, the gods have him fall in love with the reflection he himself casts upon the surface of a cold forest pool. As Narcissus reaches out again and again to touch what *he* now desires, the image of his magnificent face dissolves and disappears. The empty, cold pool into which he stares serves as a forceful representation of the absence of libidinalized representations of self and others. Alone, unloved but unable to separate from the image he himself will never possess or be loved by, Narcissus dies.

Jeff, a 7-year-old boy whose treatment I will describe in this chapter, seemed at the onset of our psychotherapeutic work to be Narcissus-like in his overtly contemptuous and controlling attitude toward me and in his self-presentations in fantasy and play, which reflected an absence of healthy narcissism and object love. Initially unable to tolerate or conduct an exchange of thoughts and feelings, Jeff insisted rather that he have absolute control over communications and play.

Jeff's modes of relating and communicating with me, and his fantasy and play, evolved in significant ways during the sixteen months of our psychotherapeutic work. I will describe three distinct phases in the treatment. Then I will discuss how I currently understand various transformations in Jeff's fantasy constructions and play. In addition, some ways in which Jeff and his mother related to each other and to me will be explored.

Consultation and History

When I first met Jeff's parents in consultation, his mother expressed anger about her son's being referred by his second-grade teachers for evaluation and treatment. "He has so much," Jeff's mother said. "Yet he always wants more. . . . It's been that way since he was born."

In many ways Jeff's parents seemed to provide most generously for their children: their two sons, then aged 7 and 4, attended prestigious school and afterschool programs, owned an abundance of toys, and, like many affluent, urban children today, participated in classes and events almost every single waking minute. Given such enrichment and indulgence, I wondered, too, what *more* Jeff might want.

Regarding his early history, I was told Jeff nursed initially, but appeared to have difficulty digesting milk. After two months he was weaned to a bottle; Jeff remained colicky during much of his first year. Developmental milestones were within normal limits.

Various caretakers had been employed by this family. Apparently, no sitter stayed longer than one year. Jeff had experienced no separations from his parents overnight until he was 3 years and 1 month old, when his mother gave birth to his brother Jack. She remained in hospital for three days. Six months later when Jeff was 3½ years of age, Jack had had to be hospitalized for a near-fatal respiratory illness. While Jack remained in hospital with his mother, now for six days, Jeff was cared for by his father and a babysitter.

Jeff lives with his parents and with his brother Jack. His mother and father, both successful architects, work moderately long hours. Neuropsychological evaluation done prior to consultation revealed no evidence of learning difficulties, although reading skills (6 months delayed) were not consistent with Jeff's superior and very superior scores on the WISC-III (a Verbal IQ Score of 139, and a Performance Score of 130).

Perceived by his teachers as creative and bright, Jeff did mostly mediocre work. He frequently interrupted his teachers during class and tattled on and insulted his classmates. Jeff complained that he was attacked and treated unfairly in school. He denied provoking other children. The teachers described Jeff's mother as aggressive and critical in her interactions with them, while she (Jeff's mother) reported feeling criticized and unappreciated by teachers and staff. Clearly, Jeff and his mother held strikingly similar views about experiences with other people in Jeff's school; both felt maligned, misunderstood, and mistreated. Neither seemed aware of how their behavior affected other people.

The First Year of Treatment

Jeff and I worked twice weekly in psychotherapy for sixteen months. He began his first session with an anxious request: "Tell me what to do." When I explained that he was free to decide and asked if there were something he would like to do, Jeff said he wanted tracing paper. Hearing that I had drawing materials but no tracing paper, he searched his backpack for tracing paper of his own. He then struggled to reproduce animals which he traced from pages of magazines and books in my office. Jeff expressed disappointment with his reproductions, and he tore and threw out every single drawing.

The second and third sessions proceeded in a similar way, with Jeff's bringing in additional tracing paper, his reproducing animals from my books and magazines, and his eventually throwing everything out. In the fourth session he agreed to play the squiggle game (Winnicott 1971). Jeff drew forms which he identified as an alien and two dinosaurs, including one with very large teeth. I commented that Jeff had drawn some interesting, powerful-looking creatures. Jeff answered that his dinosaurs were not as good as those he'd seen in my books, and he proceeded to tear up this work, too. I commented to Jeff about how he seemed unhappy with every single thing that he made, whether he had traced from a book or drawn on his own. I said we would try to understand how he had come to dislike everything he did.

In the fifth session, after more tracing and throwing away, Jeff asked if he might draw on my face and body. He *really* wanted, he said, to put charcoal on my hands and my face. When I answered that he could draw a picture of me and could paint or draw on that as he wished, he asked if he could at least put tape over my eyes and lips. I asked if Jeff wanted me neither to see nor to speak, and he responded loudly: "*Yes!*" I said I would not ask about nor look at what Jeff was doing (drawing), unless he wanted. With his back to me, Jeff then drew what I imagine were bold charcoal shapes which he eventually covered over with so much charcoal that he left his pages almost totally black. I commented that Jeff seemed to enjoy drawing on his own — without having to think or worry about me. When I said it was time to put things away and to stop, Jeff took his work, crumpled each page, threw everything into my wastebasket and smiled at me on his way out.

During subsequent sessions, Jeff now and then expressed desires to draw on my face and body and to cover my eyes and lips with tape. I think he asked, in part, to hear me restate what I had said before about such requests: that he seemed to want to keep me out—out of his thinking and deciding about what to make and to do. I said he seemed to worry that I would try to decide *for him*, unless he by force kept my eyes shut and my lips sealed. In addition, I interpreted Jeff's wish to cover my face and hands with charcoal as his perhaps wanting me to know what it is like to *not* have a say about what to make and to do. Jeff listened, but did not answer. Rather, he continued drawing without letting me see his work, and he persisted in throwing his finished sketches into my wastebasket. I wondered whether Jeff wanted me to look at his drawings after he left his sessions, but he never inquired as to whether I had.

After drawing on his own for three months—in my presence, but without my being invited to look at his work, Jeff began to relate to me with more spontaneity and trust. He routinely showed me drawings which contained abstract designs now only partially covered over with heavy dark lines. Jeff occasionally drew dinosaurs and animals, which were well-formed and endowed with impressive teeth and bony plates.

During the fourth month of treatment, Jeff began asking me to play *with* him. He assigned himself and me roles. In his favorite game, he set up soldiers, superheroes, or GI Joe figures, and he had them fight ferociously in battle after battle until all perished. During these sessions I commented now and then that not *one* hero nor *one* soldier was allowed to live, and I asked whether these men were being killed *because* they had been aggressive, fierce fighters. Nodding in agreement, Jeff continued to play out his scenes of destruction. Eventually, he allowed some of his and my superheroes to survive.

During a session in the sixth month of treatment, Jeff asked if he might use a soft, stuffed, green "Hulk" doll slightly over two feet in length, a doll which he heretofore had left in my toy closet. A popular comic book and TV character, Hulk is actually Bruce Banner, a scientist. Through accidental exposure to radiation, Dr. Banner intermittently and involuntarily transforms into Hulk, a larger-than-life strongman. As Hulk, Banner is ruled by aggressive impulses over which he has virtually no control. A Dr. Jekyll–Mr. Hyde character type, Banner–Hulk is noble and generous in his usual human form, but explosive and often destructive as Hulk.

When I responded that he might use Hulk if he wanted, Jeff scrutinized, squeezed, and pummelled Hulk with his fists. He threw, kicked and stomped on the doll, as he yelled "You Wimp!! You weakling! *Girl!*" Next Jeff pierced the Hulk with a thin, plastic pick-up stick: first his eyes, then the nose, mouth, heart, and groin, where penis and testicles would be. Hulk is bare-chested and wears green pants cut off at the knees. When the pick-up stick went through the green fabric and emerged on Hulk's backside, Jeff said: "It's coming out his bum. Look! The weakling! The wimp!"

Eventually, I said that Jeff had pierced the parts of Hulk that let him see, eat, speak, and breathe. Jeff continued to poke, pierce, and pummel the Hulk. I added that Jeff also had pierced Hulk where his penis and testicles would be — parts of the body needed for pissing, for sex, and for making babies. Jeff yelled at the Hulk: "You wimp! You girl!" I said I thought Jeff was showing me how he wanted to turn Hulk, a powerful superhero, a huge man with a big penis, into a wimpy girl-creature without a penis.

Jeff smiled and continued to pierce and to pummel the Hulk. Then he ordered: "*You* be Hulk's mother!" And shaking Hulk, Jeff spoke to him in a singsong sort of way: "You green, mean canine! You undress your mother, and you suck her clean!"

Next, Jeff tossed the doll to me: "You are Hulk's wife! Sit next to your husband on the couch!" Jeff said I was to pretend that Hulk and I were watching a triple-X video. "The Hulk sucks you," he said, and he took Hulk, threw him back onto the floor, sat on and began pummelling him again. Jeff then asked me to move off the sofa, and he picked Hulk up and sat next to him himself. I asked if he and Hulk were now watching the triple-X video. He said, "Yes." Jeff then threw Hulk onto the floor and asked me to hit, to kick, and to call the latter "a wimp" and a "stupid girl!"

I observed that Jeff had had us change places: first *I* was sitting and watching the triple-X show with Hulk, and then *Jeff* was sitting and watching. I said I wondered if he wanted to know what it would be like to sit and watch the sexy show, *and* if he wanted me to know what it felt like to be left out of the watching, like when children are left out of grown-up shows and grown-up sex.

"They can't watch it!" Jeff said. Then, placing Hulk on my skirt, he continued: "He wants to see what's there, to see what's *under* there!" I asked if Hulk wanted to see a woman's body. And Jeff answered, anxiously: "What *do* they have there?"

When I asked if Jeff had ideas about what women have, he said nothing. Eventually, I said that women and girls have a vagina and a uterus, and I explained in a few words what these are and where they are located. Jeff frowned, moved away from me, and said Hulk should be punished. I asked if he thought Hulk should be punished for wanting to see and to know about a woman's body? Ignoring my question, Jeff took the Hulk, walked to my desk, pulled back the chair, and threw Hulk into a square space beneath the desk.

"He's going to jail! To *baby jail!*" Jeff said, and he told me to get into the jail with Hulk. He said we had been "bad." I asked whether Jeff was punishing Hulk and me for thinking and talking about a penis and a vagina, and I noted that Jeff nonetheless had put us close together in the very small space beneath my desk.

In many subsequent sessions, Jeff had the Hulk fight with soldiers and superheroes who attacked, mutilated, and sometimes destroyed him. Jeff intermittently used a pick-up stick to mutilate and murder Hulk, who at other times was left alive, but put in the baby jail.

One day I said Jeff's sending Hulk and me to jail and his insisting we stay together in this very small space made me think about Jeff's having called this place a *"baby jail."* I asked whether Jeff wanted Hulk and me to make a baby there? A silence followed; Jeff's eyes filled with tears. Although he would not let himself fully cry, Jeff explained in a quiet, sad voice that during the night Jack was born, he (Jeff) had awakened and walked into his parents' bedroom to ask his mother to turn over an audiotape. Instead of finding his mother and father, Jeff had discovered a family friend asleep in his parents' bed. In a mournful tone, Jeff said: "She (his mother) never told me she was going; she was gone and I didn't know."

When I answered that I could see it must have been very, very hard for Jeff to find his mother gone, he said softly, "It was really hard." For awhile, I felt Jeff was reexperiencing and allowing us both to look empathically at his acutely painful feelings. Then, abruptly and seemingly out of the blue, Jeff coldly commanded me to return to jail with Hulk. He yelled: "Put him back in there! Stay in there!" After awhile, I spoke about how strong Jeff's wish to put his brother back inside the hospital or back into his mother's womb might have been and about how Jeff probably had wanted to have back the time before his brother's birth, when he was the only child in his family. His eyes welling up, Jeff answered again that it was "really hard," and he repeated what he had said to me before about the night of Jack's birth.

Jeff's mention of his brother's birth led to intensely aggressive outbursts and play. In subsequent sessions, Jeff described emphatically how he wanted to shut me up, to blacken my face, to hit, and to kill me! I said I thought Jeff was letting me see what he had once and still sometimes wanted to do—to me and to his parents—*because* his mother and father had made Jack and *because* they had done so without Jeff's knowing or being included in what they did. Jeff told me his mother used to wash his mouth out with soap when he was angry (later, she corroborated this). I was reminded of the charcoal which Jeff had wanted to put over my face and hands, and I answered that Jeff had not been able to speak about his hurt and anger to his mother. I said I could understand Jeff's trying to shut me up and to cover over and get rid of what we had learned.

During the next six months, Jeff was particularly provocative and aggressive. I often said I thought he was showing me how enraged he felt still about having to have a brother. In his play, Jeff put baby dolls, superheroes, Hulk, and me into jail for being "bad," for being "stupid," and for "no particular reason." I interpreted that Jeff wanted to punish me, his parents, and Jack, and that if he put his brother back into jail or, better yet, back into his mother's womb, baby Jack would die. During this phase of our work, Jeff invited and enjoyed my descriptions of babies as creatures who inevitably mess, intrude, and deeply trouble their older siblings. I spoke about how I think older children feel over *not* having a say regarding who gets added to their families. Jeff usually welcomed my speaking in this general way about life with siblings.

Collateral Meetings with Jeff's Parents

I met with Jeff's parents once every two or three weeks during the first six months of treatment. Then we met intermittently, usually once every two months until termination. In my ongoing work with Jeff's parents, I encouraged them to give Jeff space and opportunity to experience thoughts and emotions on his own, without their involvement or commentary.

During the fifth month, when I tried to obtain more specific information regarding this family's morning and evening routines, I discovered that Jeff's mother closely monitored practically every single thing Jeff did in the afternoons and evenings! She said, for example, that she had to assist him with homework assignments, as she wanted Jeff to live up to his potential.

I strongly urged that Jeff be left to do his homework himself, and that his parents openly acknowledge his efforts and work as being valuable and good enough, without his mother's corrections and revisions. In addition, I suggested Jeff's father spend more time with Jeff before bedtime, while his mother would spend more time with Jack. Though Jeff's mother found changing her evening routine difficult, over time Jeff was given more freedom to think and work on his own.

I suspect that his parents portrayed themselves (to Jeff) as living in a Machiavellian universe in which personal interests and desires dictated moral and ethical decisions. I learned, for example, that Jeff's father discussed business deals with his wife in front of their children—deals in which he had made enormous profit through others' ignorance and gullibility. In a session with Jeff during the seventh month of treatment, when I challenged his assertion that he ought to be able to cheat in card games with peers, Jeff said: "Why should I care how *he* (the other boy) feels? My dad says: 'What the other guy doesn't know is *his* problem!'"

The Second Year of Treatment

During this phase of our work, Jeff developed various new story lines. In one of these he was a shopkeeper who priced and sold toys, foods, and household goods. I played the part of a customer, and Jeff told me what to buy for my children. One day, he asked me to help him take out all the dolls from my toy closet. After my buying some of these, Jeff directed me to purchase one additional doll which is large and anatomically male. He sang joyfully: "This one's real! He's for sale! The baby's for sale!"

In subsequent sessions, I was instructed to buy the boy baby, who then was attacked and killed by various monsters. In one scenario, Jeff had a monster invade the shopkeeper's (Jeff's) body, and Jeff (as shopkeeper/monster) attacked and killed the baby. In a further development of this story line, Jeff regained possession of his body, the monster was caged and killed, the shopkeeper and I became friends, and the baby was left alive though gravely wounded.

During the thirteenth month of treatment, Jeff began a session with a creative rendition of "Rub-a-Dub-Dub." In Jeff's verse, a butcher, baker, and candlestick maker all go out to sea. These three travel in a boat with a baby and his mother, both of whom are attacked, butchered, and roasted! The tradesmen feast upon the bodies of the mother and her baby. When he retold this story on one occasion, Jeff added monkeys who chased and bit the butcher and his two friends. I reminded Jeff of a nightmare he had reported, in which a monkey tried to bite off Jeff's fingers. I said Jeff's story about butchering, burning, and eating a mother and her baby made me think about how frightened Jeff had been of being bitten—of being punished because of his wishes to hurt and to kill the mother and her baby.

In sessions during the thirteenth through the fifteenth months of treatment, Jeff revised other verses he knew or found in my office. Then he asked me to read *Alice in Wonderland*. As I read, Jeff listened quietly. With obvious pleasure, he asked interesting questions about the characters and the verse. I commented that I had heard Jeff's mother sometimes read to him before he went to bed. Jeff acknowledged that he enjoyed hearing his mother read.

Jeff and I met for sixteen months altogether. His mother then insisted that we end, ostensibly because (she reported) his behavior had improved significantly and because I had moved my office twenty blocks north (a less convenient location for her, as my old office was two blocks from Jeff's school). I recommended that Jeff continue in psychotherapy, but his mother was determined that we end.

When Jeff arrived for our last session, his family had just returned from a summer vacation. Looking over toys he had used during the past sixteen months, Jeff said he missed my old office and wished we were back there. I said I wished we were back there, too, as we might then have been able to continue our work. He said he had had a good vacation.

Jeff then took out the Brio train set and connected bits of track and tunnel and bridge in an intricate, elegant design which covered much of my carpet. At one end of his track he arranged people, houses, and trees. At the opposite end, he created a scene with apartment buildings, shops, park benches, people, and cars. I said I thought Jeff was letting me see how well he was making connections on his own — connections between some of his experiences in the country (where he had been on vacation) and in the city (where he lives), as well as connections between what we had learned in my old office and what he could do on his own when he left my new place. He smiled and said, "I like the country *and* the city now" (he used to say he hated the city).

At some point, I asked how Jack (his brother) was doing. Jeff laughed: "He's okay. I haven't killed him yet. If I do, I'll let you know." I said I was impressed that Jeff could now make jokes about having a brother, and that to be able to joke about something that had been so incredibly hard was a real achievement. Beaming, Jeff said he got along better with Jack now.

With little time remaining, Jeff asked for the superheroes: "Let's have a battle." He divided the figures and their weapons equally between us. I commented that battling in this way was exciting: Jeff had equipped us both with enough manpower and weaponry that a battle could be waged for real — one in which neither of us was sure to win. In one long conflict waged over my analytic couch, both Jeff and I lost some, but not all our heroes. I complimented Jeff on his being a worthy opponent. Moments before he left,

Jeff told me it was hard to leave the old dump (his name for my old office). I told him it was hard for me to see Jeff leave. We agreed that he would tell his parents if he wanted and needed to come back, but I think we both knew Jeff's mother would not readily allow Jeff to return.

Discussion: Transformations in Fantasy and Play During the Course of Psychotherapy

Opening Phase

"Tell Me What To Do!"
From Imitation to Self-Expression

Within minutes after we first met, Jeff pleaded that I tell him what to do. Using his own tracing paper, he anxiously reproduced images of people and animals from books and magazines in my office. Rather than expressing something of his own, Jeff seemed driven to reproduce images linked to me and my possessions. I suspect he was demonstrating how he typically interacted with his mother: trying to do and present what she appeared to want and expect. As Jeff then criticized and threw out all his reproductions, I believe he was letting me know that in spite of his anxious efforts to please, he never experienced what he did as good or fine enough.

In this opening phase of our work, Jeff behaved as if only one or the other of us could actively think and be expressive. After anxiously trying to trace things he found in my office, Jeff told me in the fifth session that he wanted me neither to look at nor speak about what he was doing. Presumably because he might then feel protected from potential intrusions, I readily agreed that Jeff could work separately. Only then did he seem free enough to let his thoughts and feelings dictate what he drew (and covered over) with heavy charcoal. In not allowing me to see or speak about what he was doing, Jeff perhaps also wanted me to know firsthand what he had experienced in relation to his mother: the silencing and suppression of sensations, thoughts, and feelings.

Jeff's structuring sessions as he did reminds me of a passage in Winnicott's (1958) paper, "The Capacity to be Alone":

> Although many types of experience go to the establishment of the capacity to be alone, there is one that is basic. . . . *This experience is that of being alone, as an*

infant and small child, in the presence of mother. . . . Ego-relatedness refers to the relationship between two people, one of whom at any rate is alone; perhaps both are alone, yet the presence of each is important to the other. [pp. 30–31]

I believe Jeff wanted to draw in my presence without interference or impingement. In my neither directing nor controlling his work, I think he experienced me as implicitly supporting his becoming and being *self-expressive*. At any rate, Jeff began to express himself spontaneously in my office, and for several months he continued to draw without letting me see or respond to what he was doing. Perhaps as he came to believe he could draw freely, Jeff felt secure enough to show me his drawings. At some point he seemed to enjoy letting me see and comment on his work, particularly the ferocious dinosaurs and aliens with spiny plates and sharp teeth. In this context, Jeff now appeared able to tolerate both his and my experiencing and expressing individual thoughts and feelings.

Middle Phase

Hulk and the Baby
Expressing the Inexpressible through Play

During this period of treatment, Jeff's modes of communication and play evolved dramatically. Rather than pleading to be told "what to do" or needing to draw apart from me, Jeff now requested that I join him in play. He usually demanded exact or fairly strict adherence to his wishes, however, when I assisted him in setting up scenes, placing toy figures, and speaking for characters.

During the early middle phase, Jeff regularly staged confrontations in which two or more figures (superheroes or GI Joe soldiers) fought and died. Over time, he agreed with my idea that the men were being injured, mutilated, and/or annihilated *because* of their aggressive intentions and actions. Following my expressions of empathy for his fierce fighters, Jeff eventually allowed some of his and my heroes to survive. I believe Jeff became more accepting of aggressive impulses and behaviors (projected into soldiers and superheroes), as he identified with my empathic feelings. I suspect that neither parent had been able to empathize with or assist Jeff in *his* developing empathy for or understanding of his aggression. Since the beginning of our work, Jeff had moved from drawing alone with charcoal, to complex play in which he and I manipulated toy figures who battled with one another. In effect, he was beginning to use highly symbolic, interactive play to become acquainted with and to communicate about aggressive fantasies and impulses.

During the sixth month of treatment, Jeff began playing with Hulk. Our work focused then on Jeff's fantasies about Hulk, Hulk's wife, and the Hulk-baby. Jeff attacked, mutilated, and symbolically destroyed Hulk — either directly with his fists, hands, and feet, or indirectly through his arranging that I or various superheroes attack and kill Hulk. When he sent Hulk to baby jail, Jeff struggled (with my encouragement) to express feelings and thoughts about baby-making and babies. His Hulk scenarios were accompanied by the expression of intense affects, which Jeff and I linked eventually to old feelings of hurt, humiliation, and anger over his parents' conceiving and giving birth to his brother. Thus, some analysis of his symbolic play with Hulk ultimately provided Jeff with access to previously repressed, profoundly painful ideas and feelings. Jeff and I explored old desires to possess his mother solely and old anger about her involvement with his father and his brother.

Although Jeff seemed preoccupied during this middle phase of treatment with sexual anxieties and fantasies—his desire to see the triple-X video and to have Hulk look under my skirt, his fantasies of attacking, mutilating, and destroying Hulk, and his curiosity about making babies—there was no evidence of development of typically oedipal fantasies and object-relationships. Regarding the oedipal phase, Freud (1923) wrote the following:

> At a very early age the little boy develops an object-cathexis for his mother . . . the boy deals with his father by identifying himself with him. For a time these two relationships proceed side by side, until the boy's sexual wishes in regard to his mother become more intense and his father is perceived as an obstacle to them; from this the Oedipus complex originates. His identification with his father then takes on a hostile colouring and changes into a wish to get rid of his father in order to take his place with his mother. . . . An *ambivalent attitude* to his father and an object-relation of a solely affectionate kind to his mother make up the content of the simple positive Oedipus complex in a boy. [pp. 31–32]

Rather than displaying an "ambivalent attitude," Jeff seemed simply enraged toward Hulk, and, I think, toward his father. Jeff did not appear to admire or identify with his father as a genitally active, potent male, a man with powers potentially available to Jeff at some future time. There was no indication that Jeff identified with his mother and father as creators, or with his father as a loving genital partner for mother. Jeff never expressed a wish that *he* and I create a baby together, or that he and Hulk do so.

Rather, I think Jeff struggled with hurt, humiliated, and rageful fantasies and feelings associated with his brother's conception and birth. Hurt over the perceived loss of his mother to Jack, and anger over his parents having procreated without his participation or control, remained the predominant foci of our work. What *was* achieved during this middle phase of treatment was the development of a capacity to think and feel empathically about his situation as the older brother—the boy who experienced profound betrayal, humiliation, and hurt with the birth of a baby brother. Indeed, it was my identification with Jeff's plight, my communication of empathic thoughts and feelings about his situation to him, and Jeff's identification with and internalization of my understanding of and empathy with him that seems to me to have been most therapeutic! Unlike the clear, cold pool into which Narcissus stared, Jeff seemed during this phase to internalize positive, empathically felt self-representations. In this way, a healthy narcissism seemed to me to be building.

Jeff's apparent failure to form oedipal identifications with his father seems extremely significant. Just as his parents had apparently not been able to empathize or identify with *his* humiliation, rage, and hurt over his brother's birth, Jeff (perhaps as a direct consequence of his parents' unempathic stance) seemed unable to form empathic identifications with *them* as genitally active, potent lovers and procreators. I suspect Jeff felt too left alone with his own anger and humiliation to identify with and yearn to be like the father who could impregnate and create! Jeff's father seemed fairly remote and reproachful in his parenting, which also did not facilitate the development of oedipal identifications. One of my goals in working with Jeff's parents was to encourage and support the development of stronger, more loving, and less critical relationships with Jeff.

Final Phase

Babies Burned, Butchered, Left Alive
Sublimation and Partial Reconciliation

In this last phase of treatment, which extended over five months, Jeff developed scenarios in which old, familiar themes appeared now in more fully sublimated forms. In one play scenario, Jeff was a shopkeeper who sold babies that were tortured and killed, but then ultimately left alive. And in his spontaneously transformed popular verse, Jeff created poems about a baby and his mother who are cut up, burned, and eaten!

Jeff now seemed truly to enjoy his play. Apparently no longer anxious about censorship or intrusion. Jeff derived obvious satisfaction and pleasure from constructing his stories and verse. Play incorporating symbolic representations of primitive aggressive and sadistic wishes was to some extent liberating: in the last several months of our work, Jeff expressed desires that some of the superheroes and babies live. Such reparative, life-preserving acts suggest that Jeff was developing what Winnicott (1963) called "the capacity for concern."

Loewald's (1988) writing on sublimation also comes to mind:

> *Sublimation* is passion transformed. . . . In contrast to what is the case with repression, in sublimation instinctual impulses are said not to be averted, but to be diverted from their aim of satisfaction in immediate discharge. Their corresponding percepts, memories, and fantasies are not repressed (as occurs in countercathexis) but instead, according to this viewpoint, are made more acceptable by some disguise or embellishment. . . . It is as if in true sublimation the vital power of passion shines through in the very perfection of mastery. . . . [pp. 9, 37–38]

Along with his sublimation of aggressive and sadistic impulses and desires, Jeff was beginning simultaneously to express concern and even love. He seemed to be struggling to come to terms with—to become reconciled to—painful necessities, particularly his brother's birth and existence. When treatment ended, Jeff seemed considerably more accepting of his brother. He was noticeably more flexible and spontaneous in play with peers and with me. In our last session, Jeff granted both himself *and* me *partial* victories in one final battle with superheroes and soldiers. In his play with Brio trains and track, Jeff demonstrated that he could now make connections *on his own* among experiences he had had with me and away from me—in the country and the city, in the past and the present.

Collateral Work with Jeff's Parents

While Jeff's father was receptive to many of my ideas about how Jeff and his parents might relate more comfortably and constructively, Jeff's mother seemed perturbed and distressed by some of my recommendations. On various occasions I praised and expressed appreciation for her having raised two exceedingly bright, engaging boys, and I tried to be gentle in suggesting changes in family routines. But I suspect she felt injured by my saying *anything* which implied she had not already done *everything* vis-à-vis Jeff in an absolutely exemplary way. Not surprisingly, Jeff's mother experienced my charging for sessions with her and her husband as an insult (she said she had thought these meetings were for *my* sake).

Prior to a collateral meeting in the fifth month of treatment, when I learned very specifically about evening and bedtime routines, I had not realized exactly how aggressively overinvolved Jeff's mother was with him. In retrospect, I imagine she found it enormously painful and difficult to hear me say I felt her son urgently needed more physical space and opportunity to experience his talents and capabilities *as his*. Jeff's development of significantly more differentiated, positive, and benign self-representations (a result of our work) probably induced in his mother anxiety and dread (unconsciously experienced, at least) over loss of the more primitive object relationship she had had with Jeff. While her son's behavior in school and in other public settings had caused her immense embarrassment and worry, I believe her domination and control over Jeff were very significant in *her* psychic equilibrium.

Shortly before insisting upon termination for Jeff, his mother had begun in a collateral session to describe a traumatic experience in her adolescence. This event had left her feeling abandoned psychically by both parents and physically by one. I suspect she had been determined to keep Jeff close to her, so as not to reexperience (passively) traumatic losses of her adolescence. We had barely begun to discuss this material when the family left for a long summer vacation.

When they returned, Jeff's mother said his behavior was so much improved that she wanted his sessions to end. Her insistence suggests she had been disturbed by my recommendation (made before their vacation) that she continue to meet with me or with someone else (either in individual or couple's work) on a more frequent basis to discuss the adolescent trauma she had endured and its links to ongoing conflicts within her family. While Jeff's mother denied being upset by recommendations, I suspect she was anxious about pursuing a psychotherapeutic inquiry of her own. Perhaps she wanted to leave me while Jeff was in relatively cooperative, good humor. I heard from a colleague that Jeff's parents eventually began couple's therapy about twelve months following Jeff's termination with me. Perhaps they were able to act on my recommendation about treatment for *them* only after Jeff had left *me*!

Summary and Conclusions

Poor Narcissus was made to desire what would neither nourish nor satisfy him—the cold, reflected image of his own face. Likewise, at the onset of treatment, Jeff seemed wedded to self- and object representations that interfered wilth his potential to experience self love (healthy narcissism) and object love. He was unable to tolerate our exchanging thoughts and feelings; he needed rather to exert absolute control over communication and play.

Initially, Jeff anxiously traced images of animals and people from my books and magazines. Over time he was able to form and express his own ideas and images in drawings, in play with superheroes and Hulk, and eventually in complex narration and verse. During his dramatic play with Hulk, Jeff, at first spontaneously and then in collaboration with me, linked images and themes in his play *directly* to his experience of his brother's conception, birth, and babyhood. Through his elaboration and ultimate softening of aggressive scenarios in poetry and play during the last months of treatment, Jeff seemed to be working through some of his rage and humiliation.

In retrospect, I think Jeff's impulsive, provocative behavior in school was driven, at least in part, by anxiety over his not having his mother available to tell him "what to do," along with his not feeling confident abut deciding on his own. His impulsive, aggressive behavior had led to his being characterized by his teachers as being ADD (attention deficit disordered). To my mind, Jeff's disruptive behaviors were at least partially linked to anxiety over being separated from his mother and then being expected to perform independently, while he deeply doubted his capacity to think and act with success *on his own*.

Jeff eventually was able to tolerate and enjoy my experiencing and describing him as a boy capable of independent, creative, cruel, *and* considerate thoughts and acts. As a result of our work, Jeff was able to develop, sustain, and use relatively more realistic self-representations which were affirmative and empowering. Ultimately, Jeff was able to put himself into my emotional shoes: he provided me in play with what he imagined I needed to feel powerful and good. At the very end of treatment, Jeff seemed able to nourish me back: to express appreciation and affection reciprocally.

References

Freud, S. (1923). The ego and the id. *Standard Edition* 19:12–66.

Loewald, H. (1988). *Sublimation: Inquiries into Theoretical Psychoanalysis.* New Haven, CT: Yale University Press.

Winnicott, D. W. (1958). The capacity to be alone. In *The Maturational Processes and the Facilitating Environment*, pp. 29–36. New York: International Universities Press, 1965.

———— (1963). The development of the capacity for concern. In *The Maturational Processes and the Facilitating Environment*, pp. 73–82. New York: International Universities Press, 1965.

———— (1971). *Therapeutic Consultations in Child Psychiatry.* New York: Basic Books.

11

The Role of Auditory Defenses in the Treatment of a Narcissistic Boy

Phyllis L. Sloate

Children and adults engrossed in intensely pleasurable or creative activities such as play, reading, watching television, or daydreaming may be deaf to increasingly exasperated calls for dinner, bedtime, and assorted family obligations. The response "But I didn't hear you," said in a plaintive tone of injured innocence, seems both familiar and predictable. We understand these moments of self-absorption as temporary and restricted phenomena, part of the normal regressions of everyday life.

In pathological narcissistic states, withdrawal of auditory and/or perceptual attention from the external world is used defensively, in an effort to fend off or regulate an object relation, while preserving the illusion of personal omnipotence, compensatory grandiosity, and the object's ideal qualities. This connection between perception, sound, and pathological narcissism was intuitively appreciated by the ancient Greeks, and poignantly depicted in the myth of Narcissus and the nymph Echo. Rebuffed by Narcissus, Echo withdraws from the world; all that remains is the decontextualized sound of her distress expressed in repetitive word fragments denuded of meaning. Self-absorbed, Narcissus cannot tolerate hearing the echo of her anguish. His punishment is to fall in love with his own image. Unable to move beyond the pain of self-love and idealization, he too is lost to life and life-giving relationships.

While preoedipal disturbances may have far-reaching implications for later personality development, this chapter is not an attempt to explain all of this child's subsequent pathology by recourse to events that transpired during the first two years of life. I am proposing that severe disruptions of early object relations, in which self and mutual affect regulation plays a central communicative role, may promote a pre-symbolic substructure that predisposes to the pathogenesis of narcissistic disorders. Audition, like gaze, may then undergo developmental distortions that will later become part of an entrenched defense organization.

To illustrate the role of early developmental processes in the anlage of pathological narcissism and the genesis of auditory defenses, I shall briefly review some findings from the empirical infancy and attachment research literature. Although these contributions have not yet been integrated within the mainstream of psychoanalytic theory (Silverman 1991), they seem especially useful for expanding our understanding of those precursors around which later narcissistic disturbance may crystallize. For detailed reviews, the reader is referred to Beebe and Lachmann 1994, Belsky and Nezworski 1988, Silverman 1992, and Sroufe 1988. Psychoanalytic explorations of the early role of audition follow. Using material from a long-term case, I shall then describe the partial resolution of a severe narcissistic disturbance in a young boy where audition played a prominent and pervasive role in the child's defensive repertoire.

Selected Review of the Literature

Attachment theory addresses the innately programmed features of infancy that, under "good enough" circumstances, potentiate interactive social relations and attachment to others. These attachment patterns, or "working models" (Bowlby 1988), eventually achieve representational status. Working within this paradigm, researchers have now classified four main infant attachment styles: B, securely attached; A, avoidantly attached; C, ambivalently attached, and D, disorganized attached. Unless modified by subsequent experience, these "working models" are stable, self-perpetuating, and have been shown to be robust predictors of later developmental trends. Children classified as avoidant conceal their affective distress, manifest depressive symptoms, and tend to manipulate and exploit others, personality characteristics associated with narcissistic disturbance.

The infant research literature has similarly described the infant's innate capacities for social relatedness and discrimination of its primary objects across sensory modalities. The parent–infant dialogue is conceptualized as an interactive process of mutual regulation, in which each participant influences and is influenced by the other's responses. These interactive patterns that constitute the infant's experience of relatedness are, over time, presymbolically represented (Beebe and Lachmann 1992, Stern 1985). Importantly, both attachment and infancy research have demonstrated the infant's active regulation of incoming stimulation and states of internal arousal, as well as an early capacity to represent interactive relationships that will contribute to the emerging organization of self- and object representations.

Infants are exquisitely sensitive to their mother's affective communications, and rapidly identify and orient to those states that are shareable and hold special emotional valence for her. Attuning to states or moments when mother is emotionally available may preserve fragile connections and closeness (A. Freud 1965, Winnicott 1971), but at a price. If maternal disturbance interferes with mother's ability to correctly read and respond to her infant's cues, the archaic matrix of nonverbally shared meanings will be distorted, and the communicative function of later language may be impaired.

Psychoanalysis has long known that depressed mothers are generally preoccupied with their own inner concerns and have great difficulty relating appropriately and affirming their infant's affective experience (A. Freud 1965). Recent investigations have delineated the timetable of influence and range of developmental deviations with greater precision. Specific sequelae of the infant's experience of failed initiatives and a lack of control over mother's complementary affective response are disturbed affect, inattentiveness, and tendencies toward passivity, observable as early as 3 months of age (Field et al. 1988).

Infants discriminate affectively disconnected maternal interactions and adjust their responses accordingly. Stern (1995) notes that an infant may strive mightily to evoke some response from a depressed mother, taking on the role of the "reanimator"; later this child may excell at being the charmer or the entertainer. He also observed that infants seem to discriminate between a forced maternal response and a spontaneous flow; if nothing else is available, they will respond with a forced communication of their own. If an infant is repeatedly compelled to overattune and/or modify spontaneous affective expression, experiences of intentionality and efficacy are further vitiated and impoverished. When not modified by later experiences, such trends may contribute to the later formation of a compliant, "false self" (Winnicott 1960).

Disturbances in maternal affective response and communication create states of helplessness and confusion in infants, and may precipitate a retreat inward to endogenously created and controlled stimulation (Murray 1991). In essence, this comprises a beginning turn away from external reality which, if not modified, may create a predisposition to seek solace in fantasy solutions rather than activity in the external world. The early failure of efficacy has also been linked to the later predisposition to develop shame reactions, an affect frequently associated with narcissistic pathology (Wurmser 1987).

Both the voluminous psychoanalytic and infant research literature on normal gaze emphasize how mother's libidinized visual engagement infuses the dyad with pleasure, as it conveys an affectively alive, meaningful notion of himself to the infant. The organization and sequelae of extensive infantile gaze aversion as a regulatory response to maternal overstimulation in less well functioning dyads is also well documented (Beebe and Sloate 1982, Beebe and Stern 1977). Abrams (1991) has discussed deviant gaze interactions in a borderline adolescent as symptomatic of a preoedipal splitting process. P. Kernberg (1989) noted a pattern of defensive gaze aversion in narcissistic children which she regards as pathognomonic for the disorder.

Although infants hear in utero long before they can see, relatively less attention has been given to this more archaic modality. Optimally, mother's voice functions similarly to her loving gaze and is most often described in musical metaphors. Psychoanalysts recognize how the melody of mother's reciprocal vocalizations to her infant's babblings is rapidly libidinized, fostering ego growth and object relatedness. The experimental literature similarly speaks of a harmonious, mutually resonant dyad in which the melody— mother's vocal tone, tempo, and pitch—powerfully conveys maternal affect.

Contemporary empirical investigations of the infant's innate capacity for cross-modal perception have recently yielded a more fine-grained understanding of the role of selective inattention. Immersed in the melody of maternal vocalizations, infants are also exquisitely sensitive to their temporal dimensions (Stern 1995). These nonverbal, temporal patterns of sounds and silences constitute an organizing medium for the infant's attachment and quality of object relatedness. The degree to which an infant over- or undertracks maternal vocalizations at 4 months has been found to predict patterns of attachment, temperament, and cognition at 1 year (Beebe et al. 1992).

Oedipally based auditory disturbances, with their connections to the primal scene, beating fantasies, and the voice of the superego are familiar clinical phenomena. Psychoanalytic investigations of audition and the early communication of affects are relatively few; hence the preoedipal base and early use of this sensory dimension for defensive purposes and their subsequent pathogenic transformations are a less well understood process.

Within the psychoanalytic literature, the significance of early auditory experiences was emphasized by Niederland (1958), who noticed how the immaturity of the infantile auditory apparatus lends sound a physical, contact quality, so that mother's voice might be experienced as an extension of her comforting touch. Terhune (1979) suggested the infant's capacity for delay on hearing mother's voice be considered the first indication of an ego function. Noy (1968) distinguished between the infantile ego's overdevelopment of auditory capacities to transform painful stimuli into pleasurable ones as a defense against auditory oversensitivity, from dyadic preferences for one channel of communication over another. The inherent ambiguity of the auditory channel, which may narrow or maintain the object's distance and lessen the boundaries between internal and external events, was highlighted by Nass (1971). He further suggested that if early auditory experiences are drawn into conflict, audition might then become an adaptive means of mastery and influence later cognitive style. Speculating, Nass proposed that this ambiguity of experience stimulates a flow of imprecise imagery, and fosters conditions favorable to its fantasy elaboration. This highly pleasurable amalgam of auditory fluidity and extensively detailed, shifting fantasy imagery is often reported by adult narcissistic patients as a preferred mode of creating an omnipotently controlled, perfect universe. Perceptual distortions that further blur distinctions between subjective and objective realms often accompany this defensive activity. It may be that the finely tuned control over external reality possible with auditory defenses is especially congenial to the narcissistic world view — the facade of living in reality is maintained, without the necessity of having to be fully contextualized in it.

With these developmental considerations in mind, I will now turn to the clinical material.

Clinical Material

Presenting Problem and Family History

Mike was referred for treatment at 5 years of age, in a time of crisis. His father had been awarded temporary custody; permanent custody and visitation rights became focal issues of an extremely bitter divorce.

Turmoil and object loss had been Mike's constant companions during his first five years. Marital discord marred his early months; heated, chronic parental battles overshadowed his practicing subphase (Mahler et al. 1975). Simultaneously, mother's depression and emotional disorganization intensified, and was accompanied by occasional disappearances from home for brief periods of time. During rapprochement, when Mike was between 17 and 20 months of age, at the height of parental battles and mother's depression, she left home precipitously for three months. Father then became quite depressed. The couple separated permanently when Mike was 30 months old. Shortly after Mike's third birthday, mother disappeared with him for ten days; father was then awarded temporary custody. Loss followed upon loss. Mother's visitation with Mike became increasingly erratic, and custody of two half-siblings from her previous marriage was awarded to their father. Her escalating instability led to a two-month psychiatric hospitalization shortly before Mike's fifth birthday. He was told that mommy was "away," and would return at some future time. To his father's surprise, Mike did not ask for her during this separation.

According to both parents, Mike's development had followed a normal course. Mother's idealization of Mike was as pervasive and unshakable as her obliviousness to the profound impact of her depression, disorganization, and abandonments on his development. Delighted by his "goodness," she characterized him as a "delicious," "always smiling," "irresistible" infant and toddler who "never gave a moment's trouble." Father was intuitively troubled by the chaos of Mike's early years and the effects of mother's emotional problems. It was Mike's excessive "goodness," however, that worried father most, and was the presenting complaint.

At our first meeting, father, depressed and exhausted, said "I'm at the end of my rope, trying to be a mother and father to Mike." Tormented by self-reproaches for having made a poor choice of spouse, his guilt left him uncertain about setting more age-appropriate limits for Mike. He worried about his son's development, and was determined to maintain custody and to protect him from mother's serious character pathology.

During the consultation, father appeared to have an overly protective, idealizing, perfectionistically demanding relationship with Mike. His fantasy—that Mike would either be seduced by mother and reject him, or become utterly enmeshed in mother's fantasies and lose touch with reality— led him to actively disparage Mike's age-appropriate fantasy life. This attempt to maintain Mike as his idealized object miscarried; unwittingly, he was creating the very situation he dreaded. Denigration of Mike's fantasy life and attachment to mother heightened Mike's idealization of her. In father's presence, however, Mike complied with his wishes. Mike's rage at father's efforts to obliterate his world of fantasies and dreams was dissociated, a solution that contributed to his internal fragmentation.

Mother projected her fragility and sense of entitlement onto Mike, whom she infantilized and idealized in a restitutive attempt to nurture her damaged child-self and to mitigate her current losses. Consciously well-intentioned, she lacked perspective on Mike's predicament, and viewed him as an enhancing extension whose small accomplishments were consistently overvalued. When preoccupied with her own work, she seemed oblivious to the sadistic, teasing play that occurred when Mike was left in the care of his visiting half-brothers. If Mike had a restless night, she welcomed him to her bed, where he served as a living transitional object, to assuage her emptiness and loneliness. She plied him with "softies," lovingly sewn blankets that conveyed her fantasy that clinging to a part of her was essential for his survival.

Although suspicious of me as her husband's agent, mother agreed to join one of Mike's weekly sessions, and also to meet individually with me once weekly. Ostensibly, her participation suggested positive maternal strivings. It also constituted a fantasied manipulation of me; her compliance would help her regain custody of Mike.

The Opening Phase

Mike, a handsome, sturdy child was accompanied by father to his first session. To my surprise, he entered the office without hesitation, and returned my greeting as though we were old friends. His engaging, pseudo-mature facade soon collapsed, revealing narcissistic selfobject needs. Constant eye contact and approving nods from father were necessary preconditions for Mike's cautious inquisitiveness and intellectually precocious remarks. His search for instant validation subsided within a month, at which point Mike seemed instead to use father in the service of refueling. Father could then remain in the waiting room with the office door ajar. A separation process was worked through during the next six months.

Mother's domination and subversion of Mike's play suggested a long-standing pattern of pathological communication. Often, as soon as Mike arranged toy soldiers, mother preempted him, and intrusively offered her fantasy as to why they were fighting, or made a competitive "interpretation." At other moments, she appeared to attune herself to his fantasy play, but then altered it in accordance with her internal needs. Her pseudo-attunements not only added to Mike's confusion over where he left off and she began, but also negated his initiative and creativity. As she appropriated and transformed the affective meaning of his experience, mother also destroyed the meaningful links between his experience and her words. This intense envelopment of

Mike could shift unpredictably within seconds to a self-absorbed state in which she was present, but emotionally absent. Mike then identified with her affective state and withdrew into silent, self-absorbed play, as deaf to my comments as mother was to his.

At best, mother's words frequently made no sense, as they were unrelated to who Mike was. At worst, they were destructive, insofar as they did not help him to make sense of his inner world, even as they undermined his autonomy and identity. Not hearing adaptively insulated Mike from these painful experiences. Silence contained and expressed his rage, and maintained his defensive invulnerability, in which there was no space for longings and loss. Several months would pass before mother could sustain a more participant—observer role.

Mike's compliance was at the heart of their enmeshment; to play spontaneously and enjoy his fantasies seemed to be equated with losing mother and his sense of self. Any expression of aggression was terrifying. If he tried to play "Hulk, the bad guy," Hulk's punishment was death by bloody dismemberment. In retreats from this, Mike would apply formless blobs of paint to paper, or draw stereotypic rainbows, to deny and reverse his misery with a pseudo-cheery picture that mother might approve. While the Hulk embodied his dissociated rage and "badness," this interesting projection of the self also sustained a hidden tie to Mike's phallic strivings and identifications with father; the Hulk's alter ego is a sensitive, socially appropriate, intelligent man.

Continuous parental intrusion into Mike's fantasy life and spontaneous play had undermined its use as an organizing medium for the transformation of trauma. Language, the child's other primary means for reflecting on and integrating affective experience, had been significantly interfered with. Self-regulation in the service of self-satisfaction had been impaired; dissociation and splitting were increasingly the means to contain painful affects and memories that could not be otherwise mastered.

As Mike became more engaged in treatment, I was incorporated into his new war play as the "backup guard." The following poignant fantasy was expressed: "The good guys died while waiting for the war to end. They starved to death." An accurate reflection of the depth of his anxiety and oral longing, this fantasy also expressed Mike's anguish over his parents' absorption in their ongoing custody war. My countertransference alerted me to Mike's fundamental remoteness, artfully concealed beneath a veneer of exquisite manners, charm, and "good boy" behavior; I could not experience Mike as affectively present. Although he smiled and said "yes," my words went unheard and were silently dismissed. This powerful identification with mother's pseudo-attunements nullified my initiatives, and preserved his omnipotence. Alternately, he withdrew completely. In school, his not hearing gained special attention from his teachers, while gratifying his wish for a relationship with a powerful selfobject (Kohut 1972). Silent in small group meetings, Mike was unable to risk spontaneous expression of thoughts and feelings, and so frightened of making mistakes that he refused to answer questions. He could not share toys or join the fantasy play of his classmates; his unpredictable aggressive outbursts further alienated them.

Maternal Abandonment

After eight months of treatment, Mike's mother informed me that she had accepted a one-year work transfer far from the New York area and would be leaving in approximately one and one-half months. While she professed despair over the loss of Mike, mother thoroughly denied the consequences this further abandonment would have for her son. Having just begun to find a better relationship with his mother, Mike was now much more vulnerable to such a loss, and a profound regression took place.

In school, he stopped signing his work with his own name, sometimes using his father's, in a vivid depiction of his identity problems and need for a sustaining selfobject. A hair-combing compulsion emerged, tuning out increased, and new learning ceased. School dismissals were very difficult; if father wasn't immediately in view, Mike became frantic.

In our sessions, his pain found expression through games of connect-the-dots played out over dot drawings of himself and mother, superimposed on "maps" of the United States. This game and numerous variations of peekaboo encompassed Mike's attempts to stabilize more libidinally toned representations of self and mother. A repetitive game of store, in which Mike "cheerfully" supplied mother's every need so she wouldn't go away spoke to his conflict between inner neediness and defensive self-sufficiency. As we worked on his feelings of helpless rage, loss, and worthlessness, father's sensitive, loving input was a powerful counterforce to Mike's belief that adults could not be trusted to reliably provide safety and comfort.

During the second year of treatment, aspects of the maternal abandonment were displaced to the school setting. Teachers' complaints escalated regarding Mike's defiant rule-breaking, demands for attention, resistance to following directions, and difficulties comprehending and remembering what he had read. They concluded that he was a learning disabled child with an attentional deficit. In effect, Mike had turned the passive experience of his needs going unheard into an active refusal to hear his teacher's requirements, responding with meaningless, fragmented echoes. Sophisticated diagnostic testing designed to clarify the origins of Mike's learning problems included intelligence, neuropsychological, and projective measures. The tests ruled out organicity, and revealed an IQ in the Very Superior range and a severe depression. The findings confirmed my impression that Mike's learning problems were rooted in narcissistically impaired object relations and defenses.

Mike told me that school was "boring"; he would attend only when and if something interested him. His unwillingness to try new work was in part associated with his defensive omniscient posture, insofar as he expected to know without having to learn. Obtaining his teacher's attention by tuning out her directions was often a conscious, sadistic manipulation of her good will; at the same time, he felt contemptuous of adults who were easily fooled by his playacting. This multidetermined symptom of not hearing also enacted his wish to compel mother to return, and appeared to be a significant identification with her perceived arbitrariness, tuning him in and out, turning him on and off, enticing and abandoning, forcing him to wait on her pleasure.

Mother was unresponsive to my attempts to sustain contact, and continued her pattern of frequent disappointment and abandonment after seductive enticement of her son. Weekend visits were abruptly cancelled with demands for rescheduling at her convenience, or she kept Mike and his father dangling by not confirming plans until the last minute.

As Mike worked on the loss of mother, he slowly began to define a sense of an independent self. In many sessions, however, he was not yet able to freely verbalize feelings of disappointment or anger with mother or with me, and instead communicated through repetitive drawings of mountains of TNT, bombs, and jailed men. These silences made explicit Mike's fears of using his mouth lest he say or do something terrible with it, and tempered the threat posed by becoming more dependant on me.

The learning of simple games was also fraught with difficulty; again, he found it humiliating to admit he didn't know it all. Mike could neither hear, remember, nor synthesize explanations of impersonal rules. Difficulties were not eased when he wrote the rules, because in either situation, his inability to modulate aggression associated with competitive conflicts left him a diffusely unfocused loser. Only tic-tac-toe, a variation on the identity-sustaining connect-the-dots, seemed to provide him with a powerful affective link to mother, and offered a modicum of safety and success.

A turning point occurred after months of consistent work with these issues. Mike angrily used bright markers to execute a jumble of jagged lines, proudly labeled this drawing with his name, and clearly wrote: "This is the sound of a person!" Mike's silent exuberance eloquently depicted his progress toward a more autonomous self, and indicated some diminution of his narcissistic defenses and oral-aggressive conflicts.

This partial integration freed Mike from the crippling affects associated with his need and longing for mother. A series of illustrated booklets, "gifts" for her promised return, filled many sessions. Moving stories of his abandonment told of the isolation and enforced self-sufficiency of small boats struggling through shark-infested waters and stormy seas. The big boats, indifferent to the plight of the little boats, were rescued by them.

Mike mentioned Susan, father's new love interest, with some anxiety. Wishes for each of them to pay exclusive attention to him were mingled with oedipal concerns, such as not having as big a gift for Susan's birthday as father did. Father and Susan's relationship was deepening: they began a couple's treatment as a sign of their mutual love and commitment, while continuing their individual therapies. Susan, a sensitive, insightful woman, became an important stabilizing force in Mike's life, and an active participant in his treatment process.

Retraumatization, Abandonment, and Working Through

Mike was increasingly present, alive, and experiencing pleasure with his expanded functioning in the world. In school, he was moved to the advanced English and Math groups, and participated in group discussions. However, after almost two years of treatment, consolidation of Mike's gains was again undermined by life events which influenced the course of therapy in unforeseen ways. Mother abruptly broke her promise to return to New York, and settled permanently in another state. Once more, Mike was faced with a profoundly painful loss that resonated with the traumatic abandonment of his practicing and rapprochement subphases.

Feeling betrayed, rejected, and helpless led to a resurgence and realignment of Mike's narcissistic defenses. His massive rage with mother was denied and displaced onto father and Susan, while mother was idealized. This intense re-fusion and identification with mother interfered with emerging paternal idealizations; progress toward oedipal conflict also came to a standstill. Mother's penchant for "getting away with it," already part of Mike's faulty ideal development (Kennedy and Yorke 1982), was revitalized by her betrayal. Working through the complicated sequelae of this final maternal abandonment was thereafter at the heart of the therapeutic process.

In his anguish and rage, Mike sought refuge behind an impenetrable wall of silence, as compulsive, stereotyped war-play and drawings of Ninjas flooded our sessions. My comments fell on deaf ears; contact seemed unwanted and unbearable. It felt too hard to trust, for my words might be as manipulative and hurtful as mother's were; better to rely on himself and need no one. That I was shut out and failing Mike were my countertransference reactions to his hostility and conviction that, like mother, anything I did could neither ameliorate nor eradicate his pain. Understanding this enabled me to remain empathically available, and to provide an accepting, holding environment that I hoped would allow Mike sufficient psychic space to restore his ever-tenuous sense of safety and trust. The transference enactment and his anger that I couldn't make things right for him were interpreted. I also told Mike that I understood he was showing me how hard it was to trust or feel safe with me, and how feeling so hurt and betrayed made him want to hurt back. Unlike mommy, I wasn't going away, but would wait until he felt ready to speak and hear my words. This communication was gently repeated over a series of largely silent sessions. Mike's hostile, self-protective silence was imperceptibly transformed into a silence of comfort (Winnicott 1958), until I was gradually re-involved in his play.

Contact was fully renewed in a moving session where Mike initiated a brief game of connect-the-dots, and a game of store. The Hulk growled and menaced me, because I was not powerful enough to supply all the pizza and cookies he wanted. Mike, however, possessed a magical umbrella that might undo my failure to satisfy his deep hunger. Although damaged in a storm, it was still the most powerful secret weapon in the world. Moreover, he could fly with it and thereby satisfy himself. This "secret" concealed yet another fantasy about an alligator from outer space who was so hungry that he devoured all the pens, pencils, crayons, and markers in the world.

Before long, Mike voiced his helplessness; mother's words could not be used to make sense of his inner affective experience. He observed that when things went wrong with mommy, she became very upset. Mike then felt guilty and compelled to comfort her while his own distress went unacknowledged. This important communication was interpreted around the confusion and rage he felt about becoming the mother he needed for himself, and his confusion and rage with both parents for having created the mess that deprived him of a normal family life. Mike confirmed my comments with the following vengeful fantasy. With the aid of his super powerful spaceship, he would set up a giant clothesline amid the stars, and "hang them both out to dry in the universe." Despite this progress, the subject of mother's betrayal remained largely taboo, with Mike firmly stating "I don't want to talk about that."

As we began our fourth year of work, Mike insistently turned me on and off, enticed me, forced me to wait on his pleasure, and then abandoned me to the experience of being with someone who was absent when present. This highly charged aspect of his identifications with mother was simultaneously enacted with friends. Mike eagerly anticipated and enjoyed playdates, but refused to either initiate or return calls. His fantasied rejection by friends and struggles with mutuality were repeatedly linked with mother's abandonments and with his need for the sense of power and control. When I felt that Mike was ready, father was counseled to encourage him to risk reaching out. Mike's burgeoning social life rapidly became an important arena of success, where initiative led toward feelings of competence and pleasure in the real world and a diminution of his omnipotence.

The full impact of his mother's traumatic betrayal and abandonment emerged during this time of heightened maternal transference, as Mike enacted that which he had passively endured. This ego syntonic repetition, sadomasochistically and narcissistically gratifying, was highly resistant to change. Self-destructive aspects of his identification with mother, such as his entitlement to lie, cheat, manipulate, and disown responsibility for his aggression, were now more accessible to the therapeutic process.

Lying came to my attention when Mike described the destruction of a school project that he and a friend had worked on. When his friend called to claim his part of the work, Mike told him that it was on the top shelf of a closet. He was not in the least remorseful about his lie, but was humiliated at the prospect of being found out. Moreover, he anticipated that I, like mother, would provide further lies that would maintain his deception.

A few weeks later, Susan discovered broken glass on a framed photograph of the couple. She questioned Mike, who tearfully denied involvement. Enraged by her challenge to his omnipotence, he presented himself to me as the innocent victim of her unwarranted attack. When I confronted him, he furiously denied his role but subsequently admitted responsibility. He felt justified in his behavior. Since father and Susan did as they pleased and excluded him, he was certainly entitled to do as he pleased.

Then Mike bit a classmate who had jostled him during recess. Returning home, he said nothing to his father, who had already been contacted by the school. Saddened by his son's behavior, the father spoke of how lies destroy trust. Mike responded with denial: after all, he hadn't lied, he had merely concealed the truth. In his sessions, Mike made explicit his contempt for all adults who were "dopes" he could easily manipulate, and his gleeful triumph when he thought he had "gotten away with it."

These repetitions and identifications were also understood in the context of the regressive impact of visits with mother, which contributed to sadomasochistic aspects of his character development. Mike's Christmas vacation was disastrous. Not only was Mike faced with a major narcissistic injury—mother's involvement with a new man—but he was also cared for by his two half-siblings who verbally tormented and physically hurt him. In a moment of uncontrolled rage, mother slapped him across the face, screaming that he had lied to her to conceal his brother's misdeeds from her fury. In fact, this time he had told the truth. In a temper, she brought him to the airport a day early, then denied her hostility and pretended her misperception was an intentional joke.

Work on Mike's humiliation about having a mother whom he could neither rely on nor feel proud of was accompanied by many nightmares. Her hurtful actions refuted his fantasy of their special oneness, and Mike wished for "paybacks" that would cause mother to suffer as he did. Additional anger was evoked by her tearful apologies, as Mike again felt riddled with guilt and responsible for her pain. Over time, he described mother's behavior as "weird," stating "something's wrong with her." Finally, inquiry about her medication allowed open discussion of her inability to be the mother he wished her to be. It seemed the combination of the agonizing reality of his vacation, mother's strange behavior, and my then confronting his identifications and defenses had finally begun to have some impact. Though painful, these new perceptions facilitated his separateness and sense of identity, and diminished the burden of omnipotence that had previously left him feeling guilty for everything and responsibile for nothing.

Mike's identification with and idealization of mother's disregard for rules and limits continued to unfold. Accounts of her sociopathic behavior were linked with his lies, cheating, and contempt for friends and adults. Questioning his pervasive glossing over details clarified the frequently manufactured explanations he presented as facts, to avoid acknowledgment of ignorance. Omniscience importantly served to maintain denials and idealizations, shielding him from disappointments such as the unbearable pain of mother's essential unavailability. One surprising consequence of this work was Mike's request that I define some quite ordinary words. It seemed that his defenses had disguised significant meaning lacunae. These appeared related to the infusion of aggression into the early dyadic relationship and difficulties experiencing mother's voice as a source of comfort, as well as his later tuning out her senseless and hurtful way of using words. Trusting my words speaks to the libidinized, new object quality of our relationship, in which words had meaning and made sense.

The gradual lessening of his defenses allowed space for reality-based, pleasurable accomplishments, highly effective antidotes to his fantasied omnipotence. As he could risk taking in, he could learn, and the give and take of the peer group was becoming tolerable. By year-end, Mike had made dramatic progress in school, where he was more consistently a straight A student. He contributed to class discussions in a lively, spontaneous manner, became interested in science, and, most importantly, he had begun to make friends.

Toward Resolution of the Narcissistic Dilemma

The next fall, as our fifth year of work began, narcissistically tinged oedipal issues unfolded in greater depth. Thus, when Susan and father began a home redecorating project, Mike felt acutely diminished, agonized over his exclusion, but neither withdrew nor became destructive. After his winter vacation, Mike angrily mentioned Ryan, mother's new man, and in the same breath insisted that if he wasn't at the center of mother's affections he felt insignificant. Despite these feelings, he had demanded more attention from mother without fear his rage would destroy their relationship. This new emotional openness and vulnerability in sessions and with his parents, without a catastrophic loss of self-esteem, along with his greater capacity for concentrated therapeutic work, presaged a significant internal shift.

Mike soon asked me to teach him to play a game for the first time; his choice of double solitaire illustrates the interplay of regressive and progressive forces. At first, Mike transformed the game into a mutually cooperative venture played on both hands. Questioning this brought a dismissive, "I'm not competitive. It's only a card game anyway." When he did play competitively, Mike visually tuned out winning possibilities, a phallic level variation of his earlier auditory defense. I wondered aloud if seeing how to be a winner was hard, when he felt like a loser inside. Mike retorted: "Just play cards." Playful comments like "oops" and "uh oh" in response to this defense helped Mike reconsider his denial. Over time, he played to win, but if the outcome turned in my favor, he visually tuned out and arranged to lose. At that point he could hear my interpretation that control of the outcome might be less painful than the feeling of helplessness he experienced as a loser. As the school year ended, Mike, more involved in reciprocal friendships, asked me to teach him gin rummy, "cause all the kids are playing and I want to be part of things."

A transition toward a more affectively engaged, object-related position emerged after his spring vacation. Mike spoke of feeling he always came last, and wondered why mother didn't set aside specific time just for the two of them. Susan and father's mutual love was compared with mother's affairs and judged "better." In a sad, accepting tone, he also shared that mother had tried to cheat father out of an airplane ticket refund, adding, "My dad would never do that."

This progressive movement was also apparent in Mike's evolving use of our relationship, as this vignette indicates:

Mike began his session by comparing his father's small office with the luxurious, large space of a senior colleague. Rather abuptly he said: "My life is ruined. I feel like everything is falling apart. It was ruined by two people, Susan and Ryan. They took away the two most important people in my life, Mom and Dad."

I said, "You sound very angry and sad."

Mike replied, "I am. And Susan is so critical because I forgot one homework. I did it, it was buried under papers, so I had to bring a note home. But I didn't forget, I was crying."

"It really hurt your feelings when she criticized one part of you; it left all of you feeling so small."

"Yes, because I'd made it up and brought it in. And it's the feeling about my dad too, I was crying about, because he pays attention to Susan."

"It sounds like there are two parts to this—feeling like no matter what you do you can't win, and an old feeling—if you're not perfect you're not desirable."

Mike fantasizes that Susan might cancel an upcoming sleepover, and giggles when I wonder if he'd like to cancel her.

Regressive trends are also apparent in the externalization of his rage with both parents onto their respective love objects to avoid the pain of facing their inadequacies. While understandable in the context of his conflicts with them, this distortion speaks to his ongoing difficulties with taking the other in fully, and hints at his sociopathic tendencies. Even so, Mike's emerging capacity to hear and derive comfort from my words, and then use them for further self-reflection deepened; classical and rock music soon became important sources of solace that likely served a transitional object function. This subli-mation also reflected further pleasurably toned identifications with father and his peer group.

Summer approached, and Mike excitedly prepared for his first sleepaway camp. Mother cancelled their planned week-long visit at the last minute, and saw Mike briefly at a relative's home. Mike assured me he was "glad" to be on his own. His omnipotent flight was interpreted as a protection against the pain of needing her so badly, and his anger that she couldn't be the mom for whom he longed. With tear-filled eyes, Mike said: "I think you're right. I don't want to talk about Mommy anymore."

Not a week later, Mike began his session with a tirade of rage and grief. Mother had called, sobbing, and she apologized for having lied about being ill. Mike stated: "She lied to me and it feels horrible. I'm so angry I feel like I never want to see her again. It's what you say. I feel responsible, like I'm her mother, like I did something, like it's all my fault. It's not my fault, it's not." Interpretations directed to the generational blurring, and guilt related to his rage, relieved Mike's anguish and torment, and promoted further differentiation and integration.

Three years after the final traumatic maternal abandonment, the narcissistically determined introjective constellation that had bound Mike to mother was moving toward resolution. Since then, Mike's sense of identity and separateness has been secure enough to enable him to cope with mother's behavior and tolerate ambivalence toward her without the repeated, regressive re-enmeshment that had previously characterized their relationshp.

Discussion

In this case, I have inferred that mother's severe character pathology and arbitrary alternation between intense absorption and inattentiveness substantially disrupted the reciprocal rhythms of the early mutual regulation process, interfering with Mike's experience of attachment and object relations. Given mother's denial, idealization, inability to notice and separate Mike's needs from hers, and use of pseudo-attunements to enhance her narcissism, it seems unlikely that she facilitated Mike's emerging initiative, autonomy, and competence (Mahler and Kaplan 1977) in ways that encouraged pleasurable investment in his functioning for his own sake.

Opportunities for healthy narcissistic gratification during his differentiation and practicing subphases were relatively few (Mahler et al. 1975). Mother's emotional absences of the first year shaded into repetitious, unpredictable abandonments and reunions during his second year, set against a backdrop of massive parental conflict. The early pleasurable sense of "we go" and an "executive we" (Emde 1988) and the security of benign, consistent caretaking and limits were lacking (Furer 1967), as were opportunities to identify with mother's predictably attuned care. This latter process of identification prepares the soil for the later flowering of empathic concern for others, and fosters important parental idealizations which will contribute to superego formation.

Increasingly, Mike's normal egocentrism would interpret mother's unpredictable abandonments and alternation of intense absorption with instant decathexis as talion punishments for his libidinal and aggressive strivings, further influencing the content and tone of self- and object representations in a negative direction. The need to be the child his mother wished him to be likely intensified as her disturbance worsened, further distorting the developmental picture.

Neither parent could easily tolerate age-appropriate expressions of aggression, so that negative affects were not readily included in the realm of shareable experiences which could then be modulated by parental regulating and organizing functions. Mike's sense of being recognized, known, and intrinsically valued for himself was again rendered vulnerable.

The chronic strain trauma of his early months was followed by a traumatic abandonment. Mother suddenly disappeared between his seventeenth and twentieth months, and father became depressed, leaving Mike without the emotional nutrient vital to a successful resolution of rapprochement (Mahler et al. 1975). Sustaining the background sense of a good self in the face of the aggressive surges of this subphase without empathic parental support is a virtually insurmountable task for the toddler (McDevitt 1975). Mike had entered rapprochement without being ready for it, and emerged with a structuralized "false self" (Winnicott 1960), which continued the early pattern of passivity and compliance, and jeopardized his capacity to negotiate subsequent developmental tasks. Becoming a parental echo perpetuated dyadic relations, and ensured his identification with those ideal aspects of himself deemed worthy of admiration and love. The development of self- and object constancy, the consolidation of early ideals and an autonomous identity, the achievement of reciprocal relations and self-reflective awareness (Bach 1985) were very partial accomplishments.

Modell (1984) has proposed that early, chronic strain trauma and severe trauma may promote the formation of a false-self organization based on an omnipotent fantasy of self-sufficiency designed to restore a sense of well-being and safety. For Mike, this comforting omnipotent illusion was clearly reparative, insofar as the early loss of mother (through repeated emotional and physical abandonment) and father (through depression) was likely experienced as the loss of a self-function. His compensatory grandiosity then coalesced into a pervasive maladaptive compromise designed to stabilize self-esteem, encapsulate aggression, and insulate him from further sadness and pain associated with closeness to his love objects.

Mike successfully exploited his grandiosity and entitlement by fulfilling parental fantasies, which further libidinized the earlier malformations and accorded them a significance that resonated across his development. His accurate perceptions of mother's reliance on him to complete and stabilize her fueled his fantasies of specialness and omnipotence. Both parents' selective responses overvalued intellectual accomplishments, further stifling initiative, spontaneity, and individuality. This situation seemed to promote a markedly sadistic superego, an ego ideal suffused with grandiosity (Kernberg 1975, Zimmerman 1982) and object relations characterized by sadomasochistic control and submission.

Mike's parents, like those of other narcissistically disordered patients, were limited by their own difficulties; understandably, their parenting functions were compromised. This circumstance, in itself, explains neither his profound inner devastation, nor the depth of his protracted struggle. I believe that consideration of the following two real and relatively constant features of Mike's experience may further our understanding of his predicament. The impact of repeated maternal abandonment followed by seductive re-enmeshment was far-reaching, and reverberated throughout his treatment. Solnit (1982) has discussed how multiple abandonments may utterly deplete the young child's emotional and cognitive ability to sustain a predominantly libidinized cathexis of the primary parents. If this life-giving connection and the sense of love, safety, and self-worth it provides is impaired or destroyed, the consequences for ego development and object relations are profound. As he notes, abandonment does violence to emerging structures, while each successive abandonment renders the healing process more problematic. Moreover, Mike's parents' hostile post-divorce relationship to each other was a deeply felt, chronic strain trauma. Their wish that Mike love each of them exclusively placed him in a constant emotional double-bind. To love either parent too openly, especially in the presence of the other parent, was for many years experienced as a guilt-laden act of betrayal that could only lead to further abandonment. This ongoing situation favored splitting trends and contributed to the congealed quality of his "false self" resolution.

Audition and Narcissism

Like many adult patients with this personality disorder, Mike relied extensively on narcissistic withdrawal (Bach 1985, Beren 1992, Kohut 1972, Modell
1984) to preserve his tenuous self-esteem. Unlike the narcissistically disordered children described by P. Kernberg (1989), his eye contact was within
normal limits when treatment began; however, the auditory sphere was
enmeshed in conflict. Mike's selective auditory blocking, a defense frequently
encountered during the early stages of analytic work with adult narcissistic
patients, is a significant deviation that merits separate discussion.

I have inferred that Mike's identification with mother's alternating style
and his selective auditory blocking originated in the archaic maternal matrix
as an adaptive means of regulating mother's intrusiveness and withdrawal, as
well as a way of being with her that allowed preverbal development to
proceed. Affectional bonds were not embedded in a context of mutuality and
consistent enough emotional availability; the melody of mother's voice was
insufficiently imbued with a sense of a comforting, responsive presence. In his
early relation to his mother, hearing and not hearing became a significant
aspect of Mike's emergent psychic structure. This pre-symbolic, nonverbal
template influenced the organization of later self- and object representations,
contributed to his later tendency to withdraw into fantasy, and affected the
content of his fantasies. Early traumatic experiences were then symbolized
and structuralized at the anal-rapprochement level with the formation of a
consolidated "false self." Although conjecture, it is perhaps not such a big step
from identifying with a mother who turned him on and off to compensatory
narcissistic fantasies of omnipotence and omniscience which provide an illusory sense of safety and power. The world (mother) now marches to the child's
rhythms or ceases to exist.

Mike's failure to fully invest the sound of words with meaning, and his use
of language to regulate the affective distance between us suggests continuing
dissonance at the anal-rapprochement level, a time in which he suffered
both emotional and physical abandonment. There, the emerging symbolic
process—particularly language—is a powerful element in facilitating the
transition from external relations to internalized conflict. During normal
development, adult language provides an empathically resonant organizing
function which conveys the sense that the child's inner states are real, know-
able, and potentially shareable. The child's private world is transformed
through the pleasurably expanding expression of a unique system of personal

meanings and intentions, as words are invested with ownership. Given the massive trauma of his first two years, and mother's disturbed communications, language had remained a partially integrated function. Within his treatment, derivatives of the early miscommunication were everywhere apparent; patterns of sound and silence were still being used for purposes of affect regulation and control of self and object.

Mother's words were often a source of narcissistic injury as they conveyed emotionally unrelated, cruel meanings whose content made no sense within Mike's psychic reality. To the extent that he perceived her damage, what had begun as an affective adaptation of infancy was transformed over development into a central, defensive constellation designed to not take in that which was hurtful and bizarre. Mother's lies, in particular, invalidated the use of language as a meaningful symbolic vehicle for human relatedness. Hearing her words became an experience of pain and destruction as opposed to a sense of being acknowledged and responded to by an emotionally available other.

Along with language, emerging fantasy and play constitute the child's basic, adaptive means of mastery over ongoing trauma, and a resource for the regulation of self-satisfactions. Mother's pseudo-attunements, part of her general system of damaging communications, and father's negation of Mike's fantasies, had left him with a paucity of opportunities to develop this crucial set of ego functions which were instead enmeshed in conflict. Hearing the other again became an experience of painful intrusion into Mike's personal world, to be shut out. Absorbing himself in fantasy was also a highly adaptive means of shutting out mother's hurtful and disturbed words. To have heard her fully would have interfered with the idealizing fantasies Mike had constructed which protected her from his rage.

Within his treatment, Mike's pervasive auditory tuning out functioned as a symptom equivalent to the deviant eye gaze described by P. Kernberg (1989), and served similar defensive functions. This elaborate, multidetermined compromise formation and identification with the aggressor both expressed and defended against his narcissistic vulnerabilities. Initially, tuning out protected his grandiosity as it warded off painful aspects of reality, expressed his rage over not being heard and acknowledged, mediated distance, was a link with mother and a form of providing mothering for himself, omnipotently reversed his helpless anger with a mother who turned him on and off, and enacted his wish that mother come to him. Later on, tuning out visually and arranging to lose as we played cards expressed oedipal longings, fears, and fantasied masochistic control.

Mike's "learning problems" vividly illustrate how the narcissistically disordered child is especially vulnerable. Despite the outstanding intellectual potential revealed on intelligence tests, auditory defenses that protected his grandiosity undermined his school performance to a point where he appeared highly distractible and unable to take in, integrate and synthesize new information. Like Narcissus, he was unable to hear the echo of his therapist, his teacher, or his own anguish. I wish to emphasize the dramatic remission of his "learning problems" by means of interpretation alone, and the crucial importance of sophisticated diagnostic assessment. Currently, it has become far too easy to ignore early narcissistic injuries in favor of neurological deficits, and to refer the child to a remediation program. The consequences of misdiagnosis and inappropriate treatment can be utterly disastrous for the narcissistically impaired child.

Aftermath

Notwithstanding the progress I have described, Mike's sociopathy and idealization of mother diminished, but did not disappear for some time. It was not until Mike felt the stirrings of adolescent development that he spoke freely of how "weird" mother could be, acknowledged her pattern of seduction and abandonment, and sadly admitted that, despite his fantasy, he really didn't want to live with her. Interestingly enough, as his ego boundaries coalesced, Mike's sociopathic enactments also ceased; a reliable, internal superego signal was firmly in place. The length of time it took Mike to acknowledge, mourn, and accept mother's considerable limitations speaks to how impossible it can be for a younger child, who needs both parents desperately, to view them more objectively. This also raises questions of to what degree our work was a preparation for this later point in time, when disengagement from parents is part of a normal developmental progression.

The new object quality of our relationship enabled Mike to experience himself as a person and to use me as a stable anchor in reality. As I ascribed real meanings to words, language was libidinized and connected to feelings and silent affects in ways that allowed him to begin to hear. My emerging role as the meaning-giver (Bach 1994) was an extremely important aspect of the background of holding that his treatment provided. Language became a vitally alive means to express and explore his own inner life; externalizations gave way to a deepening transference in which Mike was better able to bear and own his feelings. As formerly unacceptable aspects of himself were integrated, ongoing work on exhibitionistic and competitive conflicts further released Mike's considerable intellectual gifts. Listening to music blossomed into the study and mastery of a musical instrument, a fitting metaphor for his inner growth and investment in life. Unlike mother, I neither disappeared emotionally nor retaliated by discarding him as he continued to individuate; closeness no longer implied castration.

The main thesis of this chapter has been the role of early trauma in the genesis of pathological narcissism and associated auditory defenses. However plausible my thoughts on early development may seem, I do not mean to imply that early interactive events wholly determined the complicated clinical picture when Mike was 5. His deviant object relations, ego and superego deformations, and ego syntonic narcissistic defenses were multiply determined compromise solutions to conflicts, deficits, and chronic strain trauma at various developmental levels. This case does suggest that such deviant structures may originate in traumatic deformations and compensatory adaptations made during the first two years of life and be consolidated during rapprochement. It seems that further study of the powerful nonverbal and anal-rapprochement phase determinants I have discussed and their transformations in later verbal phases of development may enrich and expand our understanding of early pathogenesis and later intrapsychic conflict. It may also mitigate certain countertransference responses as it deepens our appreciation of the tenacity of narcissistic conflicts and defenses, and the magnitude of the clinical task when we undertake such treatments.

References

Abrams, D. (1991). Looking at and looking away. *Psychoanalytic Study of the Child* 46:277–304. New Haven, CT: International Universities Press.

Bach, S. (1985). *Narcissistic States and the Therapeutic Process.* New York: Jason Aronson.

———— (1994). *The Language of Perversion and the Language of Love.* Northvale, NJ: Jason Aronson.

Beebe, B., Jaffe, J., and Feldstein, S. (1992). Mother–infant vocal dialogues. *Infant Behavior and Development*: Abstracts, May, 15.

Beebe, B., and Lachmann, F. M. (1992). The contribution of mother–infant mutual influence to the origins of self- and object representations. In *Relational Perspectives in Psychoanalysis*, ed. N. Skolnick and S. Warshaw, pp. 83–117. Hillsdale, NJ: Analytic Press.

———— (1994). Representation and internalization in infancy: three principles of salience. *Psychoanalytic Psychology* 11(2): 127–166. Hillsdale, NJ: Lawrence Erlbaum.

Beebe, B., and Sloate, P. (1982). Assessment and treatment of difficulties in mother–infant attunement in the first three years of life: a case history. *Psychoanalytic Inquiry* 1(4):601–623.

Beebe, B., and Stern, D. (1977). Engagement–disengagement and early object experiences. In *Communicative Structures and Psychic Structures*, ed. N. Freedman, and S. Grand, pp. 35–58. New York: Plenum.

Belsky, J., and Nezworski, T. (1988). Clinical implications of attachment. In *Clinical Implications of Attachment*, ed. J. Belsky and T. Nezworski, pp. 18–38. Hillsdale, NJ: Lawrence Erlbaum.

Beren, P. (1992). Narcissistic disorders in children. *Psychoanalytic Study of the Child* 47:265–278. New Haven, CT: Yale Uuniversity Press.

Bowlby, J. (1988). *A Secure Base*. New York: Basic Books.

Emde, R. (1988). Development terminable and interminable. *International Journal of Psycho-Analysis* 69:23–42.

Field, T., Healy, B., Goldstein, S., et al. (1988). Infants of depressed mothers show "depressed" behavior even with nondepressed adults. *Child Development* Society for Research in Child Development 59:1569–1579.

Freud, A. (1965). *Normality and Pathology in Childhood: Assessments of Development*. New York: International Universities Press.

Furer, M. (1967). Some developmental aspects of the superego. *International Journal of Psycho-Analysis* 48:277–280.

Kennedy, H., and Yorke, C. (1982). Steps from outer to inner conflict. *Psychoanalytic Study of the Child* 37:221–228. New Haven, CT: Yale University Press.

Kernberg, O. (1975). *Borderline Conditions and Pathological Narcissism*. New York: Jason Aronson.

Kernberg, P. (1989). Narcissistic personality disorder in childhood. *Psychiatric Clinics of North America* 12:671–694.

Kohut, H. (1972). Thoughts on narcissism and narcissistic rage. *Psychoanalytic Study of the Child* 27:360–400. New Haven, CT: Yale University Press.

Mahler, M., Pine, F., and Bergman, A. (1975). *The Psychological Birth of the Human Infant*. New York: Basic Books.

Mahler, M. S., and Kaplan, L. (1977). Developmental aspects in the assessment of narcissistic and so-called borderline personalities. In *Borderline Personality Disorders*, ed. P. Hartocollis, pp. 71–85. New York: International Universities Press.

McDevitt, J. (1975). Separation-individuation and object constancy. *Journal of the American Psychoanalytic Association* 23:713–743.

Modell, A. (1984). *Psychoanalysis in a New Context*. New York: International Universities Press.

Murray, L. (1991). Effects of postnatal depression on infant development: direct studies of early mother–infant interaction. In *Motherhood and Mental Illness*, vol. 2, ed. R. Kumar, and I. F. Brockington, pp. 159–190. London: Wright.

Nass, M. L. (1971). Some considerations of a psychoanalytic interpretation of music. *Psychoanalytic Quarterly* 40:303–316.

Niederland, W. (1958). Early auditory experiences, beating fantasies, and primal scene. *Psychoanalytic Study of the Child* 13:471–504. New York: International Universities Press.

Noy, P. (1968). The development of musical ability. *Psychoanalytic Study of the Child* 23:332–347. New York: International Universities Press.

Silverman, D. (1991). Attachment patterns and Freudian theory: an integrative proposal. *Psychoanalytic Psychology* 8:169–193.

———— (1992). Attachment research: an approach to a developmental relational perspective. In *Relational Perspectives in Psychoanalysis*, ed. N. Skolnick, and S. Warshaw, pp. 195–216. Hillsdale, NY: Analytic Press.

Solnit, A. J. (1982). Developmental perspectives on self and object constancy. *Psychoanalytic Study of the Child* 37:201–218. New Haven, CT: Yale University Press.

Sroufe, L. A. (1988). The role of infant–caregiver attachment in development. In *Clinical Implications of Attachment*, ed. J. Belsky, and T. Nezworski, pp. 18–38. Hillsdale, NJ: Lawrence Erlbaum.

Stern, D. (1985). *The Interpersonal World of the Infant*. New York: Basic Books.

———— (1995). *The Motherhood Constellation*. New York: Basic Books.

Terhune, C. B. (1979). The role of hearing in early ego organization. *Psychoanalytic Study of the Child* 34:371–383. New Haven, CT: Yale University Press.

Winnicott, D. W. (1958). The capacity to be alone. In *The Maturational Processes and the Facilitating Environment*, pp. 29–36. New York: International Universities Press, 1965.

———— (1960). Ego distortion in terms of true and false self. In *The Maturational Processes and the Facilitating Environment*, pp. 140–152. New York: International Universities Press, 1965.

———— (1971). The mirror-role of mother and family in child development. In *Playing and Reality*, pp. 130–138. New York: Basic Books.

Wurmser, L. (1987). Shame: The veiled companion of narcissism. In *The Many Faces of Shame*, ed. D. L. Nathanson. New York: Guilford.

Zimmerman, M. (1982). The repetition compulsion and object relations theory. In *Object and Self: A Developmental Approach*, ed. S. Tuttman, C. Kay, and M. Zimmerman, pp. 291–300. New York: International Universities Press.

12

Narcissistic Children's Use of Action

Susannah Falk Shopsin

Child therapists perforce deal more in the currency of action than in that exclusively of words, and have long been aware of the therapeutic space as a "playground" (Freud 1914) where they and their child patients can freely explore and try out many imaginative possibilities in the relationship between them.

Currently the adult analytic literature (Busch 1995, Chused 1991 [also, Chapter 13, this volume], McLaughlin 1991, Ogden 1994, Roughton 1993) has been focusing more attention on the action elements in the analytic relationship, since it has become increasingly clear that adult patients often express their early narcissistic problems in these actions or enactments. As analysts now frequently treat patients with early narcissistic pathology, their interest has been engaged by the importance of the action component in the interactions between their adult patients and themselves.

Anna Freud (1965) noted that very early memories are formed outside of the ego, and can only be remembered through action or affect, rather than cognitively. Greenacre (1952) observed that, because of the close emotional-somatic linking in the immature ego, the earlier the trauma, the greater the somatic components of its imprint. Coming from a slightly different angle Piaget (Piaget and Inhelder 1969) has described the child's earliest forms of thinking as action oriented. During this period when the child's thinking is primarily made up of action schemes, the child is unable to conceptualize in a more abstract way about the nature of his own thinking processes. What

Anna Freud, Greenacre, and Piaget are all observing is that very early experience states do not become encoded in thought, but in action and affect schema. To communicate early experience to the therapist both the child and the adult patient need to use a form of action.

I think that the actions of narcissistic children with their therapists are analagous to the enactments defined and discussed in the literature addressing narcissism in adult patients. Both the actions of the narcissistic child patients and the enactments of the adult analysands are ways of showing the therapist narcissistic difficulties in early object relations.

In my experience as a child therapist and as a supervisor of child therapists I have observed that narcissistic children establish a unique pattern of interaction with their therapist as their principal mode of communicating their distress. With most other child patients, play material is used to express in symbolic terms the child's inner conflicts, wishes, and fears. The arena of conflict can be the child's own body, his feelings about himself, and/or his relations with his family and peers. All these issues can be expressed through different play modalities such as clay and painting, role playing, and board games. However, the actions that I will focus on in this chapter have a different emphasis. The main work of the therapy takes place in the here and now between the child and the therapist. The actions do not so much symbolically portray underlying conflicts—as would be expressed in play—as graphically describe or enact these conflicts directly in the relationship with the therapist.

As has been discussed in the literature (Modell 1976, 1980), narcissistic patients often enter treatment protecting their "narcissistic cocoon." By erecting such a cocoon, these patients defensively present the illusion of self-sufficiency. In fact they are fearful of the intimacy of the therapeutic relationship, and are unable to experience the playroom as a safe space. The child patient occupies him- or herself in a way that excludes or even negates the presence of the therapist. Often the therapist's boredom, feelings of helplessness, or frustration in not being able to communicate with the patient is the first clue that this is a child with a narcissistic disorder (Beren 1992). Establishing a sense of safety in the therapeutic environment and with the therapist is a recurring and ongoing issue in the course of the treatment of such patients.

This chapter explores the particular nature of the actions of the narcissistic child, beginning with a brief clinical example and following with a more theoretical discussion that examines and suggests why these children need to elucidate their problems in this manner.

John

John was a 6-year-old boy who was brought to treatment for his generally oppositional behavior which concerned both his mother and his school. During the first two months of treatment he barely acknowledged the presence of the therapist and denied having any problems. He played Connect Four, a board game, by himself in an idiosyncratic way as though filling up the board was the object of the game. He also talked as if he were in mid-sentence or mid-thought, so that the therapist had difficulty understanding what he was trying to communicate. This style of communication gave the therapist another indication that she was treating a child with narcissistic pathology. In addition, John allowed little interaction between the therapist and himself, often not responding to her comments and deliberately turning his back to her as he played. The therapist restricted her remarks to noting John's activities in the session or to simple greetings at the beginning or end of the session. Even these minimal statements were warded off by John's not acknowledging the comment with any change in expression or with even the simplest of verbal rejoinders, such as goodbye in response to the therapist's goodbye. Narcissistic children often act in this defensive, self-protective manner before they have been able to establish a feeling of safety in the play space or a sense of trust that the therapist won't overwhelm or intrude on them.

After two months of consistently shutting out the therapist, John initiated two new and what were to become typical behaviors. The first was his playing basketball or nerf softball. Initially he played in an exhibitionistic way and assigned the therapist the role of the appreciative audience; he wanted to be admired, rather than to engage in any mutually reciprocal play. Gradually John began to order the therapist around during the game, saying "pick it up," "you get it," and so on, and showed great pleasure in his ability to completely control his surroundings. This behavior escalated to messing up the room, throwing toys off the shelves, and ordering the therapist to clean it up. The wish for admiration gradually changed into a wish for omnipotent control of the playroom and the therapist, and when John couldn't achieve that, he became furious.

The second behavior involved John's darting out of the room at the slightest noise in the hall, ostensibly to check it out. While in the hall he would flirt with danger, climbing coatracks or standing on the windowsill to look out. Often he would go down the hall, ending up in the waiting room with his mother.

The therapist understood the darting behavior as expressing his anxiety about and fear of intimacy with his therapist, and his wish to omnipotently control the closeness and distance between them, as well as expressing his difficulties with his mother and father. Throughout the parents' marriage the father had lived on the West Coast and the mother in New York. The only time the parents had lived together for any protracted period was during the year following John's birth. When John began treatment, his parents were involved in an acrimonious and protracted divorce proceeding. While visitation was still regularly maintained, with John seeing his father for a month in the summer at the father's home and several times during the school year in New York, the mother made all contacts with the father difficult for John, and enlisted him on her side in the divorce dealings. One obvious meaning of the darting behavior was John's feelings about being flown and flung between two parents, two homes, two coasts; he felt helpless, and defended against this feeling by turning passive into active. But equally important were his underlying anxieties as to whether his parents would continue to love him as he traveled from parent to parent, or, in the therapy, whether his therapist would still care for him as he darted from the room.

His forays down the hall to see his mother underlined another central issue—his insecurity about her continuing attachment and emotional availability. While on the surface he seemed to separate easily from his mother, underneath he felt anxious about leaving her, perhaps indicating that he had not established a secure internal representation of her. While the major separation difficulty observed was in John's relation with his mother, as she was the parent who brought him to treatment, his separation anxieties vis-à-vis the father were also expressed upon returning to the mother. John clearly felt abandoned, longed for his father to be more available, and was equally anxious about the father's continuing attachment to him.

In order to deal with John's darting behavior, the therapist tried to find a way to keep him in the room. She spoke to John about their keeping "their stuff" in the room. She explained that they could learn more about his thoughts and feelings if he could stay in the room. She attempted to deal with his darting behavior by speaking to his anxiety, and trying to understand its meanings with him. Sometimes this worked; other times John found ways to trick her, running past her out the door. The therapist gradually became able to read the signals John gave her that indicated he was about to leave the room. She observed that his anxiety mounted either when he heard a noise in the corridor, as if it intruded into his omnipotent control of the playroom and had to be investigated, or when his own inner tensions, especially angry ones, felt too great. Despite the therapist's acknowledgment and verbalization of the feelings underlying the behavior, the darting continued for some time.

Initially John was wary of the relationship with his therapist and did everything he could to avoid any direct interaction. The therapist speculated that he might be anticipating that she would not understand his needs, or that she might enter his play space in an intrusive way. As he gradually began to feel safer in the therapeutic setting, he initiated activities that more directly involved his therapist and seemed aimed at evoking a direct response from her. Sometimes the response he needed was admiration, while at other times he tested out the limits of her tolerance of his misbehavior. He repeatedly needed to reassure himself of her admiring gaze, as well as to explore her anger toward him and his own anger and wish to control her. These are the two typical types of interaction that narcissistic children initiate: one in which admiration is the goal, and the other in which issues of power and control are prominent.

John played basketball or nerf baseball primarily to gain admiration. Regardless of his level of performance, John wanted to be admired. Often children like John seem to maintain a blatant disregard of reality about their performance. They show no awareness of their limitations and no interest in seriously working on improving their skills. They act as if they were gifted performers, as if by magic. Obviously this recalls the way a much younger child presents himself to his parents, both needing and wanting to be valued just for being himself. The therapist has to become part of this internal world, and her praise is needed to shore up the child's fragile self-esteem. However, the therapist's role must be understood as more than just an improved version of the parent.

John needed his feelings of perfection to maintain his fragile sense of self. In treatment, the therapist had to ally herself with his grandiose defenses to enable him to maintain his unstable equilibrium. John's need for admiration, coupled with his need to maintain his sense of self as strong and powerful, naturally led to his need to control the environment, especially his therapist, as it was she who most threatened his narcissistic universe. Understood in this way, John's need for admiration, and his move toward bossiness, became comprehensible. The play space became a microcosm of John's world; as long as he could control everything in it, he could maintain his illusion of omnipotence and self-sufficiency. His therapist, just by being separate and independent of him, even if she tried her very hardest to comply with his every wish, still remained outside of his orbit of total authority. When his need to maintain distance from and control of the therapist was understood in this way, his outbursts of rage also became understandable. The play space, the therapist, and the entire treatment environment suddenly became a threat to his autonomy, strength, and power. No wonder John had to defend himself with every means available, even darting out of the room.

His hypervigilance toward sounds outside the room was another manifestation of his anxiety about not being in complete control of his environment. Not only did he try to totally control everything *inside* the therapy room, including the therapist, but he also tried to control the world *outside*, because he no longer felt in control of the room. Perhaps the sounds painfully reminded John of the existence of people in his life, especially his mother sitting in the waiting room, whom he desperately wanted to control yet felt powerless to influence, just as he couldn't completely control the therapist inside the room. John could not depend on his mother's being consistently emotionally available and attuned to his needs. Without a sense of trust in interpersonal relationships, John substituted either total isolation and self-sufficiency or an attempt at total control of the environment and the people in it.

John's daredevil antics were another way of showing he could master the dangers of the world, represented by the sounds outside the door. If he really was omnipotent, he could climb great heights or flirt with dangerous falls with impudence.

Discussion

Narcissistic children like this have difficulty hearing interpretations without feeling narcissistically injured and needing to react defensively. To allow the interpretation to be heard, some general techniques prove helpful. When the therapist phrases her interpretations as guesses, hypotheses or "maybes," it gives the child room to question the adult's formulation, thus preserving his sense of self-esteem. Another way of achieving this is by framing the interpretation in terms of "you know, as a therapist I have to say these kinds of things" or "here comes that annoying therapist again." This formulation creates a split between the person of the therapist and the function of the therapist, permitting the child to be angry at the therapist qua therapist, while still preserving positive feelings toward her as a person (Beren 1992). When the therapist shows an understanding of how the child might feel, this, in and of itself, may help the child begin to tolerate ambivalence in object relations, and to modify his aggressive feelings by tempering them with more libidinal ones toward the same object.

Often in the beginning of the interactive process the child's need for total control is more important than his anxiety about the separate existence of the therapist. Then the therapist has to support the child's omnipotence, and only very gradually and tentatively question it or offer herself as a separate object. The child's defense of grandiosity has to be empathized with—even sympathetically acknowledged and accepted—for the child to feel safe and secure. Only after that emotional exchange has taken place—often over and over again—is the child able to tolerate any questioning of his stance.

When John's need for the therapist's admiration was prominent, the therapist might have said, "I can see how you are showing me what a wonderful ballplayer you are." In such a statement she could introduce herself into the action of the session. As the theme developed, she might have ventured, "Perhaps you worry that if you aren't the very best ballplayer, I won't like you so much any more." Now she has begun to address more genetic worries that the parents overvalue the child's achievements, while not loving the child sufficiently (in the child's eyes) for himself. Another day the therapist might introduce issues of self-esteem, saying, "I wonder if you had a specially hard day today and don't feel so good about yourself, and if it isn't especially important today to be the best ballplayer in my eyes to help yourself feel better." Addressing the feelings of helplessness that underly the child's bravado, the therapist could have said, "You need to feel like an all-powerful ballplayer, because sometimes you feel like only the grown-ups have power."

One of the goals of interpretations like this was to enable John to feel safe enough in the treatment situation to be able at a later point to acknowledge the therapist as a separate object. The therapist brought this change about in many ways. First, over time John learned that the therapist was a consistent, reliable person. She was always there waiting for him for his sessions, and, more important, always emotionally available to him. While John initially walled out the therapist, ignoring her in the same way he felt ignored and maintaining his isolation and self-sufficiency, gradually he allowed her to become part of his play, but in a specific way. He wanted her to be a narcissistic extension of himself, his wishes for admiration, his demands to perform perfectly, and his desire for total control of his environment. While his therapist tried to comply with his demands, of course she couldn't do what he wanted *exactly* as he wanted it to be done. This disjunction between the patient's fantasy and the therapist's reality, no matter how hard the therapist tries to conform to the patient's wishes, is a major factor in forcing the patient to recognize the therapist's separateness.

John did not want to see his therapist as separate. But once he acknowledged her existence at all, her separateness eventually had to emerge as an aspect of their relationship. As an independent person, the therapist was not only not fully under John's control, but was also capable of initiating actions herself. With John's increasing awareness of his therapist's autonomy, his overwhelming anxiety and defensive rage at not being in control emerged and he began to vent his fury on her. Though this development can be extremely difficult for the therapist to withstand, in fact it is a forward move in the treatment. Only then is the child ready to tolerate the therapist as an object outside of his narcissistic orbit.

What is the child trying to achieve with his angry outbursts? Winnicott, in his paper "The Use of an Object and Relating through Identifications" (1971), describes the narcissistic child's need to try to destroy the object and to experience the object's survival despite these destructive attacks before the object can truly exist in the real world for the child. In other words, initially the child relates to the object only as an extension of his own wishes and needs. The first part of John's play where he cast the therapist in the role of admiring audience exemplifies this. However, it is only after the child can provoke the therapist's anger with his own anger or misbehavior, often repeatedly, and experience both the therapist's continuing caring and the survival of the relationship between them, that the child can develop enough trust to tolerate the therapist's being an independent person in the world.

Another aspect of John's provocations was his darting behavior, which seemed to be directly related to his separation difficulties with his parents and inability to fully control the therapist. When he visited his mother in the waiting room, he seemed to be directly checking on her continuing availability, and pointing to his anxiety about her being a consistently reliable person for him. As the darting also involved the therapist's chasing after John, it expressed his wish for the therapist to actively pursue him the way he wished his mother would. Individuation became a scary developmental task for John. As long as he could maintain the illusion of being narcissistically connected to his mother, he could experience her in fantasy as there for him. As he allowed himself to hatch out of this narcissistic orbit and experience his mother as differentiated from himself, he felt alone, abandoned, unprotected, and angry. His rage was his only means of protecting himself from such terrors.

The handling of these aggressively charged interactions with the narcissistic child is crucial. To move the treatment forward, the therapist must find a way to preserve the child's narcissism while at the same time presenting herself as a separate object. The therapist must frame her interpretations in a manner that both acknowledges the child's need and wish to do just what he wants with total disregard for anyone else, and at the same time suggest he might also care about the therapist and how she feels.

Focusing again on the darting behavior, the therapist needed to address this interaction in several different ways, as it served multiple purposes for the child. The therapist might say, "It must feel so good to have me go after you when you suddenly leave the room." The therapist also wanted to address John's anxiety about doing something he felt was against the rules of the treatment. Here, addressing John's underlying fears of object attachment, the therapist might say, "I think you may be worried that when you dart out of the room, I may be annoyed with you. But I'm concerned about why you need to dart out of the room, and want to understand what this behavior means. And that's something you and I can work together on." By including John in the work of the treatment and creating a safe space between them, the therapist acknowledges the child's worth and his ability to help direct the flow of the treatment. The therapist could then follow up that line of thinking (perhaps on another occasion) by wondering, "I can see that when something makes you nervous or anxious, you just want to run out of the room and leave those feelings behind you. But maybe just a little part of you would like to stay in this room with me and try to learn what those feelings are about."

Another aspect of the darting, as well as the messing of the room, is the child's need to express his angry feelings. To prepare John for a more detailed interpretation, the therapist might have wondered about the messing, saying, "When you get excited, you want to throw all the toys off the shelf and order me to pick them all up. This makes you feel so strong and powerful. But you might also wonder if that therapist of yours will keep following your orders without butting into your thoughts with all her annoying questions." Or maybe the therapist, while she's cleaning up the mess, might just jokingly say, "Here I come again having to act like a therapist. I wonder what you're showing me by dumping all the toys off the shelf and ordering me to clean them up?" In this interpretation the therapist, through her action, was accepting John's need to have her follow his orders, while offering him the opportunity to explore his underlying feelings. Often these children not only need to test out the therapist's continually caring about them even if they act "badly," but also need to actively provoke the therapist's anger at them so that they can justify their own angry feelings. The therapist might query, "I wonder if you need to make me feel angry at you, so that you don't feel so badly about feeling angry at me?"

Roughton (1993), in discussing narcissistic patients' need to communicate their problems in action and interaction with the analyst, has offered a new understanding of the concept of corrective emotional experience. In these charged interactions, the patient tries to get the analyst to fulfill a complementary role which will gratify an unconscious wish of the patient. The analyst needs to understand the thrust of the patient's action, and must tailor his response both in action and in words to be consonant with the direction of the interpretive work of the treatment. In this way the analyst is not just a better version of the parent, but a new and uniquely therapeutic object for the patient.

Continuing in this line of thinking, Ogden (1994) further elaborates on what happens between the analyst and patient in these interactions. He suggests that the analyst responds with "interpretations-in-action" or "interpretative actions" (pp. 219–220). These interpretative actions generate a play space between reality and fantasy, where emotional issues can be explored *without having to be resolved.* In this play space the patient, and this is especially important with child patients, can feel free to try out different solutions to a conflict without feeling he is breaking the law of the parents or the analyst. The interpretative action itself conveys the analyst's understanding and acceptance of the patient's conflict without pushing for a resolution. That unique, nonjudgmental understanding is the interpretation.

Perhaps the use of fantasy play, lacking in children with an inability to use the more traditional avenues of play, is present in their very presentations of themselves. They act as if they are great performers, rulers of the playroom, or in Sam's case superb ballplayers, disregarding all evidence of reality to the contrary. They also behave as if they can control the whole environment, perhaps even the whole world in which they live! As Beren (1992) has observed, sometimes when one comments on these narcissistic features in a playful manner certain children can tolerate hearing this questioning of their need for grandiosity. In such cases the therapist, rather than the child, has to introduce the playful element into the treatment situation. This playful element allows the child to think more imaginatively and creatively about his behavior without having to make firm value judgments about it, sidestepping the superego so to speak. More important, in the way she creates her interpretations the therapist can also create that fluid play space between the child and herself in which the child can try on and explore new ways of thinking about himself.

References

Beren, P. (1992). Narcissistic disorders in children. *Psychoanalytic Study of the Child* 47:265–278. New Haven, CT: Yale University Press.

Busch, F. (1995). Do actions speak louder than words? *Journal of the American Psychoanalytic Association* 43(1):61–82.

Chused, J. F. (1991). "The evocative power of enactment." *Journal of the American Psychoanalytic Association* 39(3):615–640.

Freud, A. (1965). *Normality and Pathology in Childhood: Assessments of Development.* New York: International Universities Press.

Freud, S. (1914). Remembering, repeating and working-through. *Standard Edition* 12:145–173.

Greenacre, P. (1952). Some factors producing different types of genital and pregenital organization. In *Trauma, Growth and Personality*, pp. 293–302. New York: International Universities Press.

Johan, M., reporter. (1992). Enactments in psychoanalysis. *Journal of the American Psychoanalytic Association* 40(3):827–841.

Marans, S. (1993). From enactment to play to discussion: the analysis of a young girl. In *The Many Meanings of Play*, ed. A. J. Solnit, D. J. Cohen, and P. B. Neubauer, pp. 183–200. New Haven, CT: Yale University Press.

McLaughlin, J. T. (1991). Clinical and theoretical aspects of enactment. *Journal of the American Psychoanalytic Association* 39(3):595–614.

Modell, A. H. (1976). The holding environment and the therapeutic action of psychoanalysis. *Journal of the American Psychoanalytic Association* 24:285–307.

——— (1980). The narcissistic character and disturbances in the holding environment. In *The Course of Life: Psychoanalytic Contributions toward Understanding Personality Development.* Vol. III: *Adulthood and the Aging Process.* Ed. S. I. Greenspan, and G. H. Pollock, pp. 367–379. Bethesda, MD: National Institutes of Mental Health.

Ogden, T. H. (1994). The concept of interpretive action. *Psychoanalytic Quarterly* 63(2):219–245.

Piaget, J., and Inhelder, B. (1969). *The Psychology of the Child*. New York: Harper Torchbooks.

Roughton, R. E. (1993). Useful aspects of acting out: repetition, enactment, and actualization. *Journal of the American Psychoanalytic Association* 41(2):443–472.

Winnicott, D. W. (1971). The use of an object and relating through identifications. In *Playing and Reality*, pp. 86–94. London: Routledge.

13

The Evocative Power
of Enactments

Judith Fingert Chused

Although we think of words as the primary modality of communication in analysis, patients do more than talk to us. They also communicate with other forms of behavior—with actions, attempts at actualizations (Boesky 1982), and with enactments. The role of these behaviors during an analysis, in particular the role of enactments, has provoked much discussion, including a panel presentation (Panel 1989). Most of the analysts who participated in that discussion, both panelists and members of the audience, agreed that enactments in analysis are inevitable. What remained unsettled was the question of whether and how enactments could beneficially contribute to the analytic process.

Enactments are symbolic interactions between analyst and patient which have unconscious meaning to *both*. During an analysis, they are usually initiated by the patient's actions or by the covert communication in his words (Poland 1988). Enactments also may originate with the analyst (Jacobs 1986), although in these instances it is often the analyst's countertransference response to the patient's material that leads to the enactment.

Throughout an analysis, patients engage in symbolic action (both verbal and nonverbal) which generates a corresponding impulse for action in the analyst. In the best of all possible worlds, an analyst is sensitive to his patient's transference, as expressed in either words or action, but does not act. Sympathetic with a patient's pitiful state, he does not nurture; temporarily aroused by a patient's seductive attacks, he does not counterattack. An analyst contains his impulses, examines them, and uses the information gained to enrich his interpretive work.

This best of all possible worlds is the ideal, something we strive for, but often fail to achieve. In the second best possible world, where most of us dwell, an analyst reacts to his patient—but catches himself in the act, so to speak, regains his analytic stance, and, in observing himself and the patient, increases his understanding of the unconscious fantasies and conflicts in the patient and himself which have prompted him to action. As Sandler (1976) notes, the analyst will "tend to comply with the role demanded of him [but] may only become aware of it through observing his own behavior, responses, and attitudes, *after these have been carried over into action*" (p. 47).

It is written into our job description that in "doing analysis" we must contain ourselves yet still experience the impulse to action. But when actions are forbidden, often the experiencing of the impulse also feels forbidden. I believe at times it may be more useful for an analyst to act on an impulse, catch himself, and thereby learn about the impulse and its stimulus, than to be so constricted that he is never stimulated or so defended that he is not aware of his behavior. I do not think that enactments are therapeutic in themselves, and I do not advocate consciously gratifying a patient's wish for mutual enactment. However, unconsciously determined enactments, if observed, can inform the analyst in a new way.[1] They provide information as to the content of the fantasy, memory, or impulse that is being enacted, and lead to affects that can enrich the analytic process. The value lies not in the enactments themselves, but in the observation, description, and eventual understanding of their transferential meaning.

---

1. Enactments have been used in support of various clinical theories. For example, Alexander (1950) presented a clinical vignette containing an enactment to support the therapeutic value of the "corrective emotional experience." He described a patient who *unconsciously* provoked his analyst into disliking him in order to reinforce a defensively distorted memory of his relationship with his father. In the discussion, Alexander noted, "The analyst's reaction was not calculated to be different from that of the patient's father. He simply lost, for a moment, the type of control which we consider so important in psychoanalytic therapy" (p. 491). In essence, Alexander *unconsciously participated* in an enactment of a defensively distorted object relationship. He makes clear that it was his subsequent awareness and articulation of this that enabled the patient to gain from the experience. Nonetheless, based on this observation, Alexander made a recommendation for a *consciously manipulated* experience for his patients.

The potential for enactments is omnipresent throughout an analysis; as soon as there are transference distortions of the analyst and the process, any exchange within the relationship may lead to an enactment. A patient who "imagines" that the analyst is critical or seductive has some distance from his experience—which permits the analyst to have distance from the experience. There is no such distance during an enactment. During an enactment, the patient has a conviction about the accuracy of his perceptions *and* behaves so as to induce behavior in the analyst which supports his conviction. Even if an analyst is neither angry nor critical, a patient's accusations can still induce guilt, defense, and retaliative anger. This is one aspect of the evocative power of enactments.

In addition, all object-related wishes and fantasies (including the wishes and fantasies of the analyst) are evocative of relationships with the primary objects. Both gratification and frustration contain a potential for regression which exposes the individual to dormant internal conflicts and the possibility of maladaptive compromise formations. Every time a person has a wish within an object relationship—in this case, the therapist's wish to be of help to his patient—he exposes himself to the possibility that the interaction will evoke an earlier object relationship, that is, will become laden with transference. To want anything from patients, to want to cure, to help, even to be listened to or understood accurately, is to be vulnerable to the experience of one's own transference and thus be susceptible to an enactment.

Communication is always a two-person procedure; what is intended to be said is altered by the person and the context in which the information is received. When patient or analyst speaks, the meaning and intent of the words are altered by how the other hears him, altered for the speaker as well as for the listener.

If an analyst accepts the inevitability of his contribution to enactments and analyzes them to separate his participation from the patient's understanding of his participation, to distinguish the determinants based on his psychology from those arising from the patient's, the work can only be enhanced. As illustration, I shall present material from the analysis of Debra, a latency-age girl. Much of the work with Debra can be related to work with adults; I find it useful to focus on her analysis because so much of a child's communication is through action—and so many of Debra's actions led to enactments.

Debra

Debra was 8 years old when she was referred for treatment. She was an exceptionally intelligent child who was working at that time with an educational consultant regarding school placement. Debra had already attended three private elementary schools but had been unhappy at each, ostensibly because they "failed to stimulate" her. She had applied to and was accepted at a fourth school, one of the best available in the city, but the consultant feared that without psychological help Debra would continue to be unhappy.

Before I had even seen her, the parents' pride-filled description of Debra created an image in my mind of a very talented, somewhat vulnerable child whose environment continually reinforced whatever grandiosity already existed. My expectation proved correct—as far as it went—for Debra was very talented and very grandiose. What I was not prepared for was the intensity of her rage, the totality of her isolation, and her utter contempt and lack of empathy for others.

Debra, on first meeting, was a physically beautiful, totally self-absorbed, angry, sullen child. She had taken gymnastics since age 4, and as she posed gracefully and motionless in the chair opposite me, with no evidence of discomfort or anxious chatter, I felt as if I were part of the stage set for a movie of "Debra's visit to a psychiatrist's office." There was no apprehension in the gaze of this incredibly self-possessed child as she communicated that I, not she, was expected to perform. She did say she had no idea why her parents had wanted her to see me and that, as far as she was concerned, the whole idea of talking to someone about her private life was ridiculous—"After all, it's private, isn't it?" As I struggled to find some subject with which to engage her, I was impressed with the difficulty of my task and as sense of not wishing to expose myself or my thoughts to any more of her contempt than was absolutely necessary. This concern with self-protection set the stage for my participation in the first enactment: a guardedness in approaching Debra.

Debra was the oldest of three children. She had two younger brothers who were good athletes, on whom the father spent a great deal of time as coach for their soccer teams. Her parents were upper-class, concerned about social form and status, yet quite invested in all their children. The father was well-meaning, insecure, and totally dominated by his wife. She was an imposing woman whose enormous energies were devoted to furthering peace and fellowship in the world and to achieving an atmosphere of total psychological and physical sharing in her family. She also was given to emotional storms, which were made more dramatic by their unpredictability. During my weekly meetings with the parents I often found the mother intimidating, and I was more than relieved when, after a year of Debra's analysis, the mother accepted a recommendation for therapy for herself.

Debra's development during infancy was normal. However, from early on her precocious intellectual achievements were an important focus of her parents' lives, and she was subject to constant cognitive, physical, and psychological overstimulation. By the time Debra came to analysis her mother was sharing intimate details of her own emotional, sexual, and excretory functioning with her daughter, and expected Debra to do likewise. In contrast, the father's wish to shut the door when he toileted was considered peculiar and prudish, and his "selfishness" was a family joke.

I made the recommendation for analysis reluctantly, although I believed that only an analytic experience could enable Debra to emerge from her narcissistic isolation and expose her conflictual impulses and unhappiness. Nonetheless, I felt that to engage Debra would be no easy task.

My reluctance proved fully justified. Debra began the work with her self-esteem further reduced by the recommendation for treatment, and she was enraged at me for "belittling" her. She made it clear that it was inconceivable that there would be any benefit from the treatment.

During the first hours Debra sat silently, noting only when I took a deep breath or seemed as if I wanted to speak. That was her signal that I was open to criticism and that it was time for her to begin an attack on my appearance, my smell, or my "rudeness." Rudeness was her name for my interest in talking with her, and for my curiosity about her irritation, her anger, and her desire to be left alone. It was not lost on Debra that I made a deliberate effort not to ask too many questions and restricted my interventions to responses to her or clarifications of what I perceived to be happening between us. She said, with some satisfaction, that she knew she made it hard for me to speak. Debra's awareness of this first enactment—my self-esteem-preserving caution in response to her message that I was persona non grata—made the situation all the more uncomfortable. I felt ridiculous trying to make myself inoffensive to an 8-year-old.

Although my "self-esteem-preserving caution" and "guardedness" in approaching Debra was ". . . a *compromise* between [my] own tendencies and the role-relationship which the patient is unconsciously seeking to establish" (Sandler 1976, p. 47), I found no evidence that the elements in my life that gave rise to my participation in the enactment were relevant in understanding the significance of the enactment for her. The affect evoked in me did seem to complement hers, and that I used as a clue to her *current experience* within the transference. However, the *genetic determinants* for our participation in the enactment were quite different. I believe this is important, for had I assumed that the *unconscious meaning* of the enactment was the same for Debra and for me, it might have led to inaccurate interpretations, which would have further confused an already difficult situation.

I noted, in the midst of this first enactment, that I had ceased being neutral or abstinent, and instead was engaging in a counterenactment; that is, I was using clarifications as disguised directives. This realization, that through my words I was covertly trying to control Debra's behavior, led me to a beginning understanding of what was being enacted. And so, in the midst of her protests that I was a prying busybody, intent on sticking my nose into her business, I said she had told me that she knew her complaints and criticisms made it hard for me to speak. I wondered whether this made her feel more powerful than me, as if she could control me, and whether *she* had ever felt controlled. Much to my surprise (for I had begun to question whether there would ever be a nonadversarial exchange between us), Debra responded spontaneously that the kids "picked on" her at school, but she didn't care, she just ignored them. I then asked, "Are you trying to get me to ignore you?" To this she responded, "It probably won't work; my mother never ignores me when I want her to leave me alone."

My understanding and clarifying her use of complaints to try to control me seemed useful. For a brief period, Debra was less "up-tight," and a comfortable silence, alternating with talk about her mother and school (both of which displeased her), took over the sessions. Then the next set of enactments began.

Debra became very curious about me. At first she expressed her interest through casual questions about the sweaters I wore and whether I made them. But soon the questions escalated to a belligerent inquisition of relentless intensity. She quizzed me about my taste in clothing, perfume, hairstyles, and lipstick colors. She told me my furniture wasn't "fine," my toys were old-fashioned, and my waiting-room magazines were dull and, she was sorry to say, rather tacky. But worst of all were my other patients—they were disgusting. She was particularly interested in and censorial of the bathroom manners of the 5-year-old girl whose hour preceded hers. She talked at length about the smell, dirtiness, and habits of this other patient, watching carefully for my reaction. From my protective feelings for the other child, it was clear Debra's comments had gotten to me. However, I said nothing until she began to attack me directly. Focusing on my failure to join in her criticism, she said it was proof that I was as disgusting as the other child. I asked her, as she was shouting at me for being disgusting, whether she expected me to defend myself and shout back at her. She stopped short, then, smiling rather sheepishly, she said, "No, I guess I'm not giving you a chance. Do you think I sound like my mother when I yell?"

Debra's remarks and her finicky behavior when describing the disgusting habits of others were related to conflictual anal fantasies. Her haughty self-isolation expressed both a compromise between the wish for and fear of intrusion and a defense against an awareness of this. Her anal fantasies had contributed to her low self-esteem, and during the course of the analysis, as they became less forbidden, she projected less and became able to speak about them more directly. The problem was, as with other children (and some adults) at this early stage of the treatment, evidence of her unconscious conflicts and fantasies was clear long before she had any conscious awareness of them. This made it hard to talk about her internal world in a non-threatening, nonintrusive way that did not bypass defense, was experience-near, understandable, and at the same time therapeutically useful. I found that with Debra enactments provided a ready, albeit not always welcome or comfortable, vehicle for this, for they enabled the analytic process to be a joint venture. Her awareness that I could be "touched" by our interaction seemed to make me more available to her as an object for transference projections and externalizations.

In analysis (particularly in child analysis), the inequality of the doctor–patient (or adult–child) relationship often functions as a resistance to an integration of the analyst's words with the analytic experience—the words become encrusted with authority because of the source and are discredited at the same time they are ostensibly accepted. Recognition of the potential for and occurrence of enactments, a shared experience, diminishes the authoritarian image of the doctor and the tendency of patients, particularly child patients, to fall into a (iatrogenically induced) submissive relationship with him. It is not that the analyst "confesses" his participations in enactments, but his and his patient's awareness that the process has engaged them both enhances the sense of a collaborative effort and, to the extent the analyst is nondefensive, permits the patient greater freedom to give voice to his transference-based perceptions of the analyst.

In the beginning phase, all my attempts to explore the projection in Debra's comments had led to a heated denial and further isolation. However, Debra could talk about her behavior toward me and the interaction it produced. Her initial success in inhibiting me was clarified in a way that "felt right" to her and made Debra curious about herself in a new way. To be sure, everything that was condensed in the enactment, that contributed to it, was not explored. But from our talk she began to understand how her reaction to her peers was similar to her reaction to me, how anticipating discomfort in the contact with her classmates, she retreated from any real engagement and "turned them off" just as she tried to turn me off.

When Debra first quizzed and criticized me I had worked hard not to withdraw or counterattack, but I *had* felt inhibited from commenting on the sadistic, intrusive aspect of her questioning. In my apprehension about stimulating rage in Debra, I had participated in the enactment of her fantasy that she could control me. Again, although it was my own early life experience that made me particularly vulnerable to the threat of her anger, I did not think the specifics of my experience informed me about hers. However, becoming aware of my overdetermined reaction and its origin enabled me to talk more easily about Debra's interaction with me, which led, in turn, to her first attempts to understand herself. Debra's self-scrutiny yielded only the explanation that her wish to control me was justified by my crudeness, my curiosity about things scatological. Nonetheless, her willingness to think about herself, even if only for a moment, did permit us to extend the area we talked about. Initially, in response to, "Oh, Dr. Chused, that dark-haired girl got pee on the floor again; you must be crazy to let her use your bathroom," I would simply say, "Debra, you're telling me that girl does disgusting things; are you also telling me that if *she* does something disgusting, *we* shouldn't have anything to do with her?" Now, I was able to make more exploratory comments such as, "You've said I'm interested in sex and bathroom stuff and that's disgusting, but it's not clear what it is about having sex or getting pee on the floor that's so awful." Sometimes she could follow me into this type of dialogue, but more often than not, as we began to approach her own impulses or defensive reaction formation, she would project, with remarks such as, "You're a strange grownup, always wanting to talk about sex with a kid." For a long time, no matter what I said, Debra heard guilt, defensiveness, or seduction in my response.

It was not that Debra could not understand the words, for, as Katan (1961, p. 185) has said, with analysis, "verbalization [increases] the possibility of distinguishing between wishes and fantasies on the one hand, and reality on the other," but rather that my speaking had accrued symbolic meaning. I thought I was trying hard to "say it right" because I was so invested in the work. Debra thought I was self-motivated and intrusive. My efforts to verbalize our interaction became, for a while, an enactment of her transference perception of me as intrusive. But here, too, the clarification of our differing perceptions of my talking was part of the "working through" and permitted us to better understand her attempts to control me as she had wanted to control both her mother *and* her own arousal.

Although Debra was engaged at this point, and her isolation had given way
to greater responsiveness, the anal-erotic fantasies that preoccupied her had
not yet entered the sessions in a usable fashion. Then, after about eighteen
months of analysis, Debra began to come into my office with her school
uniform unbuttoned at the waist. She also started to wear her sweater under
her skirt, with a leg in each sleeve and the neck hole over her perineum. She
stated her legs were cold and it was important for a gymnast to wear warmers,
but since her family was poor, she had to make do with her sweater. I resisted
making any comment about the sweater until it became obvious, through her
unbuttoned uniform and requests for safety pins, that she wanted me to notice
the hole. When I stated this, she told me that she liked to have her body
noticed, and described, in rather vivid detail, the tickly perineal sensations she
had when she thought someone was looking at her. She went on to volunteer
the fantasy she had of intercourse, of two ferris wheels that rose up from a
horizontal position on the ground to join together vertically, like two wheels
fusing. But just as the holes in her clothing, her showing and my seeing her
body, were to lead to an enactment, the telling of her fantasies also became
part of an enactment. The fantasies were not communicated to me as evidence
of her inner life, shared so that together we could understand them better.
Instead they were presented, like the hole over her perineum, to excite me and
titillate her with the thought of my excitement. Speech serves many functions;
affective appeal (Loewenstein 1956) rather than the communication of ideas
was often the motive force behind Debra's words.

Debra's fantasies did indeed interest me. Having spent many hours with
her, listening (as one must) to recitations of daily events, school activities,
stuck-up friends, and mean parents, I was pleased when she began to reveal
her inner life more directly. Trying to ferret out the significance of material
expressed in displacement or through play is a difficult task—direct verbal
communication of a fantasy, wish, or fear always appeals. However, this was
not the only reason for my heightened interest. My curiosity was also a
response to the covert communication of excitement, a communication that
contained critical information about Debra. I did not recognize this at first,
but it soon became apparent (from the increased pressure in her speech and
the associated gestures) that Debra's understanding of my increased attentive-
ness was not entirely the same as mine. It was through my self-scrutiny, the
recognition and integration of what was stimulated in me with what I knew
of Debra, that I began to understand what we had just enacted. And it was to
this I directed our attention. I stated rather simply that my listening to her
seemed to make her excited. With some pride and a bit of a giggle, she agreed

she wanted to see how I would respond to her story about the ferris wheels—she liked to think about it while she was in the bathroom. She went on to say, "I could tell you were interested. My mom also likes to hear me tell what I think about sex, about getting breasts and hair and all that stuff." She then asked, "Did you know I don't use the bathroom in school, only at home and now in here, while I wait for you?" Actually, during the past several months I had noted that she was always in the bathroom when I came into the waiting room to get her, but I had refrained from commenting on it (another enactment), apprehensive that a direct comment would anger her and lead to an attack. Now I said, "Was I supposed to notice? Maybe notice but not say anything?" Again she smiled slyly, then said, rather irritatedly, "But you always ruin things by talking about them." As if to prove her point, I went on to say that I thought not using the bathroom at school was like not playing with the kids—it was as if they would find out something private about her, something she wanted them to know and not know, something she wanted them to like but was afraid they would not, just as she did not like the little girl's pee on the floor. She made no response immediately, but then said, "In my family we all like to stay on the pot a long time—and we all fart a lot too; my father has the smelliest. We always talk and joke about it, but my father doesn't like that. He also doesn't like to kiss me on the lips—only on the cheek and the forehead. My mother always kisses me on the lips . . . and *she* talks about everything."

The enactment of her transference perception that I, like the mother, was sexually interested and aroused by her, but like her father, retreated from stimulating interactions, followed from my attentive silence. As we explored her understanding of my interest in her erotic fantasy and my noticing yet not saying anything about her exhibiting herself, she began to talk of her experiences with her mother (who, in regular baths with her daughter, intently examined Debra's body for evidence of pubertal development) as well as her disappointment that her father was not more involved with her physically.

There was an additional enactment that preceded Debra's acceptance of her disappointment in her father's unavailability. As Debra was explaining how she saw me, she said that even when I was silent, she knew I wanted to ask questions, that is, pursue her and intrude into her. In part Debra's perception was correct, for when she had begun to describe her interaction with her mother, I had reacted with a silence that was far from neutral. The extent of the overstimulation she described had made me uncomfortable, and I had withdrawn from the analytic process. This enactment, though initiated by Debra's attempt at transference gratification, was created by the interaction of her behavior *and* my response. My withdrawal, a countertransference response, appeared to Debra to parallel her father's, and she elaborated it into the same secret arousal she wanted to see in him. I do not know if the reaction formation of dismay which Debra's experiences aroused in me was similar to the father's reaction. I do know, however, that Debra chose to deny my withdrawal just as she denied her father's discomfort—and her own. It was the defensive denial that I addressed.

Debra's connection to her mother had been in yielding to her mother's persistent questioning about sexual and excretory functioning. This became part of the transference, as did her denial of disappointment in the exciting yet unavailable father who kissed her on the forehead rather than the lips and had the poor manners and selfishness to close the door when he was using the bathroom. Though she initially saw me as intrusive as her mother was and as she wished her father to be, the exploration of our enactments and her transference misperceptions enabled her to see both her parents more clearly, to separate her wishes from theirs, and to begin to behave more autonomously. In addition, her gradual awareness of her disappointment and sadness over her father's unavailability (which she had initially talked about only as a joke) marked the beginning appreciation of the extent of her longing for him.

Before I say more of Debra, I would like to elaborate on my understanding of enactments and how I differentiate them from "acting out" or "repetitions." Terms such as acting out and repetition refer only to the patient's behavior; they imply that the analyst is an observer of the experience, not a participant in it. Even the term "projective identification," while recognizing the analyst's responsiveness to the patient, does not acknowledge the contribution to the analytic experience which is determined by the analyst's own psychology (McLaughlin 1991, Sandler 1976).

Enactments, distinguished by the unconsciously determined affective and behavioral involvement of the analyst, result from the patient's attempt to create an interactional representation of a wished-for object relationship. Through getting the analyst to enact with him, the patient achieves a measure of reality for his transference fantasies. *Enactments occur when an attempt to actualize a transference fantasy elicits a countertransference reaction.*

Many analysts today recognize that they are both observers and participants (to a greater or lesser extent) in the analytic process; however, this was not always true (McLaughlin 1991). Even now, while there is general agreement that threats or overtly seductive gestures stimulate responses in the analyst which affect his analyzing capacity, there is still a failure to attend to the more subtle behavior, more ambiguous expressions of the patient's affective state, which can wreak havoc with analytic abstinence and neutrality and lead to enactments.

There are several possible scenarios when a patient attempts *unsuccessfully* to evoke an enactment. The analyst may recognize what is transpiring and be able to usefully interpret the process to the patient. Or, with no reaction from the analyst, the unconscious intent of the patient's behavior may be lost, to reemerge later in another form. If the patient has sufficient self-observing capacities, he may become aware of his frustrated wishes and begin to speak of them, rather than enact them. Or he may continue to provoke until he has roused the analyst to action. So it was with Debra.

After disclosing a wish that her mother were less intrusive and her father (and I) more involved, Debra stopped talking about her excitement with me, and instead turned to the play materials. Within several weeks, she had begun a repetitive game that continued for six months. Debra's pattern was not unique; many latency children (Debra was then 10) dramatize their conflicts and wishes in play rather than speaking about them directly. What made Debra's activity interesting was that not only were her conflicts expressed through the content of the play, but she also "played" to an audience (me) and the manner in which she "played" was determined by the response she wished to elicit from me.

It began with a "confession" of masturbation, which occurred while Debra was decorating a lamp in my office that is in the shape of a glass ball. She and other children I analyze have discovered that this ball (lit by an interior light bulb) melts any crayon pressed to its surface, and it has become a means for them to draw, mess, and play out conflicts. The crayon melting for Debra began as a distraction, intended, I believe, to draw off some of the motor tension she was feeling as she told me of her masturbation. This had come in the midst of discussing my prurient interests, and though *she* initiated the "confession," she began by saying there was something she did that she guessed *I* might be interested in since *I* was so nosey. Her tone made it clear she was being "forced" to talk. Somewhat defiantly, then, as she melted a crayon, she said she sometimes stuck her finger "in there" to see if she was clean.

At this point she became aware of a design left by another child, and with competitive vigor, wiped off the other child's work and took over the lamp. The next hour she returned to the lamp as soon as she entered the office, and by the end of the week crayon melting was her only activity (other than speech). Within two weeks her crayon melting had assumed the characteristics of a ritual. It was performed in an identical manner each day; her absorption was total, her movements sensual and slow. At first she pretended that the melting crayons were men trying to cross over a barrier she had to keep clean. If they dribbled across the barrier before she could wipe them away, they would do evil. If she kept the barrier clean (and destroyed the dribbles), evil would be overcome. While her total absorption in the melting crayons made it appear she did not want me to "cross the barrier" surrounding her, her comments seemed designed to provoke me to penetrate her reserve. She spoke angrily of the other children who "dared" to touch the lamp. She also said she thought *I* was angry that she messed up the lamp and did not talk much (thought I kept it hidden, she said, because I was supposed to "act" like a "good doctor"). Gradually her transference misperceptions and preoccupying sexual daydreams became interwoven, and she developed an erotic fantasy of my punishing her, spanking her again and again on her bottom for messing. She imagined that I would act in anger but claim, "it's for your own good."

Over time, as Debra began talking more directly of her fantasy, her interest in melting crayons decreased. Its function shifted from being a symbolic playing out within the transference of sadomasochistic anal fantasies (not only did she create an incredible mess on and around the lamp, but regardless of the colors other children used, after Debra's hour the lamp was always yellow-brown) to once again being a means to release enough of the affective tension associated with her aggressive and erotic fantasies to tolerate talking about them.

Of note is that during the "lamp game," when I had expressed concern for the crayon splatters on the wall, Debra did not hear me as particularly angry. Her belief that I was angry or disgusted or aroused seemed to have no relation to my behavior or affect. During this time Debra was so caught up in the analysis that within her psychic reality I was a full participant in the transference, even when I was abstinent (Bird 1972). Though our interaction during much of the lamp game does not fit my definition of enactments, it served the same function. The major difference was that when I was not "enacting" I was able to understand the determinants of Debra's behavior sooner.

However, not long after the lamp game stopped, another enactment ensued. Debra by now had become more comfortable in school and had begun to take pleasure in describing her activities there. Nonetheless, talking about friends soon became conflictual (I believe because she felt that I, like the mother, would be jealous of her relationships with others), and she gradually slipped into her "actress mode," overdramatizing scenes and events. Once again I felt excluded and began to overtalk, chasing Debra with words. When I became aware of how insistent I had become, I asked Debra if she noticed that the more I talked, the less she seemed to hear. Her response was, "You sound like me trying to talk to my mother," and she went on to speak of her helplessness in challenging her mother's opinions. Later this was elaborated into her feeling of being helpless yet excited by her mother's sexual intrusion and the sensations it stimulated.

There was one final enactment that heralded the onset of termination. Debra began to not understand my interpretations and clarifications. During the lamp game she had acknowledged that her withdrawal was motivated by a wish to have me ask questions, and together we had connected my questions with her genital "tickles" and her confused and troubled experiences with her parents. Now, over a year later, she again withdrew, ostensibly without any understanding of "why." I began once more to work hard at teasing out the determinants of her behavior, as Debra, sensitive to my desire to be helpful, unconsciously manipulated me into "playing analyst." When I regained my self-observing capacity and asked her about this, she said, "Don't you like helping me understand myself?" I replied that I did, but then asked whether she was worried that I would not like her being able to understand without me. She nodded her head in agreement.

That enactment (our joint participation in the fantasy that she still needed me) was followed by a change in her behavior, not an enactment, but a clear nonverbal communication. Debra insisted that we play card games. She knew from past experience that I generally do not play card and board games (because of their tendency to degenerate into ritualized resistance), and over the years we had been together, she had grown to accept this, with some reluctance and irritation, but with eventual tolerance for my limitations. Now there was a new insistence, and when I would not join her, she played solitaire. I tried to clarify her behavior—she did not ignore my words, nor did she disagree, but she kept on playing cards. She then brought in yarn and began knitting in the chair opposite mine (she knew that I sometimes knit while listening to patients). Again I felt frustrated—not angry, but somewhat useless. It took me a while to recognize that Debra was telling me I *was* useless to her now, that it was time for our work to be over. Why did she tell me this way? I asked her that. Her reply was, "I don't know; I wasn't sure it was time to leave. I know I feel good, that I like school and the kids, but I also like coming here. And maybe I didn't want to hurt your feelings."

Thus began Debra's termination. This initially very vulnerable, defensively isolated child was experiencing what she had avoided for so long, that once you are engaged, it hurts to become disengaged. That she saw it in terms of *my* being hurt was not a bad beginning. We had lived with our joint participation in the analytic process, through enactments and other analytic interactions, for a long time. I was certain that if she thought I had feelings, she was aware she had them too.

Debra's analysis contained many enactments, not only because she was a child, but because she was a chronically overstimulated child whose capacity to organize and contain her impulses was less than other childrens', and I was susceptible to the primitive, dramatic quality of her behavior. In addition, her isolation and hunger, as well as her previous discomfort and feeling of vulnerability in relationships, had intensified my importance to her and her susceptibility to transference misperceptions. Like other patients in analysis, when stimulated by significant regression, she attempted to actualize the transference through enactments.

Discussion

Given that enactments are inevitable during an analysis, the question remains, how can they be most effectively utilized? Words that name can reduce anxiety by organizing conflictual emotions. Enactments, in creating experience beyond words, engage the participants in a regressive experience which often *increases* anxiety and decreases ego mastery. Yet this regression can lead to a new depth of understanding of conflict, fantasy, and memory. Enactments also link current and past experiences with a vividness of affect and intersubjective relatedness that imparts enormous conviction. They are a concrete shared experience in which the opportunity for defensive denial, intellectualization, and distortion is diminished. If an analyst finds that he is unintentionally enacting with a patient, withdraws from the enactment, and then subjects his behavior and subjective sensations to analytic self-scrutiny, he often has additional information that was not available when he was not so fully engaged.

I believe enactments result from a communication via unconscious clues (Sandler 1976) that relies on an affective signaling similar to that used by (and with) very young children, before the capacity for abstraction and symbolization takes place. Both Stern (1985) and Emde et al. (1976), in their work on the affective mode of communication that antedates language, have demonstrated the appeal, clarity, and universality of such signals. However, that repressed conflictual fantasies and wishes find expression via a developmentally early mode of communication does not mean that the conflicts expressed are from a preverbal period of life—only that a more primitive channel of communication, reliant on affectively laden signals, is being called into play. Throughout our lives we all are attuned to the subtle clues contained in gesture, tone, facial expression, and rhythm. What makes analysis unique is not the analyst's reception of the clues, but his examination of them, and his effort to find the words to describe their message.

In any analytic search to understand the intrapsychic domain, much of the initial data come from the observation of interpersonal behavior; the problem during an enactment is that the analyst's power of observation is clouded. In addition, as unconscious conflicts lead to his participation in the enactment, even after he becomes aware of the enactment, the analyst's resistance to full understanding will continue. There were times during my analysis of Debra when all I was aware of was my discomfort and a feeling that the work was nonproductive. Occasionally it required taking verbatim notes immediately after the session, or discussing the process with a colleague for me to recognize when I was enacting.

Enactments do not necessarily offer an easier road to the unconscious determinants of behavior or a better way to communicate with patients. But as they occur, repeatedly, in the course of every analysis, an objectivity about them, a capacity to deal with them just as we deal with the associations or memories that are called forth by our patients' verbal communications, can only increase our technical armamentarium. To continue to track is the work of analysis, whatever the mode of communication.

Even after one enactment is recognized and interpreted, others may ensue. When a defense or resistance, impulse or fantasy, is revealed in a patient's associations and interpreted, his psychic equilibrium will shift, often with new compromise formations and the expression of the conflict in a new form. Similarly, when an enactment is interpreted, the arena of enactment may also shift, with the patient's conflicts expressed in new behavior, which again tests the analyst's vulnerabilities.

For example, after an analyst has withdrawn from participation in an enactment, integrated the experience with his cognitive understanding of the patient and the analytic process, he often wants to share his understanding of the enactment and its determinants with the patient. However, to a patient enmeshed in transference, the very act of intervening can become a vehicle for an enactment. Interpretations, heard as meaning that the analyst understands something which the patient does not, are denied. If the analyst tries harder to clarify the experience, he is heard as defensive or irritated, and his words become evidence of his authoritarian stance.

Or, after the analyst first interprets, the patient may begin to speak in such a way as to manipulate him to continue to interpret the *seemingly unconscious* connections. This too is an enactment. And though quite common, this use of words to stimulate the analyst to "act like an analyst" can be quite difficult to detect.

In the Panel on enactments (1989), Boesky said, "just about everything the patient feels, says, thinks, or does during the session is influenced by wishful tendencies which press for actualization." When we as analysts are conscious of this "press for actualization," we are able to interpret and, through our interpretations, increase our patients' awareness of their motivating impulses and fantasies. When we are not so aware, we enact. Enactments are often the first sign of a shift in a patient's transference, a shift that caught the analyst by surprise and made him a participant in an emerging transference paradigm he is not yet able to objectify and observe. The analyst does not consciously "choose" to enact; he enacts and then thinks, "Why did I say (do) that?" It is his scrutiny of the enactment, not the enactment itself, which will lead to a new understanding of the transference.

In analysis we interpret more than words; we also explore and articulate the unconscious links between what is said at one moment and what is said at the next. That these links are revealed through the process of speaking has misled many of us into assuming that the content of verbal communications is the focus of our work. This is not true. Not that the content of the patient's material is not valuable. It is, for it leads to an awareness of unconscious connections and enriches the analyst's interpretations and makes them immediate, specific, and therefore real to the patient. But in the work of making the unconscious conscious, it is the determinants of the words and their sequence, rather than the conscious thought, that we attend to.

The same process of looking for unconscious determinants is at work when we examine enactments. We look beyond the conscious intent of behavior (both ours and the patient's) and examine it within the context of the analytic situation, hoping to uncover its relation, via the transference, to unconscious processes. Jacobs (in Panel 1989) has suggested that enactments in analysis often reflect specific identifications and are essentially memories put into action—memories of actual events or events defensively distorted by the patient but retained in memory as enacted. This has not been my experience. I think that enactments, being a resultant effect of unconscious forces in *both* the analyst and the patient, are rarely so specific. However, I do agree with Jacobs that external behavior can sometimes communicate what thoughts and feelings do not quite capture. The determinants for the analyst's participation in an enactment will not be the same as for the patient, but the intrapsychic conflicts being stimulated may prove similar enough to provide a new source of empathically derived information which, when "made consonant with the patient's material according to disciplined, cognitive criteria" (Arlow 1979, pp. 204–205), can lead to an understanding that was not accessible through words alone.

Nonetheless, enactments are still seen as deterrents to analysis. Is this just because of the potential for gratification in enactments, or because they are tenacious resistances? Or is it also because our participation in enactments leads us, the analysts, to behave in ways that feel unanalytic?

Enactments will convey, from patient to analyst, knowledge of impulses and affect that may be impossible to communicate through verbal description. But enactments will also convey to the patient the analyst's participation in the process. Unlike repetitions, in which it is the patient who repeats and the analyst who witnesses, in an enactment both analyst and patient are participants.

The communication of the analyst's involvement and his vulnerability to involvement, inadvertent though it be, will have important ramifications for the course of treatment. It is different from a deliberate act by the analyst, for the latter, be it classical abstinence or Kohutian mirroring, is under the control of the analyst and carries with it a sense of his authority. There are times during an analysis when the analyst's involvement can be an important fuel, motivating the patient to continue the work. At other times, even with the same patient, it can be a significant source of resistance, or a threat to the patient's comfort with the relationship. But all reactions to enactments, including these, are information to be explored and analyzed. Not to do so is to collude with the patient's resistance.

In summary, an enactment is a nonverbal communication (often cloaked in words) so subtly presented and so attuned to the receiver that it leads to his responding inadvertently in a manner that is experienced by the patient as an actualization of a transference perception, a realization of his fantasies. Although not therapeutic in itself, an enactment can provide invaluable information and an immediacy of experience that enrich the work. Viewed as yet another source of information, greeted with curiosity and not guilt, enactments can become part of the analytic process from which we all learn.

References

Alexander, F. (1950). Analysis of the therapeutic factors in psychoanalytic treatment. *Psychoanalytic Quarterly* 19:482–500.

Arlow, J. A. (1979). The genesis of an interpretation. *Journal of the American Psychoanalytical Association* 27 (Suppl.):193–207.

Bird, B. (1972). Note on transference: universal phenomenon and hardest part of analysis. *Journal of the American Psychoanalytical Association* 20:267–301.

Boesky, D. (1982). Acting out: a reconsideration of the concept. *International Journal of Psycho-Analysis* 63:39–55.

Emde, R. Gaensbauer, T. J., and Harmon, R. J. (1976). *Emotional Expression in Infancy. Psychological Issues*, Monogr. 37. New York: International Universities Press.

Jacobs, T. (1986). Countertransference enactments. *Journal of the American Psychoanalytical Association* 34:289–308.

Katan, A. (1961). Some thoughts about the role of verbalization in early childhood. *Psychoanalytic Study of the Child* 16:183–188. New York: International Universities Press.

Loewenstein, R. M. (1956). Some remarks on the role of speech in psychoanalytic technique. *International Journal of Psycho-Analysis* 37:460–468.

McLaughlin, J. (1991). Clinical and theoretical aspects of enactment. *Journal of the American Psychoanalytical Association* 39:595–614.

McLaughlin, J., and Morton, J. (1992). Enactments in psychoanalysis. *Journal of the American Psychoanalytic Association* 40:827–841.

Poland, W. (1988). Insight and the analytic dyad. *Psychoanalytic Quarterly* 57:341–369.

Sandler, J. (1976). Countertransference and role-responsiveness. *International Journal of Psycho-Analysis* 3:43–48.

Stern, D. (1985). *The Interpersonal World of the Infant*. New York: Basic Books.

14

The Anal World
of a Six-Year-Old Boy*

John Rosegrant

A 6-year-old boy during the second year of his psychoanalysis presented the remarkable play described below. I shall analyze this play as manifesting the creation of a perverse, anal world which was central to this boy's psychic equilibrium, and which he was able to begin changing only after engaging in a certain kind of therapeutic enactment. This case demonstrates the existence at an earlier developmental level of perverse qualities which have previously been identified in adults.

Session 1.

Donald brings a board game and states that he had to wait five minutes (he was early), throwing the box on the ground and striking the lid rapidly against my leg; I tell him to stop hitting me and say "All that time to have to wait!" He swears at me briefly, then settles into playing the game, cheating outrageously. Ten minutes prior to the end, he notices me glancing at the clock, says "Oh no, you can't!" turns over the clock, and comes for my watch; I decide to let him remove it (I discuss this choice of intervention below in the section "The Therapeutic Gain.") I say that Donald wants me not to know the time so I

*For their helpful critiques of earlier drafts, I thank Drs. Katherine Rees and Irving Steingart.

can't end the session; Donald says that is exactly what he is doing. After a bit, I say I will have to guess the time; Donald hides the watch in his pocket but I catch a glimpse, see that it is time, and tell him so; Donald wrestles me and I have to half carry him to the waiting room. Donald returns the watch by sliding it a few inches up my trouser leg.

Session 2 (two sessions later).

Donald brings the same game, puts it on the floor, and flops back on the couch, limbs splayed. I say "That's a Donald collapse!" He says yes, that he is broken in a million pieces, so I say I better put him together, and play at this by rapidly moving my hands above him. With a small smile, Donald wails "Oh no, you put my penis where my nose should be and my nose where my penis should be!" I try again, but he says I put his mouth upside down, then I put his mouth on his belly and his eyes where his nipples should be. My efforts result in jumbled body parts a few more times before I finally get it right.

The rest of the session is an unusually good-natured board game. When I say it is time to stop, Donald grabs me and says that I am in a million pieces; I say that then we would be unable to stop.

Session 3 (the next session, after the weekend).

Donald shows me a loose tooth, then gets out the boy soldiers. One side is losing badly, and I have the leader say they have to try something new, they will—Donald interrupts and says "Pee in their pants!" Donald divides the soldiers into boys and girls. A boy wants to watch a girl peeing, and shows her how he can pee farther because he has a penis. He then asks the girl what she has between her legs, and as Donald refuses to speculate, I say she has a vulva and vagina. The boy also wants to see her boobs. After a little competitive urinating, they affectionately fart and poop at each other, including farting into each other's buttocks. The girl has a long vulva but the boy has a longer penis.

War starts between the boys and the girls, with artillery consisting of pooping, farting, barfing, and peeing. A girl is captured and has to show her private parts on pain of being shot. I have the girls decide to show what is between their legs because it sometimes scares boys; Donald has the boys pee on the girls so fast that they see nothing. A boy wants the captive's boobs for himself, then the boys burn the boobs off the attacking girls; I say that way they are the same and don't have to feel bad. The boys bury the girls under a pile of poop, then rescue them by using their superior peeing to wash it away. Two boys who do not know what is between a girl's legs examine the captive there, expecting to find boobs, or something big and hairy unless it is a young girl, who would have no hair. The boys shoot off the vaginas of all the girls, then Donald anxiously has them say they have done a bad thing, because now the girls can't pee, and he decides that the boys had missed. A boy sticks a gun up the captive's vagina and leaves it five hours, nervously wondering if she enjoys it. If she has a baby she can pee with her breasts. Two boys drink milk from the girls' breasts, then stretch and pull them off so that they can drink whenever they want; I say then they will never be hungry or lonely. Donald then has these boys successfully fight everyone. Sides change again, and each side has someone with long buttocks who can poop on the others; these two end up pooping into each others' buttocks. When I say it is time to stop, there is a chaotic attack with all manner of excretions and secretions.

Session 4 (the next day).

Donald eagerly says "OK, the same game of looking at private parts." The girls are using the bathroom, the boys come to spy. They enjoy smelling farts and poop, and are clearly interested in big buttocks, not genitals. A boy lets himself be seen, but only after putting on lipstick and taping back his penis so that he will be mistaken for a girl. They compare boobs, and although the boy is impressed by the girl's boobs, the boy has big ones too. They begin ingesting each other's farts, piss, poop, and vomit, commenting on how delicious it all is, like honey or flowers. The boy especially likes putting his nose in the girl's anus to smell her farts. Donald has a moony expression on his face, and off-and-on is clutching his penis. I have the girl wonder if this is what men and women do when they are in love. They then begin biting chunks out of each other's buttocks and anuses, to their mutual enjoyment. I mention that they are biting each other's private parts. Donald has the boy reveal that he is a boy, saying "What's wrong with that?" I have the girl say that nothing is wrong with that, she likes boys. Donald has her bite the boy's penis, and then has the boy nervously pee in her mouth.

This scene is essentially repeated twice more with two more pairs. Donald has them say "We'll show them what men and women do when they're in love!" After his penis is bitten, the boy says he likes it best having his nose in the girl's anus; I say that's better than having his penis bitten because he only has one penis but there are endless farts.

History and Clinical Background

Donald is the only child his parents had together, but has much older half-siblings; these are the children of his father by a previous marriage, and have always been in the custody of the father. Donald's parents have white-collar careers. Both parents have significant character problems, and his mother has begun therapy since Donald started analysis, but his father refuses. His mother is often angry and critical towards both others and herself. His father is emotionally detached and seems baffled by what it means to be a father, showing surprise at evidence that he is important to Donald. Although Donald's parents have stayed together, their marriage has been riddled with anger and resentment for most of his life and is asymmetrical in terms of emotions and power, with his father longing for a renewal of love which his mother rejects.

In addition to the strain trauma and unhelpful identificatory models Donald has experienced from his parents, two other pathogenic factors need to be noted: firstly, Donald has experienced the repeated loss of nannies who were important attachment figures. Both parents work, so after his mother returned to work when Donald was 3 months old, a significant amount of his care was provided by these nannies. Due to external factors, several had come and gone by the time Donald began treatment. Secondly, Donald was vividly confronted with the possibility of injury to the penis because, before Donald's birth, his half-brother had his legs and penis badly burned in a freak accident. With startlingly poor judgment, his father tried to assuage Donald's potential anxiety by making sure that Donald had plenty of "natural opportunity" to look at the damage, such as by urinating with his half-brother. (It may be speculated that the father was himself coping with considerable castration anxiety.) There was no other evidence of overstimulation or sexually abusive behavior.

Donald began treatment at the age of 5 at the insistence of his preschool. He was violent with other children, pushing and shoving them heedlessly, and talked back to the teachers. His parents also noted that although he used to be sweet and adorable, he was becoming increasingly sarcastic and hard to manage. Testing done by the school indicated superior intelligence.

As soon as the analysis began, Donald formed an intense attachment to me, but adamantly refused to acknowledge directly this attachment or his resulting unhappiness when sessions ended. Indeed, anger was the only emotion he would admit to—this one he admitted to proudly. He typically hurried into sessions and played eagerly, but became enraged if I did not follow his instructions precisely, and when I ended the sessions. He firmly maintained that he hated me and that I was stupid, and sometimes hit, kicked, or threw things so that I had to restrain him physically. Interpretations of this behavior in terms of sadness about separation or about his lack of power and control compared to me resulted in silence (if I was lucky) or in increased scorn and abuse. The content of our play was generally a war in which my characters were crushed by his characters, which had a variety of omnipotent powers that changed from day to day. These ranged from exceptional karate skills to magical powers such as fiery breath, flight, gigantic monsters, and so on. Interpretations within the metaphor, in which my characters bemoaned their weakness and lack of control, and longed for the admirable qualities of Donald's characters, were usually tolerated, although even these could result in reprimands that I was talking too much. In his controlling behavior, his omnipotent play, his rage at my interpretive efforts, and his refusal to acknowledge vulnerable feelings or any sort of problem, Donald resembled narcissistic children described by Beren (1992).

Donald's anxiety and anger within the sessions gradually abated. It seldom became necessary to restrain him, and the play content changed so that although war continued, characters became much less omnipotent, and Donald and I often cooperatively operated both sides. His unwillingness to refer to his relationship with me or to acknowledge any emotion other than anger continued with little moderation, however. This brings us to the material described initially.

Farty Rules

How are we to understand this unusually vivid, even lurid material? First, it is necessary to look at the consequences of these sessions. The next few sessions were quite similar. Then Donald returned to war and board games, but for weeks maintained a preoccupation with farting: he would suddenly say "Fart!" (this was not a command, but a representation of farting) or accuse me of farting. This seemed to happen most often when he cheated, so I began to say when he cheated that he was playing by "farty rules." Donald was very interested in this idea, and easily recognized the difference between farty rules and grown-up rules. I extended the concept of farty rules to include his misbehavior at the ends of sessions, which again Donald was easily able to understand. He became intensely interested in what I thought of farty rules, and tempted me to play by them myself. He also talked about my big buttocks, and tried to get me to admit that I farted in sessions, or outside of sessions. This enabled us to talk about how much Donald wished that I were like him, and that there were times that farty rules were most fun but other times that grown-up rules were most fun. We identified that farty rules were most fun when things were not working out for him in the grown-up world, for example when he was losing a game, or when he made a mistake. When next he made a mistake at checkers, instead of coldly berating himself or me, and quitting, he stood on one leg and laughed that he was a "farty chicken leg poop nose."

Thus, the material described at the beginning appears to have had a salutary effect. From it we developed a language which enabled Donald to engage in a more friendly dialogue with me, talk about wanting us to be alike, accept that he had moments when he was unhappy with himself, and begin to explore the meaning to him of being a child vis-à-vis a world of adults.

This pattern, of lurid material in the vein of that presented at the beginning immediately preceding moments of growth, has recurred. Here are two more examples:

Session 5 (almost three months later,
the session before my summer break).

I begin by reminding Donald of my vacation, and he applauds. Most of the session is a war between soldiers. Toward the end, some of the soldiers want cake to eat, but the bosses give them poop and pee instead. The soldiers, with great interest, compare the amount of their diarrhea, then use diarrhea and pee as bullets. They begin comparing the size of their penises, which they use as weapons; the best warriors have penises that reach across the room. Donald looks at me intently and says "Wouldn't it be great if we had penises that big? We could fight anybody!" This is the first time he has acknowledged affiliative feelings toward me at a moment of separation.

Session 6 (one month after the end of vacation).

We are playing football, and Donald devises coprolaliac signals from the quarterback to the hiker, for example, "The other team peed in their eyes and farted out their mouth and poop came out their nostrils and they put their eyeballs in backwards." Sometimes Donald gives these signals, sometimes he insists that I give them; I comply, although I draw the line at using actual curse words (I discuss this choice of intervention below in the section "The Thera-peutic Gain"). After a while Donald wonders if it is important to control dreams, then sits and tells me four dreams that he wants to try to understand. He is able to see how the dreams include scary feelings that he doesn't want to notice. As we discuss the fourth dream—*he was with a baby-sitter he used to have, she was washing the floor, Donald ate some of the soapy water*—he thinks it means there is something he couldn't say, but that this doesn't make sense because whenever he is mad at his mother it's easy to yell and swear at her. I suggest that nice things are what are hard to say. Donald immediately starts to play soldier, but when I point out he is changing the subject, he sits down and soberly agrees that it is much harder to say nice things than angry things.

The Anal World

To understand the clinical material, let us examine it more minutely: in Session 1, Donald tries to make time unknowable. This is relatively ordinary material, but needs to be kept in mind because I believe it is of a piece with the more shocking material, for reasons which will become clear below.

In Session 2, Donald's body parts become disconnected and difficult to reassemble properly. Although a mix-up of sexual parts is prominent, non-sexual parts also become rearrangeable. It is as though we fabricate several alternative forms of Donald before getting back to the real one.

In Session 3, Donald begins by showing me an actually detachable body part, the loose tooth. Then the badly beaten team regresses to the childish behavior of peeing in their pants. Next follow boys and girls exploring the differences in each other's sexual parts. Then they engage in friendly excre-tory play, in a way which at first underlines their differences—competitive urination—but then emphasizes their similarity, as they identically fart into each other's buttocks. Even the genital difference is lessened, by giving the girl a long vulva. Similar material ensues, but now with a strong aggressive charge, so that excretions are weapons, and the girls must show private parts on pain of being shot. The boys make ambivalent efforts to eliminate the sexual differences, by burning off boobs, shooting off vaginas, or pulling off boobs so that the boys may keep them. The physiology of motherhood is equated with that of babyhood in that mothers can pee with their breasts. Our separation instigates even greater chaos of excretions and secretions.

Donald initiates Session 4 by saying we are to play the same game of looking at private parts. For the most part this game has the quality of affectionate lovemaking, as is stated ("We'll show them what men and women do when they're in love!") and as is underscored by Donald's erotic arousal, obvious in his expression and his clutching his penis. At first, interest is in those private parts which boys and girls share—buttocks and what comes out of them—whereas private parts which are different are hidden, by the boys wearing lipstick and taping back their genitals, or denied, by the boys also having large breasts. They eat chunks of each other's buttocks, without pain or disgust, and with no evidence of any injury sustained. When the boys' penises are noticed, anxiety increases: the boys are afraid they will be disliked for having this organ, and are nervous when the penis is bitten. A boy comments that what he likes best is having his nose in the girl's anus—an interaction which does not require a penis.

Donald's fantasy world shows striking similarity to fantasies of the Marquis de Sade and of adult patients with perversions, elucidated by Bach and Schwartz (1972) and Chasseguet-Smirgel (1978, 1981) as manifestations of an anal world. Anality is obvious in much of the direct, overt content of Donald's fantasies, and I believe that the pervasive theme of interchangeability should be understood as formally anal. By this I mean that such pervasive interchangeability is an anal quality, not only when the interchangeable parts belong to the excretory system, but also when other parts are concerned. To help us keep in mind what I mean by the quality of anal interchangeability, let us revisit this aspect of Donald's play: various excretions and secretions are interchangeable among each other, and also have interchangeable uses: poop, farts, pee, vomit, and snot serve equally well as weapons and as savory foods. Buttocks and the anus themselves may serve as food in addition to serving as excretory organs, and can be bitten off as food for one person without causing pain or injury to the other person, suggesting that they have not really been lost. Sexual parts are interchangeable between the sexes: boys may wear lipstick, hide their penises, have big boobs of their own or steal boobs from girls; girls may have long (penis-like) vulvas, have their vaginas shot off, and their boobs burnt off or stolen. Sexual parts may interchange psycho-sexual meanings: buttocks may be long and penis-like, boobs may be found between a girl's legs, mothers may pee from their breasts. In fact, virtually all body parts seem to be almost infinitely interchangeable, as I discovered when I tried to reassemble Donald after his collapse in session two.

There is a twofold bodily basis for interchangeability and de-differentiation being hallmarks of the anal world: first, the anus, buttocks, and feces are common to everyone, male and female, child and adult; second, feces are fabricated through the process of digesting and reducing various substances to an identical, undifferentiated substance. Bach and Schwartz (1972) have demonstrated that the Sadean world is typified by the same kind of inter-changeability: any orifice will serve for any sexual act; all sexual acts are also aggressive; any person may serve as the sexual and aggressive object, whether idealized or degraded, stranger, acquaintance, parent, or child; not even life and death can be meaningfully differentiated, since death merely results in a trivial rearrangement of molecules into a new life. "The body contents . . . [and] the mental products . . . all become metamorphosed by the fantasy into the standardised parts of an insane anal technology." Chasseguet-Smirgel (1978) has elaborated that a crucial unconscious metaphor in Sade's writings is the passage of his characters through an alimentary canal which results in the reduction of all to feces: "The object is . . . subjected to a process of slow digestion."

Additionally, the level of cognitive development during this period of life contributes to the child's sense that things and attributes may be interchange-able. The child at this age is first developing objective self-awareness and the awareness of separate objects, and calibrating these states with subjective self-awareness; the child is also making the crucial differentiation between male and female (Bach 1994). Since these categories are not yet firmly estab-lished, de-differentiation and interchangeability of categories may easily oc-cur. Fast (1984) has elaborated on the development of sexual differentiation in this regard. She proposes that although from birth children are socialized to behave according to their gender, their cognitive apparatus originally does not allow them to understand what it means to be of one gender or the other; rather, very young children experience all gender possibilities as open to them, in an undifferentiated manner. Some time around the age of 2, cognitive maturation allows children to recognize the limits of belonging to their own gender, but the experience of interchangeability of sexual parts and attributes remains within easy "physical reach," contributing for example to fantasies of anal birth.

Another aspect common to the anal worlds of Donald and of adult perver-sions is the idealization of its creations, particularly but not exclusively anality and the anal products. For Sade, the anus is the preferred organ for inter-course, vastly superior to the vagina. Feces are idealized by Sade, whereas ideals are treated as feces (another manifestation of interchangeability in the anal world). Sexual prowess takes on psychotically grandiose proportions, with endless repetitive erections and orgasms. More generally, adult fetishes have a twofold quality, being either dirty/smelly or shiny/polished/brilliant, the former representing anality directly, the latter hiding it behind idealization (Chasseguet-Smirgel 1981). And adults with perversions often insist that their form of sexuality is not only an alternative but superior to "normal" genital sexuality. For Donald, feces are sweet as honey or flowers. Pooping and farting can go on endlessly, creating prodigious piles. Penises can be enormously elongated.

Bach and Schwartz (1972) analyzed Sade's creation of his anal world as a restitutive phenomenon, an attempt to create a self that could survive after experiences of unbearable loss and loneliness. They reconstruct severe narcissistic disillusionment and abandonment trauma in Sade's early childhood and point out that although Sade had engaged in perverse acts prior to imprisonment, the creation of his fully fledged bizarre perversions only occurred in his writings, after he was imprisoned, and may be understood as an attempt to compensate for his loneliness and humiliation. Anality is an arena for narcissistic compensatory fantasies because anality is the arena for the first major power struggles with parents, and thus potentially for first experiences of power or humiliation, and because the appreciation of the anal products themselves must change from idealization to devaluation in the course of development. In his anal world, Sade was not weak and alone; rather, he had the complete power over objects and even over reality implicit in the anal transmutations described above.

Unbearable loss and humiliation also appear to be the dangers underlying the creations of adult perversions more generally. This was of course first noted by Freud (1927), who understood fetishes to be created as symbols of the maternal penis, in order to disavow the mother's lack of a penis, and thus to disavow the possibility of castration to the man creating the perversion. McDougall (1972) and Chasseguet-Smirgel (1978, 1981) have expanded this idea by theorizing that it is not only the lack of the maternal phallus which is disavowed by perverse people; rather, what is disavowed is the lack of the maternal phallus, the presence of the actual maternal genitals, and the fact that the mature (paternal) penis is needed for sexual relations with the mother. The fetish is an idealized anal phallus that serves to disavow the importance of the genital world generally. By this is meant that the fetish stands for anality experienced as more powerful, desirable, and important than the adult genitalia or adult sexual relations. This formulation is in better accord with the observed occurrence of fetishes than is the idea that they symbolize only the female phallus, because fetishes occur not only attached to women, as we would expect for a symbol of the female phallus, but also attached to men or to the fetishist himself, or even separate from any object—again showing the nonspecificity that typifies anality.

Thus, perversions are created to deny the "double difference," the difference between the genders and the difference between the generations. Through some combination of experience and cognitive maturation, the little boy comes to recognize that he can never be of the same generation as his parents, and that his father has a sexual relationship with his mother that the little boy will never have with her. For the little boy fully to integrate the knowledge of this double difference, he must acknowledge the loss and humiliation of never truly having the mother for himself the way the father does, as well as the possibility of castration for his wishes. He must also acknowledge that he will never possess the female attributes which previously he had assumed to be available to everybody (Fast 1984). The perverse defense against these losses and humiliations is to retreat to an anal world where the double difference is dissolved along with all differences, and where the little boy idealizes his creations to protect against a sense of doubt that he might be missing something that other people have.

Donald's play, too, appears to be designed to eliminate the double difference. His elimination of the genital difference is the more obvious, seen in the many examples of interchangeability of sexual parts. His elimination of the difference between the generations, though less obvious, is also of great importance. It is hinted at in the play content of Session 3, when Donald states that a woman who has a baby can pee with her breasts (thus reducing the adult woman's secretion to a child's excretion), and in the elimination of time (necessary for generational differences) in Session 1. But I believe its presence was most important in Donald's relationship with me. He almost certainly experienced me as condoning the anal world when I did not restrict the play in Sessions 3 and 4. In Sessions 1, 5 and 6, I was directly located in the anal world, via the elimination of my knowledge of time, our sharing of omnipotent penis-weapons, and my joining in coprolaliac signal calling. Thus, Donald strove to eliminate the generational difference by pulling me into his regression.

Donald appears to have been motivated to eliminate the double difference, and qualities of mine that made me serve as its icon, because of danger situations similar to those described above for Sade and for adult patients with perversions: in his history, we see that Donald experienced significant early object loss in the form of separations from nannies; in the clinical situation, we see that Donald was enraged by the separations from me at the end of sessions and that he was highly resistant to acknowledging attachments to me or anybody else. From the history, we do not know about Donald's learning about female genitals, but it is clear from Sessions 3 and 4 that some learning has taken place in this area; we also know from the history that Donald was repeatedly exposed to the badly injured penis of his half-brother, reinforcing fantasies about possible damage and loss. In the clinical situation, a significant part of the narcissistic injury that Donald angrily experienced appears to have been simply that I was big and in charge—I scheduled, started, and stopped the sessions, I restrained him and set limits when necessary. Donald appears to have experienced my mere presence and existence as evidence of an unattainable adult state of power and strength.

The Therapeutic Gain

I believe it to be of utmost importance that each upsurge in Donald's expression of his anal world was accompanied by small therapeutic gains—by steps into the adult, genital world that I represented. Let us consider what produced these gains.

A principal factor is simply that since anality was Donald's key regression point—was "where he was at"—expressions of anality were what he needed to understand and was capable of understanding. Prior comments about Donald's not following the rules, or wanting to win so much that he changed rules, were not helpful, whereas he quickly understood and was able to use the enacted concept of "farty rules." Expressing affiliation to me as a therapist or helping person would have been too narcissistically threatening, since it would have implied the generational difference—that he was small and needy and I was big and powerful—but affiliation could be expressed as a longing for the shared anal-world attribute of grand penises during Session 5. However, the type of incipient insight into his dream which Donald showed in Session 6—recognition that he needed to defend himself from expressing nice feelings—does not seem to fit here, since this insight was expressed in an adult, not anal, idiom; other therapeutic factors must have been at work.

A second factor leading to the therapeutic gain presumably was simply an increase in the "unobjectionable positive transference" that accompanies the feeling of being understood. Donald was more disposed to understand things in my adult way because he liked me better in this nonspecific manner.

I think it may be speculated that Donald also took therapeutic steps because of more specific messages conveyed by our interaction. He invited or demanded that I enter his anal world, and I complied within the play metaphor, while I remained in the adult world insofar as I still made my own choices about what to do, commented on what was going on, and started and stopped the sessions. One specific example of this was in Session 1, when I joined Donald in enacting that time was unknowable by letting him take my watch, while nevertheless staying in the adult world by commenting that he wanted me not to be able to end the session, and then in fact ending the session on time. A second example was in Session 6 when I joined Donald in coprolaliac signal-calling but refused to join in cursing, which I judged would be over-exciting and would remove me too far from the adult world; Donald's subsequent move to affectively meaningful dream exploration suggests that my stance at that moment had been helpful.

I hypothesize that our partial enactments were therapeutic because they helped Donald with his "divergent conflict" (Kris 1985) between his regressive desire to stay in the anal world, and his progressive desire to move toward the adult world. Our interaction gave Donald opportunities to observe that the boundary between my adult world and his anal world was crossable; if I could step down and back up, he could step up. He also had the opportunity to observe that taking steps into the adult world did not have to mean totally surrendering the possibility of anal experience, since I was still able to share it. He was motivated to follow me back toward my developmental level, so to speak, to maintain the pleasure and comradeship that he had clearly felt when I accompanied him to his level. These speculations are congruent with Loewald's (1960) idea that an important therapeutic factor is the patient's sense that the therapist recognizes in him or her the possibility of attaining a higher developmental level.

Discussion

As we have seen, Donald has created an anal world in many ways analogous to those created by adults with perversions, and even analogous to the anal world of the prototypical pervert, the Marquis de Sade. This 6-year-old's anal world nicely confirms the reconstructions made in psychoanalytic investigation of perverse adults, by demonstrating the expected dynamics in statu nascendi. Donald is still very close to the age when it is developmentally optimal to experience and resolve the oedipal triangle, to recognize and accept the double difference. But instead, Donald is investing much of his psychic energy in the perverse solution identified from adult cases.

Does this mean that Donald is at risk of developing sexual perversion? Although extrapolations to the future are always very uncertain, I conjecture that the risk of sexual perversion is not high for Donald, in part because he is taking advantage of analysis, and in part because of indications that he would be unwilling to settle for perversion. Most telling is that despite his resistance to acknowledging it openly, Donald's admiration of me and of other strong men, especially sports stars, is intense and obvious. The narcissistic hurt of not already being one of us has not destroyed his drive to attain our adult strength and status, although it has interfered with realistic movements in this direction by the partial substitution of grandiose fantasies for careful schoolwork and mutual friendships. Donald's wail of dismay when I assembled him incorrectly in Session 2 indicated his conflict around the anal solution.

Furthermore, although Donald's family constellation shows an important similarity to those which are often described in the histories of adults with perversions, it also shows an important difference (although the comparative data are far from conclusive): Donald's mother is angry and domineering and his father somewhat ineffectual and retiring—a power differential that is often depicted in the history of sexual perversions—but there is no evidence that his mother is sexually seductive, as is also often reported (Bak 1968, Chasseguet-Smirgel 1978, 1981, McDougall 1972). It appears that an illusory disavowal of the double difference strong enough to require actual perversion for its maintenance is most likely to develop when both the actuality and mythology of the family in which the child grows up discount the double difference, that is, when the father is weak and uninvolved, and when the mother prefers the child to the father, particularly in a seductive way.

Therefore, Donald's anal world can better be understood as a manifestation of a *perverse play style* with no implication that it will necessarily develop into actual perversion. I intend the term *perverse play style* to indicate play which constructs a certain relationship to reality, the equivalent at an earlier developmental level of the relationship to reality constructed, in adults who are not openly sexually perverse, by means of a "perverse personality organization" (Chasseguet-Smirgel 1981) or "the language of perversion" (Bach 1994). The core of this relationship to reality is the maintenance of illusion in lieu of accepting the disillusioning realities of adult life. Such maintenance of illusion requires not only the fantasies that provide its contents—these also occur in normal and neurotic constructions (Bach 1994)—but also an experience of these fantasies which imbues them at least at times with belief that is equal to or higher than belief in reality. Steingart (1983) called this type of experience of fantasy a "meaning disturbance," and indicated that its most easily recognized manifestation in childhood is a refusal/inability to shift out of play orientation, or to shift cognitive sets back and forth between play orientation and reality orientation, regardless of reality exigencies and the expectations of objects. Donald's play style may be recognized as perverse because of the conjunction of its anality with a meaning disturbance so defined: it was with great vehemence and intensity of belief that Donald maintained his anality and rejected the adult world (as represented by my efforts at understanding and at communicating empathy), and Donald urgently insisted on enacting his anality: we did not merely play a game that time was eliminated—Donald took my watch. We did not merely play games in which I was assigned the role of a character who talked dirty—I myself had to talk dirty.

Donald would appear to be at risk for a considerably greater-than-optimal reliance on the perverse style. Nevertheless, his use of the perverse style in the absence of actual perversion should alert us to its possible presence in a wide range of people. Indeed, Bach (1994) and Chasseguet-Smirgel (1981) have indicated that the perverse style is more or less appealing to all of us at different times.

The anal world is nicely designed to defend against awareness of the double difference, but this defense would not have been so available to Donald unless he had specific fixations or developmental lags which made it so. We know that Donald was regularly exposed to the badly injured penis of his half-brother, and it may reasonably be reconstructed that such exposure during the anal period was an important determinant of his openness to the anal world. The castration anxiety accompanying such blatant confrontation with a damaged penis would stir up ambivalence about forming a masculine identity, while the observation of such a differently formed penis would magnify the age-appropriate puzzlement about what a male identity really entails. Such dynamics lead to a turn away from the phallic toward anal drives, and to less clear and definite cognitive boundaries.

The world of the classic anal character type, epitomized by the traits of orderliness, parsimony, and obstinacy (Freud 1908), is the opposite of the kind of anal world that Donald has created. Where in the classic character we find orderliness, we find Donald's world enormously chaotic and befouled; where in the classic character we find parsimony, in Donald's world we find profligate and extravagant fantasies of the exchange of huge amounts of excretions and secretions; where in the classic character we find obstinacy and rigidity, in Donald's world we find limitless flux. I believe these differences are best understood as differences in the respective organizing anal experiences: underlying the classical character is the experience of the constricted sphincter, so that people living in this manner are constantly trying to maintain control and exercise "sphincter morality" (Ferenczi 1925). Underlying Donald's anal world is the experience of the feces themselves, messy, interchangeable, and limitless in that they are ever renewable. Among other things, the classic anal character defends against the experience of the anal world; the hyper-rationality of the obsessional may in part be a repudiation of perverse illu-sional reasoning.

It is of interest to note that in Donald's playful fantasy that I had reas-sembled him so that his mouth was on his belly and his eyes were where his nipples should be, he reproduced an image discussed by Freud in his minor paper "A Mythological Parallel to a Visual Obsession" (1916). Freud described a 21-year-old male obsessional patient who was preoccupied with this visual image and Freud reported the same image depicted in a Greek myth. Freud's patient would see an image of a naked torso, with facial features painted on the abdomen but lacking genitals, whenever his father entered the room. The patient had had an unusually strong efflorescence of anal erotism, both up until his tenth year, and again during adolescence as a regression from genital sexuality. He now had refined sensibilities and high morals, and although he loved and respected his father, he saw his father as debauched. Freud under-stood the visual image as a mocking caricature of the father. I believe we can now be more precise. The son, who judging by the length of time that he had experienced a vivid anality, had probably only tenuously established controls over anal-world fantasies, created a subtle compromise-formation in which the anal world was both expressed and repudiated: the image of father castrated and with body parts rearranged disavows the double difference by means of anal-world interchangeability; at the same time, the temptation to enter the anal world is defended against by mocking its representative, the debauched father.

The mythological parallel comes from the myth of Demeter and Perse-phone. While searching for her kidnapped daughter, Demeter is too grief-stricken to eat or drink, so her hostess Baubo makes her laugh by suddenly lifting up her dress and exposing her torso to Demeter. Freud explains that ancient sculptures of Baubo show a torso lacking genitals and with a face drawn on the abdomen. Freud drew the general inference that this self-mocking interrupted Demeter's sorrow. I believe that here, too, we can now make the more precise inference that an anal-world illusion, promising that all is flux so no loss is permanent, is used to dispel Demeter's tragedy. Inspection of a drawing accompanying the paper leads even more strongly to this interpretation, because the "eyes" on the torso simultaneously appear to be nipples, but on breasts which are completely child-like, since they consist solely of nipples, with no adult definition. Therefore, the image contains not only anal interchangeability, but also a specific disavowal of the generational difference—the adult Baubo has a child's breasts.

Freud did not explain what psychological meaning underlay the parallel between his patient's image and the mythological image. I believe that the concept of the anal world provides the missing explanation. What my 6-year-old patient is creating now has been created before in Freud's Vienna and in ancient Greece.

References

Bach, S. (1994). *The Language of Perversion and the Language of Love*. Northvale, NJ: Jason Aronson.

Bach, S., and Schwartz, L. (1972). A dream of the Marquis de Sade: psychoanalytic reflections on narcissistic trauma, decompensation, and the reconstitution of a delusional self. *Journal of the American Psychoanalytic Association* 20:451–475.

Bak, R. C. (1968). The phallic woman: the ubiquitous fantasy in perversions. *Psychoanalytic Study of the Child* 23:15–36. New York: International Universities Press.

Beren, P. (1992). Narcissistic disorders in children. *Psychoanalytic Study of the Child* 47:265–278. New Haven, CT: Yale University Press.

Chasseguet-Smirgel, J. (1978). Reflexions on the connexions between perversion and sadism. *International Journal of Psycho-Analysis* 59:27–35.

——— (1981). Loss of reality in perversions—with special reference to fetishism. *Journal of the American Psychoanalytic Association* 29:511–534.

Fast, I. (1984). *Gender Identity: a Differentiation Model*. Hillsdale, NJ: Analytic Press.

Ferenczi, S. (1925). Psychoanalysis of sexual habits. In *Further Contributions to the Theory and Technique of Psychoanalysis*, pp. 259–297. London: Hogarth, 1950.

Freud, S. (1908). Characters and anal erotism. *Standard Edition* 9.

——— (1916). A mythological parallel to a visual obsession. *Standard Edition* 14.

——— (1927). Fetishism. *Standard Edition* 21.

Kris, A. (1985). Resistance in convergent and in divergent conflicts. *Psychoanalytic Quarterly* 54:537–568.

Loewald, H. (1960). On the therapeutic action of psychoanalysis. *International Journal of Psycho-Analysis* 41:16–33.

McDougall, J. (1972). Primal scene and sexual perversion. *International Journal of Psycho-Analysis* 53:371–384.

Steingart, I. (1983). *Pathological Play in Borderline and Narcissistic Personalities.* Jamaica, NY: Spectrum.

15

Narcissistic Injury and Sadomasochistic Compensation in a Latency-Age Boy

Alan Frosch

Introduction

In the opening soliloquy of *The Tragedy of King Richard III* (1593), Shakespeare tells us of Richard's narcissistic injuries: "Deformed, unfinished . . . lamely and unfashionable . . . so that dogs bark at me as I halt by them"— and his attempts at compensation: "Since I cannot prove a lover . . . I am determined to be a villain" (Act I, Scene I, p. 113). If I cannot find gratification through libido, I will find it through the exercise of my aggression. Of course, Richard is talking not only about his physical deformities (which Shakespeare may well have exaggerated, see Smith [1957]) but about his emotional reaction to them. Richard tells us that something went wrong between him and his mother: "[I was] sent before my time into this breathing world, scarce half made up, cheated of feature by dissembling nature" (p. 113). It was mother (nature) that did him wrong—sent him out of the womb before his time. Richard's physical deformities are a metaphor for feeling unloved by his mother:

A grievous burthen was thy birth to me
Tetchy and wayward was thy infancy (Act IV, Scene IV, p. 146).

If the Duchess of York had loved her son more, then Richard's school days might not have been so "frightful, desperate, wild, and furious" (p. 146). Wildness and fury are Richard's attempts to compensate for the fearfulness and desperation of feeling unloved.

In this paper I will discuss my work with David, a latency-age boy whose "wild and furious" verbal and physically aggressive behavior is clearly atypical for someone his age. One way to understand David's actions is to view them in the context of a series of narcissistic failures and the compensatory strategies (defenses and restitutional measures) for coping with these failures.

At the oral, anal, and phallic stages of his development, David's parents displayed a repetitive pattern of less than adequate response to his needs. This was most pronounced with his mother who did not seem able to devote herself to David, so that he never became the center of her interests. David's aggression would seem a reaction to this. "If I cannot be loved, valued, and cared for, then you will hate and fear me, but I will certainly be a compelling presence in your life."

The inability of David's parents (particularly his mother) to contain his aggression in the first four to five years of life led David to develop a defensive strategy characterized by the rapid mobilization of rage directed at the other. The rage functions to ward off feelings of helplessness and a sense of annihilation, but also to maintain desire and involvement vis-à-vis the other. Unlike Richard, who eliminates his objects in order to feel alive, David devalues his objects but does not relinquish his longing to obtain narcissistic supplies from them — "you must love me" screams the sadist as he beats his objects (Bach 1985).

The evolution of David's behavior into a sadomasochistic organization developed out of his attempt to get his mother (and later his father) to accept (i.e., understand the meaning of) his aggression. In the presence of his parents' failure to understand his anger, David felt more and more out of control. His sadomasochistic behavior was a way to create a sense of greater control by turning the passive experience of being engulfed by rage into the more active experience of directing the rage at others and getting a relatively predictable reaction.

In short, by making the other feel helpless and out of control, David can disavow such feelings in himself and feel more in control. For David, the movement from passively experiencing anger to actively directing it at someone — initially (and primarily) his mother — was an important step in turning unpleasure into pleasure. The anger became erotized. "How would you like it if I knocked over your bookcase?" David announced as he leaned against my bookcase on a day when he felt that "you and that bitch" (mother) were forcing him to come—"Tomorrow is the first day of my vacation. Why the fuck should I be here today?"

History of Failed Narcissistic Aspirations and David's Reactions to Them.

David is the second child born to a middle-class couple, both of whom work. His sister is four years older than David and is described by her parents as the all-American girl: an A student and excellent athlete, she is popular, personable, and "never a problem at home." When David was born, his mother had just completed her PhD and "landed the job of a lifetime." She went to work full-time when David was 2 months old. At that point she began drinking several mugs of coffee a day, as well as Coca-Cola. She continued to breast-feed David in the morning and in the evening when she returned home. She discontinued breast-feeding at 6 months when it became apparent that David was gaining only about a pound a month. In her words, "caffeine is a small molecule that goes right through to breast milk," so David's failure to thrive was a result of his mother's "bad milk."

I understand this story both as a factual piece of David's early history and as a metaphor for the mother's lack of libidinal connection to her son. The mother's involvement with her career, her excitement over her new job, and her own narcissistic issues interfered with the essential task of motherhood— what Stern (1995) calls the life-growth theme: "Can the mother keep the baby alive? Can she make him grow and thrive physically? It is this theme . . . that makes success at feeding so vital" (p. 175).

As I understand David's development, this is a crucial organizing event in his life. He is deprived of mother's good milk. What he had has been taken away. Some beginning sense of existence is threatened with annihilation and David fights for his survival. He is a "difficult" baby. He cries, has tantrums, is a "fussy" eater, and is not easily soothed. He forces the environment to attend to him. He tries to elicit from the environment that which he has been deprived of by mother.

This breach in the early libidinal relationship between David and his mother represented a pattern that was to be repeated in various forms throughout David's life—first with mother and then with both parents. For example, from the age of 2 months David spent significant amounts of time with baby-sitters. His parents report that one of the sitters was a teenage girl so preoccupied with herself that she would watch TV for hours on end and pay no attention to David, who was left to cry most of the time. The parents fired the girl after a few months, but the story raises a number of questions.

Why was this girl hired or, at the very least, why was she kept on for several months? What does it mean for a child to express frustration and anger for hours on end and not be heard? David's anger was carried over into the relationship with his mother. She describes David as an extremely difficult child who sorely tried her patience. David's mother felt that there was something wrong with him. In the comparison with his sister, he did not fare well. The mother's inadequacies are externalized and David is the one who is impaired (Novick and Novick 1987). Without the libidinal investment in her son, David's mother's judgment is seriously impaired—and it is David's fault. This was certainly the case around toilet training.

David's mother described his toilet training as relatively uneventful; none-theless it was frustrating to her because he had had more difficulty than his sister. From his mother's point of view, David had taken too long, achieving bowel control about the age of 3. Following this there was a regression and he began soiling. His parents decided not to use diapers during this period, and for three to four months David soiled his clothes. The regression seemed coincident with his mother's increased involvement with her job (which meant longer hours away from home and frequent business trips). David's father had always traveled two or three months a year, one or two weeks at a time. Now mother began to take two- or three-week trips, over the course of a year totaling some three to four months. David's reaction to his mother's traveling was intense. He would not speak to her on the phone when she called and would often be enraged at her when she returned. This was in marked contrast to his father's leave-taking, which David seemed to take more in stride. David's mother was, in her own words, "totally oblivious" to separations, and her leave-takings occasioned temper tantrums as well as soiling.

David is not the good, loving, "clean" child who has a burgeoning sense of mastery over bodily functions, drives, and objects. What we see with David is a failure of these aspirations. The failure, however, was not complete. David's longing for his mother seems to have taken the form of an intensification of his aggressive relationship with her; his anger was met by an intensification of her anger toward him. Her attempts to compensate for this anger took the form of a technical relationship toward David where the emphasis was on doing the "right thing." Doing the "right thing" without a libidinal interest in the other is a prescription for failure, and David was treated as if he did not exist. David's sense of helplessness, associated with a failure of narcissistic aspirations, is here defensively altered through a process of reversal. David is the powerful one in the relationship with his mother. She can abandon him, but he can do the same to her and, in the process, deny that her leave-takings have any meaning for him at all. Narcissistic wishes to be loving were replaced by the erotization of wishes to be "bad." David's intense longings for his mother was replaced by an angry sadomasochistic relationship with her.

During the phallic/oedipal period, David's provocative sadomasochistic behavior increased dramatically. He would go often into his parents' bedroom and jump in bed with his mother in a sexual and aggressive manner. If he were asked to leave by either parent, an argument would ensue and David would become verbally abusive. By age 6 or 7 the mixture of sex and aggression was striking: "Take off your clothes, Mom, so I can play with your tits before Daddy gets home." Following such incidents, David's father would speak to him, chastise him, or physically carry him to his room. More often than not, David's response to his father's interventions was to say "go fuck yourself."

David's father became a vivid character only when the phallic/oedipal period was reached. Up to that point he remained a passive, shadowy figure who was not a source of support for David. During the latter part of the phallic/oedipal period, and extending into the years typically associated with latency, David's father is described by both parents (and David) as a forceful, highly competitive, and sometimes angry presence in relation to his son.

For David, the competitive situation of the phallic/oedipal period is associated with an earlier time of life when he was small, weak, and helpless in relation to powerful figures who were unavailable to him in a narcissistically enhancing and life-affirming way. The situation is potentiated during this crucial developmental period, at least in part, by his father's competition and anger toward David, which is clearly fueled by David's sadomasochism.

When he was very young David's temper tantrums drew attention, thereby allowing him to be involved with the other through the exercise of his aggression. The more elaborated versions of these temper tantrums when he was 6 or 7, however, represented a restriction of ego functioning that interfered with the gratification of narcissistic aspirations in a realistic way. David could not relinquish his infantile grandiosity so that he could compete with peers and take winning or losing in stride. Losing was tantamount to feeling annihilated and an occasion for attacks of rage; winning, for a grandiose display of elation invariably accompanied by a complete devaluation (i.e., annihilation) of the other.

It is easy to see how such behavior could provoke retaliation. It is a retaliation, however, that on an unconscious level David controls. He provokes the behavior. At home he could not play a board game and lose. He might throw the game all over the room, or accuse the other of cheating and start an argument. Given David's behavior, it is easier to see how he could feel himself feared and disliked rather than admired and the center of attention in a positive, narcissistically enhancing manner.

Bibring (1953) gives the example of a narcissistically vulnerable patient who warded off feelings of helplessness by having a "fantasy of walking down the street with a large sword in her hand and cutting off the heads of the people passing by . . ." (p. 44). He makes the point that such aggressive fantasies can be narcissistically gratifying. To a significant extent this was the case with David. His sadistic behavior toward his parents defends against wishes to be loved and cared for, and provides him with a sense of pleasure and excitement associated with the discharge of aggression, and a sense of power associated with verbal and physical abuse of the other. The fantasies underlying these reversals of affects and role relations can reach grandiose proportions and compensate for a profound sense of vulnerability and helplessness. David does to others what he feels has been done to him. When he tells his mother that he would like to fuck her, or calls his father a bitch and throws cat litter all over the house, David is treating others as if they did not exist as people with needs and feelings. This was the situation that existed when David entered treatment a month or two short of his ninth birthday.

Treatment

David presented as a somewhat short and overweight boy. His parents told me that David felt very uncomfortable about his weight and would not swim without a T-shirt. In the initial sessions there was a forced maturity as he sat in a chair, crossed his legs, and chatted about this and that. One of his favorite conversations was about food. David told me that he carried prodigious amounts of jelly beans, candy bars, and other assorted treats in his backpack, and he would often open his pack during a session and devour bags of potato chips and candy. When I would make a comment about this, with the intention of exploring it a bit, David would tell me to "shut the fuck up," or he would put his hands over his ears and scream in a high-pitched voice that was deafening. When I commented on the piercing quality of the sound he seemed genuinely pleased and told me that he thought it must be deafening and that he was convinced he could eventually shatter my windows with it. All of this occurred during the first month of treatment.

The Wannabe King: An Anal-Sadistic Fantasy

In the second month of treatment David decided he wanted to make a castle out of Legos. Construction of the castle was spread over a number of sessions, and David's creativity and skill were apparent in the final product. It was a large castle, with ramps for the guards and a dungeon for prisoners. The dungeon had one prisoner in it, and the reason for this man's imprisonment never became clear. What was clear, however, was that the prisoner would escape. This was accomplished through bribing a guard and eventually killing the king who had placed him there. When this was done, the prisoner became king. He made friends with all the neighboring kings, as well as the guards of the former king, now deceased. Everyone seemed to be getting along very well. Then one day the former prisoner, now king, killed all the guards and all the kings and became king of everyone. He became all-powerful.

In David's fantasy he turns the tables on the king who imprisoned him. He does to the king what was done to him—he puts him in a hole. He kills him. In David's fantasy he is also a duplicitous person who kills his friends and colleagues. He is an anal-sadistic king, not an oedipal victor. The pleasure is in tricking and killing the other, not in being strong and victorious, or in getting the admiration of others through courageous deeds. David's victory is an empty one, and he is alone—he kills everyone, and he must go on killing. David convinces others that they have a libidinal relationship with him when in fact they don't. He charms them with his libido and destroys them with his aggression. This is a situation that is familiar to David from his early relationship with his mother where he must have felt a sense of attachment, betrayal, and ultimately helplessness. Once again he does to others what he feels has been done to him. In real life, of course, David does not kill people. But he does turn his aggression on them so that he can set up a situation in which the other ceases to be a reliable object and David therefore feels alone—the way he must have felt as a very young child in the absence of a reliable maternal object. The past is re-created in the present like similar Russian dolls nested within each other.

As the work continued, the aggressive nature of David's behavior seemed to climb at an exponential rate. With great elation he would throw his empty food wrappers all over the office and threaten to rub his bubble gum into the couch. David, like Richard, was determined to be a villain. He communicated through action, as well as words, that I had to assume the passive role in our relationship. He was preoccupied with revenge, strength, and power. He might talk, for example, about how he felt that a friend had not treated him properly and how he would get that person back. At times a toy might be thrown at me as the session came to a close, or he might threaten to push all the books off the bookcase on his way out. It was as if he were taking revenge on me for ending the session. The behavior, clearly designed to provoke, did not cross the line where David became unmanageable.

To some extent, however, his provocations were successful. In David's story of the "Wannabe King," David ultimately is left alone because of his aggression. My countertransference was such that I found myself struggling at times to stay connected to him in a positive way, and even after two years of twice-weekly psychotherapy, I often felt apprehensive about seeing David. His abusive behavior made me angry. The work, however, was made most difficult for me because I felt so helpless. I doubted whether I could help David. I often felt as if I were a prop for his foils, and felt that his self-esteem seemed to ride on how he could devalue or provoke me. When not caught up in my countertransferentially induced despair, I could reflect that my feelings of vulnerability, helplessness, anger, and guilt were similar to feelings David has had all his life, feelings he in a sense "gave to me" to hold on to during our sessions. I thought that I was able to help David by containing these feelings for him—something his parents were not able to do.

David's sadomasochistic relationship with his mother was an attempt to adapt to a relationship that, for David, was filled with fears of being hurt or annihilated. This disturbance in the libidinal relationship between David and his mother was re-created in the transference. David felt I was beating him, that is, forcing him to talk about things and treating him as a "retard" or a "psycho." His response to these attacks was to beat me: David actively engaged me through the exercise of his aggression. The Novicks (1987) point out that the therapists of children with fantasies similar to David's often found the work "arduous, joyless, and ungratifying for a long time" (p. 356). I would add to this that I also found working with David an intensely intimate experience. He was never distant or withdrawn. Although David felt I was forcing him to come, he hardly ever missed a session and only rarely did he want to end early. On the contrary, David often wanted to beat me one more time at cards before he left, even if our time was up. He wanted to leave me, as he put it, "penniless, on the street without a dime so your own wife wouldn't bother to even look at you. You're nothing, a real piece of shit." The wish is to obliterate me or, at the very least, humiliate me. David wants me to feel as he has felt so much of his life. His way of relating to me is to engage in a perverse relationship. It is an anal-sadistic relationship that is highly charged and intimate.

At card games David would cheat openly. If I commented on this obvious behavior, he would deny it, become enraged at me, and accuse me of calling him a liar. What was particularly interesting was the fact that David's superior intelligence and need to win made him an excellent cardplayer. His strategy, concentration, and investment in the game would assuredly have led to victory without any recourse to cheating. It was the cheating, abusiveness, and overall provocative behavior that was the essence of David's perverse relationship with me and everyone else, particularly his parents. I believe that this way of relating provided David a certain distance from intense longings for intimacy that were terrifying to him. Patterns of sadism and masochism were repeated at different levels and took an endless variety of forms.

The following vignette exemplifies the sadomasochistic fantasies, the underlying sense of vulnerability, and the communicative value of an enactment when the therapist is able to extricate himself from the pull of countertransference and get back to the work of understanding rather than enacting.

The Baseball Cap Enactment

During the second year of treatment, David spent a session showing me his voluminous collection of superhero cards. For the most part I listened and asked a question from time to time so that I could better understand the nature and function of each superhero. When I felt there was an opportunity to do so, I might offer a comment about the defensive and gratifying aspects of these fantasy figures, and muse aloud how anyone might feel strong and totally protected if he were like one of these superheroes or had some connection with them. My line of thought was not lost on David, and at some point he told me to "cut the cheap psychology crap, you fucking retard."

David experienced my comments as a narcissistic injury. His fragile sense of self seemed so dependent on the maintenance of grandiose fantasies of omnipotence that any suggestion of vulnerability was met by rage and devaluation. Overall, however, the session was colored in a distinctly positive, I would say libidinal, tone. David wanted to show me his card collection and clearly valued my interest in it. He was in no hurry to leave the session, and I did not feel a great need to *do* something with the material.

As the session drew to a close and David collected his things and started to leave, I noticed that he had left his baseball cap on the couch. I mentioned this to him as I picked it up and flipped it to him. He dropped it, picked it up, and left.

The next session began on the same positive note. David began to draw superheroes and asked if I had any Wite-Out he could use to correct a drawing. After he had used it, I noticed that he had left the cap off. I asked if he would put it on, and he did. The next thing I saw was the bottle of Wite-Out moving through the air at a considerable speed toward my head. I had the uncanny sensation that time had slowed down. As I watched the bottle moving toward me, I wondered how I would feel seeing patients for the rest of the day covered by Wite-Out. I put up my hand, caught the bottle, and had the sense that I might cry. I blurted out, "Why did you do that?" David calmly responded, "Because you threw my baseball cap at me."

David could not express in words the meaning of the previous day's experience. To say "because you threw my baseball cap at me" does not do justice to the intensity of the feelings he may have had. For David, throwing the Wite-Out and inducing certain feelings in me that were similar to his own was an essential step in the communicative process. Only after the action was performed could David try to approach the experience through the use of language. Freedman (1994) has written about the sequence of action followed by recollection and insight; he notes that increased levels of mental reorgani-zation are often preceded by an action, acting out, or enactment. The terms are often used interchangeably. As I understand Freedman, enactments are often related to a failure of language. Thoughts and impulses that cannot be represented through spoken language can achieve representation through action.

In a related vein, Mahon (1991) has outlined the advance from the more concrete and action-oriented thinking of the prelatency child to the more abstract thought and language of the child who has had a relatively successful resolution of the Oedipus complex and entered the psychological state of latency (Sarnoff 1976, pp. 115–121). Bach (1994) has argued that on a preoe-idpal level the "child's words must 'pass through' a receptive or attuned parent and be endowed with affect and significance in the course of this passage before they return to the child as 'meaningful words'" (p. 145). The child must be heard by the parent in an emotionally meaningful way so that words can be used as symbols to communicate to others the child's experience of the world. David's language is skewed toward primary as opposed to secondary process; in Piagetian terms, it is preoperational rather than being at the level of concrete operations (Steingart 1983). In short, because words are inadequate to convey the intensity of his feelings, David switches to a different level of representation-action.

David's reliance on action makes the therapist's task of containment more difficult. It is one thing to have an intellectual appreciation for David's narcissistic difficulties and quite another when they present as actions that lead to powerful emotional responses in the therapist.

The therapeutic process takes the form of a minidrama played out between patient and therapist, one fueled by transference and countertransference distortions. McLaughlin (1991) has described such dreams as a mix of verbal and motoric behavior of such force and intensity that they influence the other to respond in a particular way. It is only when the therapist can extricate him- or herself from the countertransference and metaphorically step back and return to the job of analyzing, rather than enacting, that he or she is in a position to understand the meaning the patient has given to the transference situation (Chused 1991, Lasky 1993). At some point, aspects of this understanding can be given to the patient in the form of a verbal intervention that can help explain, clarify, or organize the enactment. The verbalization of this action-oriented, affectively laden "thing" (i.e., enactment) is an attempt to make the unconscious conscious. For this to be successful, it must take place in an atmosphere of trust where David feels that his words and actions are important and have meaning. Only then can the words that I attach to the situation represent a new way to look at things, rather than a challenge to David's sense of reality and an invitation to continue the sadomasochistic enactment.

A necessary condition for the establishment of therapeutic trust is the therapist's ability to be attuned to the patient's inner emotional states, to think about these states, and to understand how the other views the experience before attempting to intervene. In short, the therapist must take the patient's feelings, thoughts, and actions very seriously. The therapist must avoid the establishment of a technical relationship (without minimizing the importance of good technique) and strive to libidinize the patient through the exercise of therapeutic love—a process where the therapist is "devoted" to deepening his understanding of the patient's psychic reality, his unconscious construction of the world (Steingart 1995). This is how I understand the process of containment.

David has organized the transference relationship in a way that is consistent with his unconscious representation of the world. In this situation the intricacies of personal meaning include for David his feeling that I am trying to hurt or humiliate him by throwing the baseball cap. For the work to proceed in a productive way, it is crucial that the therapist be able to use his feelings as signals that act as an affective dimension to the pattern of meaning created by the patient.

In this situation, my feeling that I might cry is crucial in understanding how I organized what went on between us. I felt hurt by someone I thought was my friend. I used these words because they help explain why I felt like crying. David had become part of my dynamic past. I did not feel like a therapist attempting to help a troubled child. I felt like a vulnerable child who had been betrayed. I became the container for David's feelings.

My initial evaluation of this situation was as follows: David dropped the baseball cap, and for him this represented a terrible humiliation. It is the emotional counterpart to beating me at cards and leaving me turned into a piece of shit on the street. Loss—the dropping of the cap, losing a board game or a game of cards—feels like an annihilation to David. Of course he felt hurt by me. Who wouldn't in such a circumstance? The word "hurt" does not even begin to capture the extent of David's unpleasure. It feels like the narcissistic humiliation experienced by a baby crying for attention only to be ignored; by a 2-year-old who feels terrible shame and humiliation when an unempathic parent scolds him over a loss of bowel control; or by a child who feels humiliated when he must walk around in soiled clothing, or ignored and filled with impotent rage when his mother leaves on a business trip. All of these childhood calamities may be condensed into the baseball cap incident.

The act of throwing the Wite-Out at me, though very dramatic, in fact follows a set pattern in David's overall behavior. The incident exemplifies David's use of aggression to defend against feelings of vulnerability and helplessness. In this case the immediacy and intensity of my own emotional response allowed me to understand that the enactment was also David's struggle for survival, a desperate attempt to be heard, to be understood. It is David's way of trying to maintain a meaningful relationship with me. He needs to let me know that I hurt his feelings in order for this relationship to have any value to him. And David must feel that I can welcome, understand, and eventually help him with these feelings—in short, that I can contain his feelings of being hurt and angry.

The Dialectic between Psychic and Material Reality

Before the therapist can help the patient understand the enactment, a crucial question concerning the nature of reality must be addressed. For example, is

David's father in actuality a monster who wants to kill his son ("break his neck") and therefore someone who David must ward off through the use of aggression? Or is it more accurate to say that David takes his fantasies about his father and turns them, through the use of projective identification, into a virtual reality that induces the other to act in a way consistent with the fantasy? (Here I refer to projective identification as an interpersonal maneuver, as opposed to limiting it to fantasy. The extension of this concept from fantasy [Klein 1946] to behavior has been elucidated by Ogden [1979]).

But I began this discussion by saying David dropped the cap. I could just as easily have asked why I threw the cap. Does the flip of the cap really represent my unconscious wish to hurt David? Or is it a friendly gesture, that is multiply determined, that may therefore contain sadistic elements that David selectively responds to because of his unconscious mental set?

It is in the heat of the transference, where the therapist can look at himself as well as at the patient, that questions concerning the nature of reality can best be answered. In this case I have no doubt that it is David's psychic reality, his unconscious organization of the world, that defines the present along the lines of the past. For David this past includes significant narcissistic insult early in life. His response to the baseball cap incident is understandable from this perspective. David's dynamic organization of the present fits into the pattern of meaning established earlier in life and is reinforced through his compensatory and defensive strategies.

It is the exercise of aggression that is David's primary and automatic defense against these narcissistic injuries. While oedipal issues are clearly present, it is David's excitement in humiliating the other, in wiping the other out, that is the primary driving force behind his fantasies and behavior.

David's anal-sadistic organization is a compromise position that defends against longings to be a passive little boy who will be loved and cared for, on the one hand, and fears of being ignored and humiliated—"Wited-Out," if you will—on the other.

For a child to begin to master the Oedipus complex and move out into the larger world and say, in effect, "this is who I am and this is what I want, and I am not all-powerful—I know that my father is bigger and stronger than me and that his relationship with my mother is different from mine," there must be some basic sense of self-worth and trust about himself and others. The development of trust and self-worth is initiated very early in life and speaks to a certain kind of relationship in which the child can receive narcissistic supplies, which leads to libidinal investment in self and object representations. This process was interfered with in David's development. To become the center of attention, he provokes the other. Thus he receives attention with a negative sign: hate not love. This is the masochistic counterpart of his sadistic behavior. This situation is very familiar to David and has, as the Novicks put it, "the smell of home" (1987, p. 363).

With David's need for love in mind, I would like to entertain another interpretation of the enactment. In this scenario David did not become upset when I flipped the baseball cap to him. His positive affect at the beginning of the next session can support such a consideration. Instead he became upset when I asked him to put the Wite-Out cap back on the bottle. Why didn't I assume that he might use the bottle again, or that he would put the cap on when he finished drawing? Was I afraid of David's aggression and treating him like a time bomb about to explode? If this is so, it is a clear example of how the past actively organizes the present through the inducement of certain feelings, attitudes, and behavior in the other that are similar to feelings, attitudes, and behaviors of significant objects from the past.

Another way of looking at this situation is to consider that my motivation for asking David about the Wite-Out cap was a maneuver on my part to push him away. Was I uncomfortable with the intensity of his positive feelings? With someone like David the narcissistic defenses (e.g., rage and devaluation) can so dominate the clinical picture that the underlying longing for love (narcissistic supplies) can fade into the background. David's need to get attention and involvement from the other is reflected by the intensity of his defenses, particularly his aggression. In my work with David I have learned that it is his libidinal feelings, his need for me to *want* to be with him (he has accused me of seeing him only because I am paid to by his parents), that is often a factor in the transference/countertransference constellation. It is David's need to be loved (i.e., his wish to be comforted, to be held in high esteem) as well as his hatred that must be contained by the therapist.

Summary

David, like Richard, was ripped out of his state of narcissistic omnipotence before his time. Mother's bad milk (factually and metaphorically) was an impingement that shattered David's fragile sense of narcissistic omnipotence and did not allow for "optimal disillusionments" and a gradual abstraction of infantile omnipotence in the form of a positively cathected ego ideal (Blos 1979, Freud 1914). It is the narcissistically enhancing sense of omnipotence of infancy and early childhood that is the "foundation on which trust in oneself and the world is built. Indeed, it is when these *experiences of omnipotence* are lacking and the object's failures impinge on the child that a reactive *defensive omnipotence* arises to deny and overcompensate for feelings of annihilation and death of the self" (Bach 1994, p. 172).

I have suggested that a failure of narcissistic aspirations in infancy and early childhood was met with by a mobilization of aggression on David's part. Initially the aggression was a way of expressing frustration and attracting his mother's attention. Over time the aggression became pleasurable in its own right and was used in the pursuit of grandiose fantasies of omnipotence. The narcissistic rage and devaluation of the other also turned passivity into activity and served to defend against longings for intimacy that threatened to reactivate feelings of helplessness and despair. The fantasy of the Wannabe King was seen as a compromise formation with primarily preoedipal determinants. In this fantasy the wish to sadistically attack the other represents an anal-sadistic organization that fuels oedipal conflicts. In this fantasy David's murderous rage puts him in a position where he is alone. It was suggested that in real life David potentially "kills off" the other by inducing aggression or fear in them; this, while exciting to David in his anal struggles, carries with it the threat of abandonment. This was particularly clear in the clinical process referred to as an enactment.

An analysis of my reaction to David can suggest that wishes to hurt David or to move away from his intense feelings, libidinal as well as aggressive, may have played a role in the baseball cap incident. I also speculated that these feelings may have been implicated in my initial reaction to the Wite-Out cap.

All patients attempt to actualize the transference by converting their wishes to actions that can induce the therapist to behave in ways that confirm the patient's psychic reality. These actions, or minidramas, are compromise formations that are related to the gratification of, or defense against, transference wishes (Boesky 1982). These issues are crucial in our work with all patients, but are accentuated with a child like David who can feel easily hurt and humiliated.

David's narcissistic vulnerability, the propensity to experience the present along the lines of failed narcissistic aspirations of the past, leads to the rapid mobilization of aggression, with a heightened potential for action. This action potential is directly related to the consistent failure of narcissistic aspirations, which has led to a less than adequate mastery of the Oedipus complex. This has a direct bearing on David's thought and language, which is skewed toward an archaic organization and cannot be used to convey the intensity of his affective state.

For David to remain in a meaningful relationship he must be able to express his feelings about the other. When this expression is organized primarily around action, the demand on the other (therapist, parent, friend) not to respond in kind becomes very great. In the therapeutic situation, the therapist's capacity to contain David's emotional expressions and tactfully convey the meaning of the transference situation is crucial to therapeutic success. With patients less narcissistically vulnerable, the process of containment can often remain in the background; it is both necessary and, for the most part, readily available. With patients like David, however, it is more likely to be the focus of the therapist's attention throughout the treatment.

Sadomasochism—Another Perspective

The theme of loss and restitution runs through David's sadomasochistic enactments. One form it takes is David's provoking the other to attack him. This would be tantamount to a loss of the reliable object, the contemporary representation of bad milk. In these enactments David does not quite go over the edge—he doesn't push the bookcase over. When he does push the other too far he is able to re-establish the libidinal aspects of the relationship. He oscillates between order and disorder, between maintaining libidinal connections, severing them, and bringing them back to life. Of course, I am describing the external manifestations of David's internal world.

David's sadomasochistic world is something he knows very well. It is a world where one is beaten or does the beating, and it represents "a perversion of reality" (Frosch 1995, Grossman 1993, Steingart 1983) where fantasy and aggression take precedence over reality and libido. The fantasies are organized around sadomasochistic constructions that hold out the promise of redemption—the mother of pain is associated with the mother of pleasure. As the protagonist in Pauline Reage's (1965) *Story of O* says—"It is only when you make me suffer that I feel safe and secure." It is only when O's sadistic "master" is about to leave her that she chooses to die. The painful blows of the sadist's whip defend against the greater pain of loss and annihilation.

In David's fantasies the suffering is typically associated with the devalued other. Narcissistic trauma and self-annihilation have been transformed into a grandiose affirmation of the self. David can do anything he wants, with anyone he wants, in any way that he wants, and particularly in ways that are forbidden. Negativism has become the object of idealization (Bach 1984, pp. 145–146). Loss and restitution take place in the destruction and restitution of the all-powerful object. In David's fantasy world of anal omnipotence, self and object are always interchangeable. Sadism and masochism are different sides of the same coin. Self and object exist as complements, or they do not exist at all. This sadomasochistic world of suffering and redemption, loss and restitution, is a reflection of the disturbance in the pleasure economy between David and his mother and is re-created in the transference.

Concluding Comments

For David thought and language are still skewed toward archaic levels of organization. Therefore his use of action instead of words allows the therapist an opportunity to see his narcissistic vulnerabilities in an emotionally charged way. This provides an occasion for containment and the potential for insight-oriented interventions. At the same time, however, the therapist's capacity for containment can be compromised during affectively charged and action-oriented dramatizations of David's internal world directed at the person of the therapist. At these times the potential for action, as opposed to analysis, on the therapist's part can be destructive to the therapeutic process. It is "a dangerous thing if reality fulfills repressed wishes. The phantasy becomes reality and all defensive measures are thereupon reinforced" (Freud 1928, p. 186). David exerts pressure on reality to bend to his fantasy expectations. That is to say, he tries to induce *material reality* (current experience with others) to fit into the pattern of expectations based on *psychic reality* — his collection of narcissistically informed archaic unconscious fantasies organized as compromise formations.

References

Bach, S. (1985). *Narcissistic States and the Therapeutic Process*. New York: Jason Aronson.

——— (1994). *The Language of Perversion and the Language of Love*. Northvale, NJ: Jason Aronson.

Bibring, E. (1953). The mechanism of depression. In *Affective Disorders*, ed. P. Greenacre, pp. 13–48. New York: International Universities Press.

Blos, P. (1979). The genealogy of the ego ideal. In *The Adolescent Passage*, pp. 43–88. New York: International Universities Press.

Boesky, D. (1982). Acting out—a reconsideration of the concept. *International Journal of Psycho-Analysis* 63:39–57.

Chused, J. (1991). The evocative power of enactments. *Journal of the American Psychoanalytic Association* 39:615–639.

Freedman, N. (1994). More on transformation: enactments in psychoanalytic space. In *Spectrum of Psychoanalysis: Essays in Honor of Martin S. Bergmann*, ed. A. K. Richards and A. D. Richards, pp. 93–110. Madison, CT: International Universities Press.

Freud, S. (1914). On narcissism: an introduction. *Standard Edition* 14:67–104.

———— (1928). Dostoevsky and parricide. *Standard Edition* 21:175–196.

Frosch, A. (1995). The preconceptual organization of emotion. *Journal of the American Psychoanalytic Association* 43(2):423–447.

Grossman, L. (1993). The perverse attitude toward reality. *Psychoanalytic Quarterly* 42(3):422–436.

Klein, M. (1946). Notes on some schizoid mechanisms. *International Journal of Psycho-Analysis* 27:99–110.

Lasky, R. (1993). *Dynamics of Development and the Therapeutic Process*. Northvale, NJ: Jason Aronson.

Mahon, E. J. (1991). The "dissolution" of the Oedipus complex: a neglected cognitive factor. *Psychoanalytic Quarterly* 50:628–636.

McLaughlin, J. T. (1991). Clinical and theoretical aspects of enactment. *Journal of the American Psychoanalytic Association* 39:595–614.

Novick, K., and Novick, J. (1987). The essence of masochism. *Psychoanalytic Study of the Child* 42:353–384. New Haven, CT: Yale University Press.

Ogden, T. (1979). On projective identification. *International Journal of Psycho-Analysis* 60:357–373.

Reage, P. (1965). *Story of O*. New York: Ballantine Books.

Sarnoff, C. (1976). *Latency*. New York: Jason Aronson.

Shakespeare, W. (1593). *The Tragedy of King Richard III*. In *The Complete Works of Shakespeare*, ed. W. Wright, pp. 111–156. Garden City, NY: Garden City Books, 1936.

Smith, G. (1957). *A History of England*. New York: Charles Scribner's Sons.

Steingart, I. (1983). *Pathological Play in Borderline and Narcissistic Personalities*. Jamaica, NY: Spectrum.

———— (1995). *A Thing Apart*. Northvale, NJ: Jason Aronson.

Stern, D. (1995). *The Motherhood Constellation: A Unified View of Parent–Infant Psychotherapy*. New York: Basic Books.

Credits

The editor gratefully acknowledges permission to reprint material from the following sources:

Index